The Worlding of Arabic Literature

The Worlding of Arabic Literature

Language, Affect, and the Ethics of Translatability

ANNA ZIAJKA STANTON

Fordham University Press
NEW YORK 2023

This book was a recipient of the American Comparative Literature Association's Helen Tartar First Book Subvention Award. Fordham University Press is grateful for the funding from this prize that helped facilitate publication.

This book is freely available in an open access edition thanks to TOME (Toward an Open Monograph Ecosystem)—a collaboration of the Association of American Universities, the Association of University Presses, and the Association of Research Libraries—and the generous support of the Pennsylvania State University. Learn more at the TOME website, available at: openmonographs.org.

Fordham University Press also publishes its books in a variety of electronic formats. Some content that appears in print may not be available in electronic books.

Visit us online at www.fordhampress.com.

Library of Congress Cataloging-in-Publication Data available online at https://catalog.loc.gov.

Printed in the United States of America

25 24 23 5 4 3 2 1

First edition

In memory of Humphrey Davies
(1947–2021), an extraordinary translator of Arabic literature
into English and a central protagonist of this book,
whose loss is quite simply irremediable.

No painter mayhap your portrait for me painted, yet
In these my verses you are portrayed; they are your guardian—
Or if a narrow grave-shelf has hid you,
For me the Earth today is the narrowest of spaces
—Al-Shidyaq, *Leg over Leg*, trans. Davies, 4:211

Contents

Note on Translations and Transliterations ix

Introduction. From Embargo to Boom: The Changing World of Arabic Literature in English 1

1 Sonics of *Lafẓ*: Translating Arabic Acoustics for Anglophone Ears 27

2 Vulgarity of *Saj*ʿ: The Scandalous Pleasures of Burton's *The Book of the Thousand Nights and a Night* 56

3 Ethics of the *Muthannā*: Caring for the Other in a Mother Tongue 83

4 *ʿAjamī* Politics and Aesthetic Experience: Translating the Body in Pain 113

Conclusion: Beyond Untranslatability 140

Acknowledgments 157

Notes 161

Bibliography 197

Index 219

Note on Translations and Transliterations

Translations throughout this book are mine unless otherwise noted. To transliterate Arabic into the Latin alphabet, I have used a modified version of the *International Journal of Middle East Studies* (IJMES) system, wherein each Arabic emphatic consonant is represented by the Latin-letter equivalent of its closest nonemphatic counterpart plus a dot underneath; the Arabic vowels *alif*, *wāw*, and *yāʾ* are represented by ā, ū, and ī respectively; and a *shaddah* is indicated with a doubled consonant. I have rendered the Arabic feminine marker *tāʾ marbūṭah* as *-ah* (or *-at* when it occurs in a possessive structure). Although no separate uppercase letter forms exist in Arabic, I have capitalized proper nouns throughout the transliterations to aid Anglophone readers in comparing between the transliterated version of a passage and its English translation. I have represented all short vowels only when transliterating passages from *Alf laylah wa-laylah* or the Qur'an or, in one case, lines of metered Arabic poetry. Finally, when referring to an author who publishes at least sometimes in Arabic, I have generally preferred to utilize the transliterated spelling of his or her name throughout the main text of the book, even if I also refer to work by that author in English; in the notes, however, the spelling of each author's name appears as it does in the cited source.

The Worlding of Arabic Literature

Introduction. From Embargo to Boom: The Changing World of Arabic Literature in English

Toward the close of the twentieth century, the Palestinian American critic Edward Said published an essay in *The Nation* decrying the absence of translated Arabic literature from the Anglo-American literary field. At a time when non-Western fiction overall was increasingly finding an audience among globally minded American readers, Said observed, Arabic literature remained uniquely "embargoed" from circulating in the United States. To explain this situation, Said pointed to the enduring prejudices of American readers and the publishing industry that served them, citing as evidence the case of a New York publisher who, in the early 1980s, had refused to commission translations of novels by the Egyptian future Nobel laureate Nagīb Maḥfūẓ because he deemed the Arabic language too "controversial" for its literature to be able to attain any kind of critical or commercial success in English.[1]

Over the decades since Said's essay appeared in print, it has become a touchstone for scholars studying the translation and reception of Arabic literature in the Anglophone West. In particular, it has been interpreted as extending Said's diagnosis of the Orientalist attitudes and epistemologies that have informed Euro-American engagements with the Arabophone Middle East since the colonial era—a diagnosis seminally articulated in his reputation-making 1978 volume *Orientalism*—to elucidate the plight of translated Arabic literature in English-language book markets in the present day.[2] By this account, that Arabic literature should be doubly excluded from circulating in English by its foreign provenance and its untranslatable language not only underscores the practical obstacles that it faces in the Anglophone literary field but also indicates its essential incommensurability to the predominant values, tastes, and habits that define this field.

The Worlding of Arabic Literature represents an attempt to think beyond this understanding of Arabic literature's relationship to Anglophone readers, the Anglophone literary field, and the English language itself. To reexamine the situation of Arabic literature in English translation today is both a timely and a much-needed endeavor. Most obviously, such a rethinking is called for by the fact that so many new works of translated Arabic literature have been published recently in the United States that the scholar Waïl Hassan, writing in the 2014–2015 State of the Discipline report for the American Comparative Literature Association, identified "an unprecedented boom in literary translation from Arabic" as among the marquee features of a twenty-first-century "age of globalization" presently overtaking the U.S. cultural field.[3] According to figures from a database maintained by the Three Percent initiative and Open Letter Books at the University of Rochester, 328 original English translations of works of Arabic fiction and poetry were published in the United States between 2008 and 2022.[4] The majority of these were released by independent and academic presses, traditionally the mainstay of translated literature in the United States; and yet notably during this period, several larger commercial trade publishers began to add works of translated Arabic literature to their catalogs as well.[5]

Various explanations have been proposed for these developments. In Hassan's view, the recent manifold increase in the number of translated Arabic literary works arriving in the U.S. market follows from "the logic of 'Know Your Enemy' [that] imposed itself [in the United States] on the heels of the Second Intifada of September 2000 and the terrorist attacks of September 2001," as Americans continue to seek out information about the Arabophone region that could help them better understand its apparently congenital hostility toward the West and antipathy toward Western ideals.[6] Along similar lines, Robyn Creswell has argued that any receptivity to translated Arabic literature that the U.S. literary field evinces today relative to the late twentieth century cannot be dissociated from the array of newsworthy happenings—beginning with the attacks of September 11, 2001—that have kept the Arabic-speaking Middle East perennially in the thoughts of the American public in the current era.[7] For this reason, Creswell maintains, although Arabic literature is "no longer embargoed" from the U.S. market, "to translate anything from the Arabic" remains "an act with immediate and often explicit political significance."[8] More optimistically, the literary critic Claudia Roth Pierpont has suggested that

Americans are drawn to reading translated Arabic literature because it provides "a marvellous array of answers to questions we did not know we wanted to ask," about "how people live in Cairo or Beirut or Riyadh" and "think and work and suffer and fall in love and make enemies and sometimes make revolutions."[9]

It is not the goal of this book to adjudicate among these multiple rationales for translated Arabic literature's newfound prominence in the United States, nor do I hazard an alternative explanation for this situation, other than in provisional terms in the conclusion. There are undoubtedly many motivations that might drive a U.S. publisher to acquire translation rights for a work of Arabic fiction or a member of the American public to purchase a work of Arabic literature in translation to read—some admirable, and some more troubling. Without surveying a plurality of actual publishers and readers as to why they have done these things or might do them in the future, I can say nothing more on this point.

Instead, this book proposes that when Arabic literature ceases to be embargoed, new typologies of worldliness are opened up to it by the mere fact of its circulation in English. Arabic literature that can be read in English translation is positioned to distribute the resonances of Arabic literary language across a new linguistic field. It does so, this book contends, via concrescences of body and text that refigure the dialectics of self and other that Said envisaged into a range of embodied encounters between an Anglophone translator or reader, on the one hand, and the material formations of Arabic's own literariness, on the other. A concrescence marks a coming together and a burgeoning outward of two unlike but entwined things, an event of becoming-worldly that leads to gains in capacity and extension for both parties involved. (To think of worldliness as an eventual state—the achievement of a process of "becoming" in Gilles Deleuze and Félix Guattari's sense—is once again to differentiate my approach from Said's, for whom a text's worldliness is a circumstantially, contextually, historically "incorporated" given, "an infrangible part of its capacity for conveying and producing meaning.")[10] As the body of an Anglophone translator or reader rubs up against, conjoins with, or is impinged upon by the linguistic material of an Arabic literary text—and as Arabic and English themselves are brought into arrangements of contiguity, coalescence, and co-implication by an act of literary translation—Arabic literature is affirmed as mattering in the world affectively, aesthetically, and as *literature.*

Such mattering could not be reduced to that of a commodity that travels through international networks of reception and consumption as an avatar of a monolithic cultural identity: Arabic literature in translation acting as a prosthetic for an Orient that has long served as the "cultural contestant" of the Euro-American West, and simultaneously as "one of its deepest and most recurring images of the Other," as Said put it in *Orientalism*.[11] Nor can translation itself in this regard be viewed principally as a procedure of "cross-cultural interpretation," to quote from Lydia Liu's critique of postcolonial theory's account of translingual interactions between Western and non-Western societies that end up "treating the concrete language issue . . . as a superfluity or merely part of a critique of the effects of colonialism and imperialism."[12] Following Liu's example, I offer here an alternative to postcolonial theory–inflected models for studying the translation of Arabic literature into English, one that is premised not upon sweeping assessments of the cultural encounters that translation facilitates but instead upon recovering a "dynamic history of the relationship between words, concepts, categories, and discourse" that translation mobilizes within and between languages.[13]

A Blooming of Ethics

In adopting this approach, I remain at the same time profoundly alert to the ethical questions that scholars grounded in postcolonial thought and its various offshoots have long posed about the otherness of non-Western literary traditions in the Anglophone literary field. Not doing away with the Saidian dichotomy of self and other so much as stretching it and augmenting it, threading it through with a multiplicity of connecting strands that pass not between civilizations but among translators and texts, readers and texts, and translators and readers, this book identifies sites and moments in the history of the translation of Arabic literature into English since the colonial era when events of translating and reading bloom into something like an ethics of engaging the other in the contingent affective spaces to which literature yields access. This genealogy of practices of translating and reading Arabic literature in English runs in parallel to the geopolitical narrative of Orientalism from the Crusades onward that Said excavated, and which has often served in the Anglophone academy as a guideline for the diachronic study of Arabic literature in Euro-American cultural contexts.[14] To the extent that the genealogy that I am proposing intersects with this narrative, as it does particularly in the second and fourth chapters of this book, it does so in ways that press upon this dominant story to become itself more capacious, more accepting of how and where the literary flourishes within and alongside the political. In this manner, I aim to continue what Hosam Aboul-Ela identified in 2010 as the work of "a new generation of scholars [of Arabic literature] in the United States" who are turning away from "the method of colonial discourse analysis as articulated by Said, his contemporaries, and his students" to focus instead on "Arab letters" as a creative corpus ripe for scholarly examination in its own right, separable from questions of how Arabic literature and culture are (mis)recognized by the Western gaze or appropriated reductively for Western use.[15]

Aamir Mufti has argued that world literature in its current conception was inaugurated through "the assimilation of vastly dispersed and heterogenous writing practices and traditions" from non-European regions, notably the Arabophone and Persophone Middle East and the Indian subcontinent, into a late eighteenth-century European literary arena structured by "rivalries between the emerging vernacular traditions" of multiple European nation-states. By Mufti's account, Arabic aesthetic writing came to be recognized historically in the West as "literature" via a related process, whereby the preexisting diversity of modes of Arabic literary expression were repackaged under a single classificatory heading consonant with the paradigms of the European bourgeois space within which it would thenceforth circulate.[16] This book embraces a basis for Arabic literature's literariness that precedes and far exceeds its absorption into Western textual schema, while nevertheless not disavowing the worldliness that it gains when it becomes recognizable also within these schema.

Each of this book's chapters takes as its focal point the translation into English of a figuration or principle of the Arabic language whose literariness I identify, in accordance with the precepts of the classical Arabic science of language (*ʿilm al-lughah*), as deriving from its manifest usages in various autochthonous linguistic contexts.[17] By choosing such "small linguistic units" around which to build my argument, I follow in a historic tradition of Arabic aesthetic theory that, as Lara Harb has noted, tended to home in on particularized "literary figures and linguistic structures" as the central aspects of a text that made it capable of provoking an aesthetic experience in an audience.[18]

The first half of this book considers the translation of material elements in the literary language of two premodern Arabic texts: Aḥmad Fāris al-Shidyāq's 1855 fictional travel narrative *al-Sāq ʿalā al-sāq fī mā huwa al-Fāriyāq*, and the *Alf laylah wa-laylah* or "Arabian Nights" stories. In chapter 1, "Sonics of *Lafẓ*: Translating Arabic Acoustics for Anglophone Ears," I examine how the linguistic form (*lafẓ*) of al-Shidyāq's literary Arabic, as differentiated from its semantic content (*maʿnā*), is translated in the auditory qualities of translator Humphrey Davies's virtuosic English writing in *Leg over Leg or, The Turtle in the Tree* (2013–2014). In chapter 2,

"Vulgarity of *Saj'*: The Scandalous Pleasures of Burton's *The Book of the Thousand Nights and a Night*," I explore how the nineteenth-century British Orientalist Sir Richard Francis Burton turned to an oral and a vulgar register of English to translate the characteristic Arabic rhymed prose (*saj'*) of the *Nights* stories in *The Book of the Thousand Nights and a Night* (1885–1888). In both cases, what cannot be translated from Arabic into English via straightforward exchanges of meaning compels the translator to activate an affective register of his own language to convey the embodied effects, if not the literal significances, of the words that he translates.

The second half of the book examines the translations of two contemporary works of Arabic literature that mobilize the affective resonances of English to intervene ethically and politically in how Arabic literature comes to circulate in the Anglophone literary field in the twenty-first century. In chapter 3, "Ethics of the *Muthannā*: Caring for the Other in a Mother Tongue," I cast a critical eye on my own translation of Lebanese author Hilāl Shūmān's 2013 novel *Līmbū Bayrūt* (*Limbo Beirut*, 2016). Identifying two elements within Shūmān's Arabic text that lack English equivalents—the Arabic *muthannā*, or dual inflection, and the Arabic alphabet—this chapter shows how I translated each with care for its aesthetic role in Shūmān's novel by deploying my body as a medium for the translation process. In chapter 4, "*'Ajamī* Politics and Aesthetic Experience: Translating the Body in Pain," I investigate the political implications of translating Arabic literature into English in light of the recent history of violence inflicted upon Arab bodies by the American state. Examining Iraqi author Sinān Anṭūn's self-translation, with Rebecca C. Johnson, of his 2004 novel *I'jām* (*I'jaam: An Iraqi Rhapsody*, 2007), which was published in the United States at the height of the Iraq War (2003–2011), this chapter explores how the English text transmutes the original text's wordplay based on the orthographic convention of *i'jām* (the dotting of letters in the Arabic alphabet) into an aesthetic experience for readers capable of unsettling a normative collective structure of feelings around the war in the American public sphere.

Exemplifying the aesthetic potential of Arabic linguistic form, phonetics, grammar, and orthography, the elements of language that I examine across these four chapters elude precisely the kinds of assimilative procedures that were employed to bring Arabic literature into line with European models and categories during the colonial era. Yet, as I show, each is nonetheless translatable into English, the hegemonic "global literary vernacular" of world literature today—if one whose hegemony is, as I argue contra Mufti, more ethically complex than its critics are often apt to acknowledge.[19] By comparing the Arabic version of each work of literature under study with its English translation to show how material elements of Arabic literary language are registered in the affective reverberations of literary English, I dispute on evidentiary grounds the notion that Arabic literature must be essentially unsuited to Anglophone modes of aesthetic expression. The collection of case studies that my book amasses not only proves the translatability of Arabic literature but also demonstrates how an account of its existence in the world literary system that begins from the premise of its translatability—rather than from an assumption of its untranslatable alterity—situates it relationally rather than differentially within this system.

The interactions between Anglophone translators and readers and Arabic literary texts that I examine function to position Arabic literature in the world relative to the responses that it triggers in a body. To engage the other in this way is not to encounter it as Gayatri Chakravorty Spivak's "quite-other" that "by definition" we cannot reach, and which, ethically, we must not reach, given that its identity as itself depends on its remaining other to us—for the other that is the Arabic text is precisely what is reached, and even touched, through the procedures of translating and reading that this book delineates.[20] These encounters transpire aurally, when a body apprehends words as "sonic edifices" whose sonority and rhythms register "enactments or embodiments of forms of life and self" taking shape within the immanent aesthetic movements of language, as Khaled Furani has described.[21] They are activated haptically, when touching and being touched by language becomes constitutive of the process of translating or reading a work of literature from a position of "meaningful adjacency" to it, in Adam Zachary Newton's formulation. "What sort of *alteration* (ethical othering) follows from being neighbored" to a text in this way, Newton wonders, "and it to me, in sensible proximity? What phenomenological meaning can be assigned to those book-holding hands" of a translator or reader, for whom to engage with Arabic literary language is to be changed by it on a physiological level?[22]

Recalling that Spivak elsewhere refers to translating as "the most intimate act of reading," it is no accident that the translators and readers of Arabic literature whose activities I study in this book are often one and the same personages.[23] To hear, touch, or otherwise interact affectively with a text while reading it *as* a translator is to perform a gesture of "world-making," as María Puig de la Bellacasa calls it, that "undermines the grounds of the invulnerable, untouched position of the master-subject agent" while simultaneously reminding us that "what we do in, to, a world can come back, re-affect someone somehow." Translating as world-making unfurls as a recursive movement that always "carries ethical resonance."[24]

Locating an ethics of translation in the bare affective ties that link a self to an other, I recognize the body as the place where the self/other relationship is negotiated, and where both self and other are unmade and remade relationally. In such minimal involvements with the other's body, such acts of reaching toward the other for the sake of becoming entangled in the net of intensities that it casts out into the world, ethical responsibility hangs as delicately as the promise of an action that just might do right by the other, an affective impulse toward the other's care.

Whereas the ethics of translation articulated in the first two chapters of this book rests on a translator's capacity to make Arabic literature's literariness legible to the bodies of Anglophone readers, in the third and fourth chapters it is the bodies within the literary texts that render the labor of translating Arabic literature into English an ethical practice. The events of translation described in this book take shape between and among the various bodies, both real and fictional, that connect Arabic literature into the world by means of the affects that Arabic literary language provokes, enables, and transmits. When the affective resonances of Arabic literary language are translated into the linguistic formations of English, Arabic makes English literary, and English makes Arabic worldly. To attend to such events of making-literary and making-worldly, as they constellate into something like a historical chronology of how Arabic and English have engaged each other aesthetically since the first English translations of the *Alf laylah wa-laylah* stories appeared in the early eighteenth century, allows me to reconceptualize the translational dynamics of such interlingual meetings. The otherness of the Arabic language serves here not as a quality of difference that either impels English to submit to its inchoate strangeness or triggers its aggression, its jingoistic hatred of what is alien to its own familiar avenues of expression. Rather than yield to this tragically binary choice (one that has underpinned so many discussions of the ethics of translating into English from supposedly marginal or minor languages), English in the translations that I examine embodies Arabic within its own affective material to produce an array of new literary configurations and conjunctions.

In making this argument, this book is indebted to the account of translation between Arabic and its colonial counterparts French and English from the late eighteenth through mid-twentieth centuries that Shaden Tageldin provides in *Disarming Words: Empire and the Seductions of Translation in Egypt*. Eschewing simplistic polarities of self and other, Tageldin reveals the asymmetrical power dynamics of translation in such circumstances to be undercut by the desire of languages and language users to seduce and be seduced by what is other to the self, betokening "a politics that welds rupture to rapture . . . by making its object believe that rupture is coterminous with the past, that subject and object are one and the same."[25] If translation always involves instances of breakage, incommensurability, and untranslatability, then Tageldin insists on the necessity also of looking to activities of intimacy, copulation, and even love that occur across the unequal sign of dissimilarity and nonequivalence that translation predicates. It is only by giving due heed to such activities, I assert here—in a gesture of solidarity with Tageldin—that a study of translation can begin to move beyond seeing only the differences between languages and attend instead to their history of inter-implication and mutually assured transformation.

Translating into English

Compared to the book markets in many other languages, the slice of the Anglophone publishing industry that is dedicated to the publication of literature in translation is vanishingly small. This is especially true in the United States, where, according to a much-lamented statistic, only around 3 percent of all new titles published annually are translations, and less than a third of these are literary translations specifically.[26] The U.S. market's resistance to translated literature has been attributed variously to xenophobia, indifference, or laziness, and in all cases is seen as revealing a culture that is "aggressively monolingual" in its preferences.[27] Moreover, there is so much English-language literature published worldwide each year that Anglophone readers desiring to expand their literary horizons can range nonexhaustively through these offerings without ever needing to turn to texts written originally in other languages.[28] Although translated literature overall has achieved modest gains in status in the U.S. literary field in the current millennium, for most U.S. Anglophone readers it remains at the peripheries of what is recognized as literature, and certainly as literature that could be enjoyed for its pleasurable aesthetic qualities.[29] Given these circumstances, translators who hang their proverbial hats on translating literature from other languages into English, so the conventional wisdom goes, must be either renegades or fools, laboring for the love of the text rather than with any expectation of reaping profit or fame from their efforts.[30]

In an academic context, however, the labors of Anglophone translators have been more often measured by their politics than by their dispensations of love and affection toward the texts and languages involved. On the one hand, Anglophone translators have been sometimes framed as innately empowered, by virtue of their role as cultural mediators, to counter the dominant ideological and economic trends of a literary field that has long devalued foreign literature. By this logic, the act of translating into English is charged automatically with the potential to acquire a "cultural political" momentum capable of "unsettling" normative hierarchies and "smashing" artistic canons within the Anglophone literary sphere, as Lawrence Venuti argues in *The Translator's Invisibility: A History of Translation*.[31] From an opposite angle, however, other critics have affiliated the politics of translating into English with the reification of the hegemonic place of English in today's global literary sphere. In this regard, Aamir Mufti contends in his memorably titled book *Forget English! Orientalisms and World Literatures* that English is the language in which all non-Anglophone literatures must be made readable today if they are to be ranked as world literature. English, Mufti writes, operates in the present as a "vanishing mediator" for the circulation of texts, ideas, and information on a transnational scale, having become so profoundly and constitutively enmeshed in the signal cultural, social, financial, political, and epistemological structures of a planetary twenty-first-century modernity that its function in these capacities has become all but imperceptible.[32]

Translators of Arabic literature into English are by no means exempt from this "double bind" of potential and risk, as Spivak might call it.[33] Arabic literature when it is translated into English has typically been understood to enter the "world republic of letters" from a language and a region that are "peripheral" to those in which this republic's primary operations are carried out.[34] For this reason, critics including Roger Allen, Marilyn Booth, Issa Boullata, Michelle Hartman, and Nirvana Tanoukhi have called for methods of translating Arabic literature into English that would confront Anglophone readers with the linguistic, cultural, and locational particularities of the source text in ways disruptive to the ease and fluency of the reading experience. Only through such a methodology, so the argument goes, can Arabic literature's deficit of cultural capital relative to the Anglophone literary field for which it is destined be at least partly surmounted.[35] Hartman, for one, building on Venuti's notion of "foreignizing" versus "domesticating" translations, has proposed that in light of "Arabic's problematic colonial relationship with English," any Anglophone translator of Arabic literature should employ "foreignizing" techniques that reverse this power dynamic, including preserving Arabic proper nouns in situ in the English text and retaining generic features of the source text that unsettle genre norms in Anglophone literary discourse. By adopting such strategies to make the translating language scan unidiomatically for Anglophone readers, Hartman suggests, the translator would "emphasize the difference of the foreign text" contra the overwhelming pressure toward conformity that obtains across the contemporary Anglophone literary field.[36]

All of these aforementioned critics view the Arabic-to-English translator as occupying a position of authority vis-à-vis the Arabic text, within a discursive regime that privileges English writing over Arabic writing, and Anglophone translators over Arabophone authors, as sources of mimetic and epistemological truth. The burden of representation that the Arabic-to-English translator thus bears, according to this model, mirrors that of the Bengali-to-English translator in Spivak's 1992 essay "The Politics of Translation," an essay whose intimate portrait of Spivak's own translation practice—described by her as a delicate process of conveying a subaltern alterity out of its indigenous linguistic context and into one alien to it, carried out at great peril to the well-being of this other for whom the translator's task had made her ethically responsible—was foundational to the discourse of translation ethics that emerged in the Euro-American academy from the 1990s onward.[37] When the translator plays the part of a "literate, institutionally empowered critic or theorist [who] seeks to articulate in writing the heretofore unheard experience, perspective, and interests located at subject positions that have not previously had access to such articulation," in Henry Staten's gloss, this scenario all but guarantees that translating should be "fundamentally an ethical task."[38]

Yet how do the coordinates of translation ethics shift when the otherness of the Arabic text is understood not as a quality inherently at odds with the fluency of Anglophone textuality, as Hartman, for example, would have it, but rather as that which has the potential to make English *more* (rather than less) aesthetically pleasing to an Anglophone reader: more expressive of its own literariness, more expansively and virtuosically itself?

In light of the charges that have been leveled against English as a translating language and as the language of world literature in the present age, my methodology that emphasizes language rather than culture, and aesthetic form rather than mimetic content, in charting the workings of literary translation from Arabic into English allows me to recuperate English from its unhappy affiliations with the politics and practices of language hegemony in the world literary system. Again following Lydia Liu's example, I invert her proposition that "a non-European language does not automatically constitute a site of resistance to European languages" to argue that English does not automatically constitute an agent of imperialist aggressions against Arabic.[39] To the contrary, I maintain that an ethical mode of translating Arabic literature into English can be divined in how English addresses itself to Arabic from *within* its role as the dominant or hegemonic language of the world literary arena, insofar as Arabic literature's literariness becomes paradigmatically worldly when it is translated into English precisely *because* English occupies this privileged position.

An ethics of translation centered on preserving the aesthetics of the source and target languages alike via embodied methods of engaging with both does more than proffer a "code of conduct" for translators, as the French translation scholar Henri Meschonnic has suggested.[40] Ethically, Meschonnic argues, "it is what a text does that must be translated; more than the meaning, its power, its affect," so that the proper object of translation is not the linguistic sign *per se*, but the "body-in-language" that signifies itself via the rhythms and movements of words.[41] Meschonnic's model of embodied translation finds echoes in the work of Douglas Robinson, who has described translating as a "primarily somatic" process in which words in two languages can be judged equivalent when they "feel the same" to a translator.[42] I engage with Robinson's arguments in more depth in chapter 3. Yet neither of these thinkers has been especially influential in molding the discourse of Anglophone translation studies in the contemporary era.[43] A vigorous academic conversation in English around the role of affects and the body in the practices and ethics of literary translation has yet to emerge.

While such scholarship remains relatively thin, however, there exists among Anglophone translators an inventory of anecdotal accounts detailing the affective and material registers in which they must operate to do right by the literariness of a source text. For Peter Cole, a translator of Hebrew and Arabic poetry, "the study of ethics in the context of literary translation should concern the ways to best realize translation's true nature as a carrier or embodiment of the highest *literary* good" (the emphasis on "literary" is Cole's own). An ethical translation practice, he insists, will thus embrace translation as "something that happens along, or under, the skin: a tangential sensation, one that is rooted not in ideology, not even in good will or fellow feeling, but in syntactical, rhythmic, and acoustic experience."[44] Elliott Colla, a scholar and translator of Arabic literature, writes of "sub-lexical aspects of language that create sense, but not at the level of denotation," and which must be translated into English as "energy, not meaning" or through dynamic processes of "transduction" and conversion. Embraced for their fullest aesthetic potential, such elements of an Arabic literary text "cast shimmering semantic auras across texts" in both languages, Colla maintains.[45] For Robyn Creswell, who like Colla is a translator as well as a scholar of Arabic literature, a good translation is one that actualizes the source text's "potential for making sense—including, of course, aesthetic sense" in the target language. In

Creswell's estimation, this outcome can be achieved only when translators are prepared to deal with language in "larger units than the word: the shape and syntax of sentences, the tone of voice, the weight of a phrase," taking "patterns rather than instances of usage" as the principal modality of their practice.[46]

Such a translation practice, Creswell continues, quoting translation theorist George Steiner, reveals "the radical generosity of the translator" who has produced it. Requiring "a gesture of 'initiative trust'" on the part of the translator "that there is 'something there'" in the source text to be translated, and therefore "that the transfer will not be void," translating for the sake of making aesthetic sense of the source language in the translating idiom enacts a translation ethics founded on the assumption of the other language's basic translatability.[47] Steiner himself writes in *After Babel: Aspects of Language and Translation* that for a translator confronted with everything in a source text that cannot "be divorced from its formal autonomy"—including "nonsense rhymes," "glossolalia," and other elements of literary language that appear "untranslatable because they are lexically non-communicative or deliberately insignificant"—the "sensation comes very close to being tactile," as though of words that have become "only themselves, blank and replete as stone."[48] The immanent materiality of language engages a translator as a bodily sensation, its tactility physically constituted to such a degree that words become things in the world.

If the body/language nexus in translation has remained underexamined within a scholarly discourse preoccupied with the politics of translation as a mechanism of intercultural or informational exchange, then this omission exposes a disjuncture between academic views of translation and a legacy of testimonial and experiential accounts from translators that assert translation as an aesthetic process grounded in the sensations of language. To acknowledge the sensorial dimensions of translating calls to mind perhaps most canonically the declaration by Saint Jerome, translator of the Bible into Latin, that he preferred to translate "not word for word, but sense for sense."[49] In justifying a translation practice based on sensory rather than literal equivalences, Jerome claimed to be following a precedent set by past Roman translators (among them the philosopher Cicero and the poet Horace) who chose not to "simply cling to the words" of their source texts but "rather [to] conserve the greater beauty and elegance" of these works in their translations.[50] The implications of these remarks by this fourth-century CE translator have been much debated by critics.[51] Maria Tymoczko interprets Jerome's notion of sense in the formulation "sense for sense" ("*sensum exprimere de sensu*") as "probably signif[ying] 'the gist' of the text" in the source language, indicating for her that Jerome and his fellow Romans held a "fairly utilitarian" view of translation as mainly a pragmatic tool for making information accessible in Latin that had previously been available exclusively in other languages.[52] Yet Tymoczko's interpretation, I would suggest, misses the extent to which a sense-based translation practice is associated specifically for Jerome with the preservation of the source text's aesthetic and material aspects: its "beauty and elegance" ("*decorem . . . et elegantiam*"), or what he refers to more generally as "the properties of other languages" ("*proprietates alterius linguae*") insofar as these can be made evident within a translator's own idiom.[53] Might it not be that what Jerome intends by "properties" in this context is not so different from the immanent qualities of literary language that give it its "formal autonomy" in Steiner's terms?

If the aesthetics of a text reside at least partly—or perhaps even essentially—in its material formations, and if this linguistic material necessitates that a translator shift into a sensorial and embodied register in order to translate it, then the translation practices that this book explores carry an ethical imperative. To translate the literariness of an Arabic text into English, and in so doing, to make this text make sense to Anglophone readers—to make it readable in English in an affective and a sensual register—is to translate Arabic literature into English with care for the text in its fullness, and with optimism as well for what literature can do in the world. This optimism, too, utopic though it may be, holds ethical potential; it is a radically generous offering from a translator or critic to the text, literary tradition, or language that stands poised for translation, an entrustment of its translatability and an affirmation of its incipient worldliness.

The Literariness of Arabic Literature

With respect to how Arabic literature has been both studied and read in an Anglophone context, it has been deaestheticized in several ways at once. As Mohamed-Salah Omri explains, because the favored paradigms employed to "articulate the difference of Arabic literature" in a comparative framework have been those "inspired by Said's critique of Orientalism and postcolonial theory"—in which "discourse is preferred over form, meaning over construction of meaning, context over text"—Arabic literature "remains almost absent" from "more specialized areas of literary studies" in the Anglophone academy.[54] More broadly, Tarek El-Ariss has noted the paucity of rigorous theoretical engagement with Arabic literary texts across a range of Anglophone academic disciplines in the present millennium, wherein these texts have "remained confined to their contexts as anthropological artifacts" rather than being read as "aesthetic objects . . . [that] bear on the way we understand general concepts."[55] It is my hope that the critical approach to examining Arabic literature in English translation that this book adopts, which gives far greater attention both to the aesthetics of these texts and to their wide-ranging and generalizable theoretical potential, can contribute to improving this situation.

Beyond making this intervention into how Arabic literature has been addressed in English-language scholarly contexts, this book derives another crucial raison d'être for its methodology from how translated Arabic literature has tended to be received by the reading public of the United States. Discussing the reception of Arabic literature in English translation in the United States, Dima Ayoub notes that because "monolingual English readers expect Arabic literature to reflect monolithic representations of the Arab world," it "has endured considerable difficulties in the Anglo-American context."[56] Chief among the challenges faced by Arabic literary texts in this regard, according to the translator and scholar Marilyn Booth, is that they have been read not as fiction but as "windows on the world" that they seem to portray.[57] In pedagogical settings, works of Arabic literature in English translation are most often circumscribed within "classroom discussions of faraway cultures," as the poet and translator Mona Kareem observes;[58] in public discourse, they are treated "not as works of art, but as ethnographic glimpses into the mind and culture of the 'Other.'"[59] Even as the sum total of Arabic literary titles translated into English increases—a trend that began at the end of the last century and has accelerated dramatically in the current millennium—this can never guarantee that "Western readers . . . have launched intellectual and aesthetic journeys into other worlds," as Jenine Abboushi Dallal wrote in the late 1990s, or that these readers will take an "interest" in individual works of Arabic literature based on more than their thematic or mimetic content.[60] In Booth's assessment, among Anglophone audiences overall, "Arabic literature is not allowed to have aesthetics."[61]

While I cannot reasonably expect that the arguments I make in this book will reach a sufficiently wide readership to alter the perceptions of Arabic literature in the Anglophone literary field on a broad scale, to a certain extent they may not need to. To rethink the reading of Arabic literature as an embodied process is to embrace the possibility that literature can affect readers at a depth level below conscious recognition, circumventing the relevance of what "interests" a reader—in Dallal's formulation—and routing around the intellectual opinions and attitudes that any particular person brings to a text. I am not claiming that

Anglophone audiences have never read, or no longer read, Arabic literature in order "to comprehend how each text 'reflects' Arab reality," as Magda Al-Nowaihi proposed in 2004. Nor would I advocate for this "mimetic model of simple reflection" to be overturned in favor of a return to a "notion of the universality of the aesthetic," a solution that Al-Nowaihi rightly critiques for being almost certain to reinforce a narrowly Eurocentric vision of what literature is or ought to be artistically.[62] Rather, I ask in this book what it is of the specifically *Arabic* aesthetics of a source text that an English translation can or should transmit, and how, in so doing, this translation might become capable of furnishing its readers with a means of access not to the "reality" within the Arabic literary work, but to its literariness.

Hosam Aboul-Ela asks "what happens when we turn our attention to the formal qualities" of literature while remaining alert to "the current dynamics of global culture" that play out in an international literary field fraught with structural and epistemic inequalities that privilege the Euro-American Global North over the postcolonial Global South. Must "geopolitical context . . . necessarily be discarded in favor of technical questions," he wonders? To the extent that "literature's very literariness tends to defer" always and already any analysis that yokes texts too bindingly to geopolitics, can an examination of literary form provide a congenial basis for exploring an Arabic literary work's imbrications in the world as it is constructed geographically, historically, economically, politically?[63] By maintaining throughout this book that the embodied experiences produced by a text engender identifiable ethical opportunities within the literary field in which it circulates, I show that the aesthetic need not be opposed to the geopolitical but can rather be constitutive of how geopolitics is lived affectively among a population of readers, for whom to read a work of Arabic literature in English translation is to participate on an affective level in the whole matrix of relations that have linked the Arabophone Middle East to the Anglophone West over the past several centuries.

Simply to read works of Arabic literature that have been translated in such a way that their literariness is transmitted into the vibrant affects of literary English, I contend, is already and inevitably to be changed by having done so. In making this claim, I take a cue from Heather Love's notion of "close" but not "deep" reading, wherein a reader sidesteps "the metaphysical and humanist concerns of hermeneutics" upon which many standard interpretative paradigms are based to move lightly instead across the surface of a text, describing rather than interpreting it, alert to its exteriorizing gestures of historical documentation or social critique. Such a mode of reading, because it "does not depend on the ethical exemplarity of the interpreter or messenger," is envisaged by Love as enabling the emergence of a resilient, egalitarian kind of critical ethics.[64] In like manner, I propose that for reading Arabic literature in English translation to produce a resonant and transformative encounter between a reader and a text does not depend on the skillsets of an especially well-intentioned or qualified Anglophone reading public, but that this comes to pass instead through the merest instances of a reader's relational affective engagements with the materiality of literary language as it is conveyed in translation.

Differently from Love, however, I see ethics working not by a reader's remaining staunchly outside the text, but by meeting the text on a level plane or "plane of consistency," as Gilles Deleuze and Félix Guattari would call it.[65] On this plane, the reading body cedes its borders to flows of affect from the text's own language, sensible manifestations of its literariness escaping outward and extensively into the world. Through these processes, iteratively and recursively, an Arabic literary text in translation is affirmed as literary insofar as its language affects readers physiologically. Literary aesthetics become a worldly phenomenon coterminous with the embodied experiences that literature purveys. Here Nicholas Dames's account of reading literature as entailing a processual series of sensible interactions with a text's formal elements, in *The Physiology of the Novel: Reading, Neural Science, and the Form of Victorian Fiction*, serves as a valuable intertext for my argument. Guided by "rhythms of attention and inattention, slow comprehension and rapid skipping ahead, buildups and discharges of affect," reading as Dames describes it unfolds as "a performance enacted in and by the nerves."[66]

In a similar regard, I have profited from Robyn Warhol's insights in *Having a Good Cry: Effeminate Feelings and Pop-Culture Forms*, which demonstrates through an examination of the particularized somatic responses that popular "forms" of fiction produce in their audiences that "whatever else it may entail, reading always happens in and to a body."[67] Gleaned through interviews, case studies, and personal experience, Warhol's findings record a choreography of tears, smiles, and wrinkled foreheads, gasps and shivers, racing heartbeats and clenched muscles that inscribe the affects of reading across the body's inner and outer surfaces. Building beyond such subjective and self-reported portraits of readerly affect as Warhol offers, Rachel Greenwald Smith argues in *Affect and American Literature in the Age of Neoliberalism* for the social and political salience of the "impersonal" affects that interlink among the "human and nonhuman beings and things" out of which a modern literary system is composed.[68] Tending to "often go unrecognized on an intuitive level," such affects, she proposes, "become visible only when traced in particular formal gestures" that literary texts employ to arrange a reading public into configurations of shared affective sensibility.[69]

Considering the affects that rebound across multiple literary systems when Arabic literature is read in English translation invites us not only to rethink how and why Arabic literature comes to matter in the world republic of letters to which translation grants it access, but also to reassess the nature of the world in which it circulates. The seventeenth-century philosopher Baruch Spinoza posited a human body extending outward into the world and thus into broadcast range of the affects of the world's other embodied inhabitants, so that when they are "affected with an affect, we are affected with a like affect." Could the world of world literature be rethought as a Spinozan world of bodies, each one "determined to motion or rest by another body, which has also been determined to motion or rest by another, and that again by another, and so on, to infinity?"[70] Building on this idea, Pierre Bourdieu's concept of "taste," indexing a text's collective reception to a hierarchized regime of cultural prestige, could be reconceived as a type of "stickiness" in Sara Ahmed's sense, designating a readership's communal *affective* positionality vis-à-vis the text in question.[71] Ahmed cites Spinoza's contemporary John Locke—according to whom, in her paraphrase, "we judge something to be good or bad according to how it affects us, whether it gives us pleasure or pain"—and doubles down on the fundamental physicality of both the pleasurable and the painful in this regard. If we recognize, as Ahmed does, an evaluative judgment implicit in "how bodies turn toward things," then affects provide a metric of reception on a worldly scale distinct from that through which literature's merits have more traditionally been measured.[72]

Drawing on a lineage of affect theory that reaches from Spinoza to Ahmed and beyond, in which affects are posited as the external forces that act on a body to suture it relationally into the sensible, material environment of things and bodies around it, my book presents a study not only of how texts become worldly but of what happens to those who translate and read these worldly texts. In accounting for how the English translations of Arabic literary texts that I examine transform the translating and reading bodies with which they come into contact, I profit from Brian Massumi's notion of affects as nonconscious autonomous intensities emancipated from the exigencies of teleological narration and cognition, as they are described in *Parables for the Virtual: Movement, Affect, Sensation*;[73] Teresa Brennan's arguments in *The Transmission of Affect* for viewing affects as transmissible energetically among bodies held in proximity through spatial and social structures; and Tarek El-Ariss's proposal to deploy affects as a heuristic alternative to mimetic approaches for studying Arabic literature, as exemplified in *Trials of Arab Modernity: Literary Affects and the New Political* and *Leaks, Hacks, and Scandals: Arab Culture in the Digital Age.*

Within the literary formations of English, the literariness of an Arabic text reverberates, if in a different language, in a host of new collective reception contexts, and within, upon, and against a range of new bodily surfaces and orifices. Mara Naaman has proposed, with reference to Bourdieu's notion of a cultural field "configured as a network of relations" between the aesthetics internal to literary texts and the external conditions of these texts' production and reception, that insofar as works of Arabic literature circulate today both locally and internationally, in Arabic as well as in translation, "one cannot disengage the[ir] literariness" from their existence in a multilingual world literary system.[74] Yet where Naaman, following Richard Jacquemond's arguments in *Conscience of the Nation: Writers, State, and Society in Modern Egypt*, advocates ultimately for the priority of national frameworks in determining the layout of a contemporary Arabic literary field embedded within the structures of the larger world republic of letters, I propose that this field is no less shaped today by forces that originate from outside an Arabophone context.[75]

My intention is not to suggest that Arabic literature in the present era becomes worldly only to the degree that individual works of Arabic literature conform to a single homogenous set of international standards or tastes, as some have argued,[76] nor to imply that the nation no longer matters in shaping the form and content of modern Arabic literary output. (Indeed, paying homage to a rich and far from obsolete tradition of scholarship that has focalized the study of Arabic literature through the prism of national histories and national imaginaries, my arguments in the third and fourth chapters of this book engage explicitly with the relationship between the literary texts under examination and the national contexts in which the events depicted in their narratives unfold.) Rather, I propose that the literariness of Arabic literature as world literature must be seen as a holistic property accruing to a collection of texts whose range now spans into many countries and languages, and as one that therefore relies not only on the aesthetic formations of Arabic but as well on those of English and the other languages into which Arabic literature is translated and in which it is read today.[77]

To the extent that I define Arabic literature's literariness in this book partly as a quality acquired by texts that are *read as* literary by various audiences and in various times and locations, my argument converges with the account that Michael Allan gives of how Arabic literature, or *adab*, "became literary" in *In the Shadow of World Literature: Sites of Reading in Colonial Egypt*. For Allan, Arabic literature derives its literariness jointly from the formal aesthetic properties of the individual works of Arabic writing that bear the label of *adab*, and from the fact that these works' passage through the world is facilitated by disciplinary and institutional frameworks that treat them as literature. The former aspect of Arabic literature's literariness can be ascertained through techniques of close reading; the latter requires a critic to be "focused not on *what* but *how* texts are read," and thus to "shift away from mimesis as the foundational category of literary theory to consider the disciplines and practices that inscribe how literature comes to matter."[78] Allan's study holds these two approaches purposefully in tension, employing a historically and geographically particularized investigation of how Arabic literature evolved in Egypt in the nineteenth and early twentieth centuries to undergird a broader exploration of what Arabic literature *is* formally and aesthetically. From tracing the singular history of Arabic literature's emergent literariness in one geographic setting, Allan telescopes outward in other parts of his book to examine how Arabic literature intersects with, is informed by, and sometimes intervenes in the material and conceptual apparatuses of a transnational, secular world literary system.

The premise that literature is constituted as such through the codeterminative operations of literary form and forms of literary praxis, especially those practices predicated on reading, is a cornerstone of Allan's argument; as a basic premise, he takes "disciplines, practices, and sensibilities to be as inseparable from the understanding of literary form as the institutions (libraries, presses, or schools) that make the concept of literature itself thinkable."[79] My inquiry into how Arabic literature's literariness is reified and made worldly as Arabic literary texts are translated into English—or, more precisely, is reified in this context *by being* made worldly—departs from Allan's study, however, in a crucial respect. Whereas Allan understands the formal aesthetics of Arabic literature and the modes of reading that it invites to continually reinforce each other throughout the processes of its worlding, I propose that the modalities of reading that matter for determining Arabic literature's position in the world are those that *follow from* the aesthetic formations of its language and are indeed produced and shaped by them.

The literary form that matters here is that of Arabic, but it is also that of English. Refuting the reductive and essentializing logics that have long governed Arabic literature's reception among Anglophone publics, an English translation of an Arabic literary work does so most powerfully, I contend, not by representing Arab societies with an enhanced degree of verisimilitude or complexity (like Allan, I, too, am alert to the ethical and epistemological limitations of privileging mimesis as literature's main contribution in the world). Instead, it does so precisely by relocating the apparatus of ethical possibility away from mimesis to the affective encounters with Arabic literary form that a translation can make possible for Anglophone readers.

Caroline Levine defines form as "an arrangement of elements—an ordering, patterning, or shaping" whose "work" it is "to make order" out of what otherwise lacks purpose and direction. Amid the seemingly contradictory properties of form that Levine lists—forms can be material or immaterial, generalizing or particular, political or historical—what remains constant is form's inherent possibility. A form's very durability—"bounded enclosures will always exclude, and rhyme will always repeat"—makes that same form plastic, movable, and capable of traveling without shedding its innate formational principles. Any given form, Levine proposes, borrowing a concept from design theory, "affords" a range of "potential uses or actions," "potentialities [that] lie latent—though not always obvious," and which become animated as forms travel from one situation to another.[80] What Levine's study of form suggests to me is that in its linguistic role as in all roles in which it serves to configure the substances that surround us, form must be translatable. If form cannot be translated via the semantic correspondences that exist between languages, as content can, then it can be translated instead through the shared affordances that two languages offer. The affordances of the various materials among which designers may choose for their creations, Levine explains—such as glass, steel, or cotton—are realized in the different ways that they shape the bodily experiences of a building or an item of clothing for the people who interact with them.[81] Form's potentiality rests in its latent promise of becoming embodied. This is no less true of forms of literary language, which, as they interface with a body, introduce this body to a host of possible sensibilities and sensual encounters. In such experiences that language affords, the aesthetics of Arabic literature become both translatable and worldly.

The Form of a Book

To posit the worldliness of Arabic literature as an ethical outcome of its translation into English is to situate my project at the intersection of several somewhat divergent strains of thinking about translation's role in an ever more globalized contemporary reality. After centuries of being relegated to the margins of Euro-American literary criticism—after all, as Walter Benjamin observes, there was no muse of translation among the nine mythical beings who personified the key modalities of artistic and humanistic expression for the ancient Greeks[82]—translation has been lately thrust to the forefront of literary studies in the United States. This may be first because "in the face of shrinking budgets, declining student numbers, and diminishing faculty positions" in humanities departments at colleges and universities across North America,[83] the presence of translated works on the syllabi of humanities courses portends gains in "global competency" for the students who take these courses, thus supposedly proving the continued relevance of the liberal arts in an increasingly corporatized but also increasingly internationally oriented higher education system.

Moreover, translation has recently gained attention for its role in facilitating the emergence of a new academic discipline of world literature and its associated methods of reading and canons of texts. For David Damrosch, translation serves as the lynchpin for a capacious study of the world's heterogenous textual traditions, as he writes in *What Is World Literature?*, by allowing literary works to circulate among audiences temporally and geographically remote from their points of origin, gaining in depth and significance as they do so.[84] For Franco Moretti, translation furnishes a means by which the "sheer enormity of the task" of reading the entirety of the world's literary output becomes even slightly feasible, given the constraints that prevent any single scholar from mastering more than a handful of languages in his or her lifetime.[85]

Translation has also been mobilized in recent years as a critical apparatus by comparatist scholars for whom its contingent claims to authority make it well suited to deconstructing dominant contemporary global structures of discourse and knowledge, including those sometimes propounded by world literature scholars. In *Against World Literature: On the Politics of Untranslatability*, Emily Apter activates this theoretical potential of translation to challenge the totalizing, "bulimic" impulses of a modern global literary system that venerates the portability of texts with too little thought for how their linguistic and ontological particularities may be compromised as they move out of their native contexts.[86] Translation's use in this heuristic capacity, according to Apter, befits its location at "the epistemological interstices of politics, poetics, logic, cybernetics, linguistics, genetics, media, and environment."[87]

Such scholarship that emphasizes the theorization of translation over its praxis has not been without its detractors. The French-to-English translator Mark Polizzotti, for one, describes this way of thinking about translation in *Sympathy for the Traitor: A Translation Manifesto* as characteristic of an "increasingly abstract strain of scholarly translation theory" whose "convoluted formulations [are] seemingly designed mainly to tickle the fancies of grad students."[88] In a similar vein, Lawrence Venuti has accused much contemporary scholarship on translation in the Euro-American academy of being unable "to say much that is useful about translation" and of veiling urgent questions about how translation is practiced across the globe today behind mystifying declarations about its metaphysics.[89]

Symptomatic for Venuti in this regard is the *Dictionary of Untranslatables: A Philosophical Lexicon*, a monumental English translation and revision of a no less massive French volume for which Apter served as a chief editor (with Jacques Lezra and Michael Wood).[90] Nearly 1,300 pages long, the *Dictionary* collates a vast assortment of terms in multiple languages that are designated as "untranslatables," according to Barbara Cassin, the French volume's editor, not because they cannot be translated but because "their translation, into one language or another, creates a problem."[91] In Rebecca's Walkowitz's gloss, such terms are "what one doesn't stop translating even though one cannot finish translating" them, or those that are "unable to be finished being translated";[92] examples include the English "Culture," "Melancholy," and "Sublime," the German "Dasein" and "Welt," and the Greek "Polis." One of Venuti's principal critiques of the *Dictionary* is that the supposed untranslatables that it collects, contrary to their "cryptic" framing by the volume's editors, in fact reveal an "eminent *translatability*" among human languages and the enduring resourcefulness of translators in making them so. By sanctifying the insufficiencies and inadequacies of translation, in Venuti's view, the *Dictionary* risks evacuating translation's history of its many successes, thus overlooking the labor of actual translators past and present to discover inventive solutions for even the thorniest problems of linguistic incommensurability.[93]

Responsive to these critiques of contemporary translation theory, my own study of translation in this book is profoundly invested in the practicalities of translating Arabic literature into English and committed to recognizing the efforts of the translators who have labored (in body as well as mind) on behalf of its translation. Yet it seems to me that the stated aim of scholars such as Apter and Cassin to leverage translation into an occasion for philosophical contemplation while establishing its "distance from a teleological history organized according to a register of gain and loss," as Cassin puts it, makes their work at the same time germane for an exploration of translation ethics that seeks to theorize it otherwise than as a measurement of semantic fidelity, representational politics, or mimetic truth.[94] The recent metaphysical turn in translation studies, while by no means novel—certainly Benjamin's portrait of translating as an asymptotic process of approximating the "pure language" of pre-Babelian humanity in his 1923 essay "The Task of the Translator" can be thought of as an antecedent[95]—is generative for my project because it offers a current academic discourse with which to engage, as I depart from binary constructs of source language and target language, writer and reader, and other and self that have been foundational for much praxis-oriented scholarship on translation over the years.[96]

More largely, as I cull from multiple and sometimes contradictory lineages of scholarship to elucidate my own arguments in this book, I contest the notion that there exists an essential opposition between theorizing translation and practicing it, as the translator David Bellos claims, and between those individuals who pursue the one enterprise or the other.[97] Can we not theorize translation's praxis from a critically informed and intellectually rigorous perspective while simultaneously activating these same theories of translation to undergird new and different modes of practice? What kind of scholar (or translator, or scholar-translator) would be up to this task? Toward these ends, I seek in this book to examine the ethics of translating and of reading translated literature via a critical apparatus that conjugates the heuristic potential of the models offered by Apter and Cassin, as well as by Spivak, Benjamin, Meschonnic, and Robinson (among other critics), with the pragmatic and subjective framework for thinking about translation exemplified in Venuti's work and in the personal anecdotes of literary translators such as those whom this introduction has already cited.

To bridge the juncture between these approaches, I center myself throughout this book—and especially in chapter 3—as a locus where theory and practice unite in the formation of a singular, irreducibly embodied figure who is both a scholar of translation and a translator. In claiming this positionality from which to write, I become not only the author of this book but at times both the object and medium of its explorations of the worldliness of Arabic literature in English translation. What risks, professional and personal, does a scholar court by writing herself into an academic monograph as I have done here? Elspeth Probyn, a cultural studies scholar who has mined her own affective experiences as an embodied being in the world as a starting point for investigating the sexuality of femaleness, the ethics of shame, and the politics of contemporary food consumption habits, among other topics, cautions that to interject accounts of the personally affecting into the depersonalized and resolutely *depersonalizing* discursive spaces of academia often meets with "sheer incomprehension" from devotees of a more serious, objective brand of intellectualism, or provokes "nervousness and embarrassment" that a scholar should so expose herself to public scrutiny.[98]

Yet it is my contention that to remain attentive across the chapters of an academic monograph to the bodies among which literary texts circulate as they move through the world, including my own, is to practice scholarship, too, as a worlding activity and an act of care for the subject matter at hand. Such a method of critique that places the critic materially amid the things that she studies—bodies, texts, languages—and renders her susceptible to the "palimpsest of force-encounters traversing the ebbs and swells of intensities that pass between" them, in Gregory Seigworth and Melissa Gregg's phrasing, leaves her never untouched herself by the affects of literature as they proliferate across a literary system.[99] This is an approach scaffolded upon a refusal of the notion that there exists an "ontological distinction between academic theory and everyday theory," as Eve Kosofsky Sedgwick puts it, or that "what one is doing and the reasons one does it" should reflect two disparate sets of priorities, commitments, or activities.[100] Critique here carries out its exploratory moves "beside" the text that it examines.[101] A monograph becomes a site of unfolding concrescences between texts and bodies, Arabic literature and the world. A scholar activates academic writing as a mode of ethical praxis.

In my personal orientations toward this project, I take inspiration from Jeffrey Sacks, who writes in *Iterations of Loss: Mutilation and Aesthetic Form, Al-Shidyaq to Darwish* of language that loses its autonomy and self-possession through acts of violence inflicted upon words and word users, texts and textual form, by the colonial and juridical systems that have shaped the history of Arabic literature in modern times. For Sacks, this loss is apparent in literary language that privileges form over meaning—language that, arrested in the iterative motions of becoming itself only as it "becomes something other than what it is," "forms the occasion for an ethical or political disruption of sense, to give place to ways of being and of being with others that occur as interrupted, interruptive events of form." Thus "bereaved," such language calls for "a responsibility in reading" that furnishes Sacks with a critical methodology for his book. As a reader and scholar, Sacks attempts to "remain with" the scenes of mourning that linguistic form stages again and again in the Arabic and Arab Jewish literature that he studies. Comparing and contrasting texts across and within languages, he himself becomes mournful.[102]

Literary language, vulnerable to estranging processes of aesthetic diminishment when it abrades against the rough surfaces of the world, is that for which Sacks's monograph cares—cannot stop caring—so that Sacks himself is caught up in the affective events that caring for another necessitates. For the Arabic literary texts that I examine, their tangible encounters with the world via translation produce not losses of aesthetic value but accumulations of literariness, gains accrued via affective networks that link up rhizomatically under and beside the official avenues of transmission, valuation, and exchange that world literature inaugurates. Not to be mourned, the iterative worlding of Arabic literature nonetheless calls forth affective responses from a scholar that carry an ethical charge, as the rhythms and refrains of the literary score her body with fleshly traces. "Refrains are a worlding," Kathleen Stewart writes, wherein

> nascent forms quicken, rinding up like the skin of an orange. Prepersonal intensities lodge in bodies. Events, relations, and impacts accumulate as the capacities to affect and to be affected. Public feelings world up as lived circuits of action and reaction.
>
> Critique attuned to the worlding of the refrain is a burrowing into the generativity of what takes form, hits the senses, shimmers.[103]

Ethics inheres in the shimmering possibility of bodies and texts worlding each other, in translation and via the routes of contact that translation makes possible.[104] Formations of language, nubs or nodes of aesthetic matter accreted in a text—"clusters of textual energy," as Philip Lewis calls them[105]—impinge on a body to incipit a change in this body's own form. Apprehended affectively rather than perceived consciously, the aesthetics of literary language retune the body to resonate at the text's own pitch, to transmit at its frequency. Through translation, a text registers aesthetic effects far from its sites of origin. A reader embodies the literariness of the other as an intensity of affects. The fulcrum of their encounter is the translator, who channels the energies of the source language into energetic writing in his or her own tongue, and whose body is repurposed in this process as the medium through which the literariness of the literary becomes translatable.

1 / Sonics of *Lafẓ*: Translating Arabic Acoustics for Anglophone Ears

In 2013–2014, a notoriously difficult work of Arabic literature became available for the first time to Anglophone readers. Translated into English by the veteran translator Humphrey Davies as *Leg over Leg or, The Turtle in the Tree, concerning The Fāriyāq; What Manner of Creature Might He Be*, Aḥmad Fāris al-Shidyāq's 1855 masterpiece *al-Sāq ʿalā al-sāq fī mā huwa al-Fāriyāq*—a prodigiously long, genre-defying text that is part narrative fiction, part social critique, and part philological commentary—was a surprise critical hit.[1] Patricia Storace in the *Times Literary Supplement* described *Leg over Leg* as "one of the most important translations of the twenty-first century," comparable to the first English translations of the Russian writer Leo Tolstoy a century earlier, and hailed Davies's achievement in translating al-Shidyāq's "labyrinthine novel" as "monumental" and "virtuosic."[2] John Yargo in the *Los Angeles Review of Books* called the translation "a triumph" and praised Davies for "skillfully render[ing the] punning, rhyming prose" of the original text "without breaking the spell."[3] Martin Riker in the *New York Times* cited *Leg over Leg* as one of several recent translations of literary works from the Middle East that "remind us that this thing called literature is much larger than our own little moment."[4] *The Guardian* included *Leg over Leg* on its list of "Best Books of 2015," with an endorsement from the critic Marina Warner declaring Davies's translation to be nothing short of "dazzling."[5]

I begin by citing these reviews because they are unusual for a work of Arabic literature translated into English. As Edward Said observed in 1990 and as many other scholars have affirmed subsequently, the

Anglophone literary field has shown itself over a period of decades to be largely indifferent, if not outright hostile, to all translated literature, and to translations from Arabic in particular.[6] Davies's translation spans four volumes with a cumulative total length just shy of eighteen hundred pages. Densely packed with rhymes and verses of poetry, obscure English vocabulary and nonce words of Davies's own invention, and irregular typographic and formatting elements, *Leg over Leg* is as far from being a "domesticating" translation in Lawrence Venuti's sense as it is imaginable for a text to be.[7] Yet, as I will argue in what follows, neither does Davies's use of what Venuti would describe as "marginal" and "nonstandard" varieties of English diction create a "foreignizing" effect for Anglophone readers as Venuti has proposed it should.[8] Indeed, *Leg over Leg* provides an apt starting point for the transhistoric examination of Arabic literature in English translation that this book as a whole undertakes precisely because of how it resists and complicates this domestication/foreignization binary.

Leg over Leg was one of the first titles released under the auspices of the Library of Arabic Literature, a joint-venture imprint of NYU Press and the New York University Abu Dhabi Institute that was launched in 2012. Overseen by a multinational editorial collective of scholars of Arabic literature, the Library has, to date, published some thirty-five works of premodern and early modern Arabic writing in parallel-text Arabic-English editions, including both prose and poetry.[9] A core rationale for the series' establishment, according to the Library's executive editor, Shawkat Toorawa, was its founders' shared perception that "modern, lucid English has not been the norm in the translation of premodern Arabic," and that this fact had contributed to a widespread lack of knowledge of, and appreciation for, the rich and multifaceted tradition of Arabic literary production before the twentieth century among an Anglophone readership.[10] What the Library hoped to provide, on the contrary, were translations of Arabic literary texts each "ideally . . . sound[ing] as if it were originally English," and which would therefore be "approachable by someone who knows nothing about the Arabic literary heritage," as another of the Library's executive editors, James Montgomery, put it.[11] If premodern Arabic literature had previously been disadvantaged by having "entered world literature in poor, inelegant, even wrong, translations," then translations like Davies's of *al-Sāq ʿalā al-sāq*—one of five inaugural projects contracted for the series—were intended to help in reversing this situation.[12]

This chapter explores what happens when an Arabic literary text is introduced into the world literary system "sounding" as if it were English. What avenues of "approach" does such a translation extend to Anglophone readers who would not read Arabic literature otherwise? With respect to the sonics of the two languages involved, what alterations must be made to the phonetic and acoustic aspects of Arabic, but also of English, for a translation of this kind to become possible? I posit in this chapter that how English sounds in *Leg over Leg* is not incidental to the success it attained in the Anglophone literary field. Judged by the standards of commercial Anglophone fiction, *Leg over Leg* has hardly been a bestseller; yet among the Library's titles released so far, it has been notable for drawing "the attention of reviewers and readers outside the field of Arabic/ME [Middle East] Studies," and during the first five years following its publication its sales outpaced those of other titles in the Library's catalog.[13] For the Arabic of *al-Sāq ʿalā al-sāq* to have been made to sound like English produced, in this case, a translation that served to introduce Arabic literature to an Anglophone audience as a corpus existing in "lucid" English—a corpus, in other words, that could be read as literature. Yet the worldliness of Arabic literature that is achieved through such methods is complex, requiring further elaboration.

Any examination of sound in *al-Sāq ʿalā al-sāq* must begin by recognizing that this work of literature addresses its readers in Arabic first and foremost with an injunction to listen:

مه صه اسكت اصمت انصت آيبس اِعقَم اسمع اِئذن اصِخ اصغَ.

This line is the first phrase in the first chapter of the Arabic text,[14] and it is composed of eleven imperatives addressed to a masculine second-person singular subject. Each command enjoins its addressee either to listen or to be silent in order to listen. Transliterated into the Latin alphabet, the sequence reads: *mah ṣah uskut uṣmut inṣit aybas iʿqam ismaʿ iʾdhin iṣikh iṣgha*. The first four words in the phrase comprise two rhyming pairs; three of the last four words begin alliteratively with the phonetic combinations *is* or *iṣ*. Rana Issa describes these semantically redundant imperatives as "onomatopoetic words" that "wheeze" from the throat and "recall the voice warming exercises a singer would do behind the scenes," evoking both the sounds of words for their own sake and the sounds that they make when they emerge from a human body.[15]

This opening, which operates dually to instruct listening and to exemplify language that must be listened to before or in addition to its being understood for its semantic content, frames how *al-Sāq ʿalā al-sāq* is supposed to be approached by readers in Arabic. This is a text that must be read "with the ears," to borrow Angela Leighton's phrasing, in order to allow for the possibility "that written words makes noises as well as shapes, calling on the ear like an after effect of being seen and understood." Such a mode of reading, Leighton proposes, requires the reader to "go . . . slower, no longer following the lines to the end in order to discover what is meant, but attending instead to any number of incidental rhythmic effects and sound combinations."[16] To read with the ears is to read unhurriedly, savoring rhythm and the sonic arrangements of language, while the meanings of individual words retreat in importance.

What will be discovered in this Arabic text for those who read it with their ears, as the first chapter's opening passage goes on to explain, is "*kull mā khaffa ʿalā al-samʿ*"—"all that is light and lovely to hear," as this phrase might be translated—which emanates from "*al-alfāẓ al-shāʾiqah al-rāʾiqah wa-al-maʿānī al-fāʾiqah al-āfiqah*," "the splendid, pure forms and superior, excellent meanings" that language proffers.[17] Forms (*alfāẓ*) and meanings (*maʿānī*): form and content, *lafẓ* (singular of *alfāẓ*) and *maʿnā* (singular of *maʿānī*). The aesthetics of *al-Sāq ʿalā al-sāq* in Arabic are constituted in the merger of what language signifies with how its significance is outwardly expressed. Characteristic of the totality of the Arabic language (*lughah*) as something that is comprehended semantically but also appreciated aurally, *lafẓ* and *maʿnā* come together in this text to produce an array of sounds that relieve, soothe, and give pleasure to the ear, "lightening" ("*khaffa*") the burden of hearing upon the one who hears them.

Of these two components that create the aesthetic experience of the text in Arabic, it is *lafẓ* that is most salient for Davies's act of translation, because he has been charged with making Arabic sound like English, and *lafẓ* is what endows language with its capacity to be heard. Serving in certain contexts as a cognate of *kalimah* (word), *lafẓ* denotes an articulated utterance or speech act: etymologically, that which is ejected or thrown (*yalfiẓ*) from the mouth.[18] Thus gesturing to the form that language takes when it emerges from one body to be apprehended sensorially by another, *lafẓ* "always indicates an actual acoustic event."[19] For Davies's translation to be not only approachable by Anglophone readers as a work of literature, but approachable by them in the same way that the Arabic text is approachable by Arabophone readers, requires sound to be as much a part of the aesthetics of English as it is of Arabic.

Yet to translate into English the *lafẓ* of an Arabic text is hardly a straightforward proposition. Since at least the age of the pioneering eighth-century grammarian Sībawayhi, whereas *maʿnā* in Arabic has been taken to refer to the comparatively stable and fixed semantic intention of a word or phrase, *lafẓ* has designated a far more aleatory aspect of language's outward manifestation: language as a sensible event, or as the realization and actualization of the potential to signify that *maʿnā* implies.[20] Together, *lafẓ* and *maʿnā* comprise the plenitude of *lughah* in its classical conception; for this reason, as D. E. Kouloughli notes, the pair has sometimes been taken as an analogue for the signifier/signified duo in Saussurian semiotics.[21] This comparison, however, fails to account for the aesthetic premium placed on *lafẓ* relative to *maʿnā* in a longstanding tradition of Arabic literary and linguistic criticism. As Ramzi Baalbaki observes, classical scholars of the Arabic language after Sībawayhi, including philologists, grammarians, and rhetoricians, were "largely preoccupied with *lafẓ* (form) at the expense of *maʿnā* (meaning)."[22] Lara Harb, citing the work of the eleventh-century literary theorist ʿAbd al-Qāhir al-Jurjānī, explains the higher aesthetic status typically accorded to *lafẓ* with reference to its role in the Qur'an, the holy text of Islam that Muslims believe to contain the unadulterated word of God as it was revealed to the Prophet Muhammad over a period of several decades in the early seventh century CE. Many of the Qur'an's suras share narrative elements with stories found in the Jewish Torah, al-Jurjānī reasoned, and yet in his view the aesthetic effect produced by the Qur'an's versions of these stories surpassed that of all other possible renditions. Thus the secret of this Arabic text's perfection or inimitability (*iʿjāz*) must lie in *how* its ideas were expressed rather than in the ideas themselves, or that is, in the form (*lafẓ*) of Qur'anic language and not in its content (*maʿnā*).[23]

In the context of an English translation of the Arabic text of *al-Sāq ʿalā al-sāq*, the content, or *maʿnā*, of the latter is translatable insofar as explanations or equivalents for even al-Shidyāq's most recondite words (of which there are many) could be found in dictionaries or glossaries. Indeed, Davies reports that he consulted any number of these volumes while translating *al-Sāq ʿalā al-sāq*, among them al-Fīrūzābādī's *al-Qāmūs al-muḥīṭ*, Ibn Manẓūr's *Lisān al-ʿArab*, and Edward William Lane's *Arabic-English Lexicon*, for without such resources the "translation would have been too time-consuming to be feasible."[24] With regard to the *lafẓ* of al-Shidyāq's Arabic, however, its transmission into English required a different set of strategies. To accomplish this feat required Davies to act as a translator but also as a reader, for reading, of course, is never only the end game of translation but also its preliminary scene and activity. If *al-Sāq ʿalā al-sāq* interpellates its Arabophone readers with a command to listen—to read with their ears—as the essential means of having a full aesthetic experience of the text, then a translator who seeks to replicate this experience for his readers must take this command doubly to heart, letting it guide his own approach to reading the literary work in Arabic while ensuring that listening remains central to the experience of reading it in English as well.

To open to *Leg over Leg*'s first chapter and find that Davies's translation begins "Gently! Hush! Silence! Quiet! Cock an ear! Listen up! Hold your tongue! Quit talking! Hear! Hark! Hearken!" is to recognize these English imperatives as both translations of al-Shidyāq's Arabic ones, and as an injunction to read with the ears that has now been redirected toward Davies's Anglophone readers.[25] When *Leg over Leg* explains that what an audience stands to gain by reading in this manner is tantamount to "all such words attractive and *fascinating* and figures admirable and *scintillating* as bring pleasure to the *ear* and to the constitution *cheer*" (the italics are Davies's), the translation at this point, too, can be understood as referring to both the aural aesthetics of the source text and those of the English text.[26] Does not every translation refer simultaneously to itself and to the other text? Here, however, the reference diverges at the body of the one who reads in Arabic versus that of the Anglophone reader of the translation. The words and figures of the English text will be pleasing to the ear of this latter reader irrespective of the fact that they are ultimately translations from Arabic, pleasing in and of themselves as literary expressions of the English language. English ceases to refer to Arabic at the moment its own literariness is constituted, when English words are heard as literary even by an Anglophone audience who may know "nothing about the Arabic literary heritage."

And yet it is precisely through this cessation of reference that the literariness of the Arabic text becomes translatable. Invited to partake in the acoustic event that is Davies's text, his audience hears English that has been produced out of the translator's hearing of Arabic. Hearing is something that happens in and to a body, the result of sound waves entering the ear canal and sending vibrations first into the eardrum, then into the bones of the middle ear, and finally into a reservoir of cochlear fluid whose ripples stimulate the auditory nerve to the brain. The translator here acts as what Deborah Kapchan calls a "sound body: a resonant body that is porous, that transforms according to the vibrations of its environment, and correspondingly transforms that environment," and which as it does so participates in "creating and conducting affect."[27] The interlingual connection here is not referential so much as it is sensory. Literariness travels not through the translation of content but through the translation of form's sensibility, wherein a text that is lovely to hear in Arabic becomes one that gives the ear pleasure in English, too. Does Arabic sound like English in Davies's translation, or does English sound like Arabic? The two halves of this question circle each other in irresolvable dialectical tension. Ethically, where do self and other, foreign and domestic, intertwine in this translation of Arabic sound, and how is the reading and listening (but also translating and writing) translator implicated affectively in their entwinement?

Formations of *Lafẓ*

What constitutes *lafẓ* in *al-Sāq ʿalā al-sāq* may be defined on several levels at once. Most broadly, with reference to the notion of *lafẓ* that predominated in the classical Arabic tradition, it can be taken as encompassing the plurality of formal elements in the text's language that cause its content to be apprehended aesthetically. In this regard, *lafẓ* is akin to form as the Russian formalist critic Victor Shklovsky defined it, comprising the aspect of a literary text that, in being made "difficult," operates accordingly "to increase the difficulty and length of perception because the process of perception is an aesthetic end in itself and must be prolonged."[28] Per René Wellek and Austin Warren's distinction "between words in themselves, aesthetically indifferent, and the manner in which individual words make up units of sound and meaning, [which is] aesthetically effective," *lafẓ*'s innate acoustic quality makes it homologous with the text's literariness as a functional outcome of how language signifies in this work of Arabic literature.[29]

By Rebecca Johnson's account, the "superabundance of formal techniques and generic modes" on display in *al-Sāq ʿalā al-sāq* include

> passages in verse (including examples of *madīḥ*, *hijāʾ*, *ghazal*, and *rithāʾ* (praise poetry, invective, amorous [poetry], and [elegiac] poetry)), prose (with passages that imitate or make reference to historical writing, sermons, aphorisms, linguistic studies, and philosophical critiques), and prosody (it includes four original *maqāmāt* . . . as well as other passages written in rhyming prose, or *sajʿ*) . . . [in addition to] selections from European authors, . . . anecdotes, typographical jokes, and lists.[30]

The text is moreover replete with what al-Shidyāq himself describes, in an authorial aside early in book 1, as "*muḥassināt*"—embellishments or beautifying ornaments—including paronomasia, linguistic parallelism, metaphor, and metonymy ("*al-tajnīs*," "*al-tarṣīʿ*," "*al-istiʿārāt*," and "*al-kināyāt*"). For al-Shidyāq, the use of such devices exemplifies how "the exteriority of form" ("*ẓāhir al-lafẓ*") holds priority over "the interiority of meaning" ("*bāṭin al-maʿnā*") as the means through which language becomes aesthetic.[31] Altogether, these defamiliarizing formal uses of language mark al-Shidyāq's text unmistakably as literature.

More exactly, they identify it as a work of Arabic literature produced during the period of cultural and intellectual renaissance across parts of the Middle East known as the Nahda (*Nahḍah*), conventionally dated as beginning with the French occupation of Egypt in 1798 and concluding with the decolonizing movements that liberated much of the region from European suzerainty by the mid-twentieth century. Throughout this period, as Sabry Hafez explains, Arab authors tested out various innovative approaches to combining traditional Arabic literary genres—such as the *maqāmah*, a type of episodic narrative composed in unmetered rhyming prose—with stylistic techniques and aesthetic modalities adapted from European literature, in an effort to cater to "the nature and needs of the new reading public" that was emerging at this time especially in urban centers like Cairo and Beirut.[32] Fruma Zachs notes the increased attention of Arab writers during this era to calibrating their language to what their readers would both understand and enjoy, resulting in the development of new varieties of literary Arabic that aimed to balance between classical Arabic (*al-fuṣḥā*) and the colloquial dialects in which everyday life in Arabic-speaking societies in the nineteenth century was primarily conducted.[33]

Born around 1805 in what is now Lebanon, al-Shidyāq was personally involved in many such endeavors to reform morphological, orthographic, and lexical aspects of the Arabic language consistent with the broader modernizing aims of the Nahda. A leading figure in the Levant's fledgling Arabic publishing industry, he opened a printing press and, bringing to bear his experience as a calligrapher and copyist, he designed several new Arabic typefaces for its use.[34] Through a practice known as *ishtiqāq* of deriving new Arabic vocabulary from preexisting alphabetic roots, he coined a number of novel Arabic words, many still used today, to name European items and concepts that had been introduced to the Levant during the preceding decades.[35] Such work brought al-Shidyāq into close proximity with the material properties of the Arabic language, whether as a graphic code substantiated in ink and metal lettering or as a mesh of words held in tension with each other and with words in other languages through the movable schema of synonymy and antonymy, etymology and derivation.

Although *al-Sāq ʿalā al-sāq* is loosely plotted around the narrative of a man named al-Fāriyāq and his wife al-Fāriyāqiyyah as they travel through the Mediterranean region and eventually to England and France, this story is interrupted frequently by digressive passages that collate words of etymological or acoustic interest, offer al-Shidyāq's own observations on various elements of Arabic grammar and lexicography, or comment meta-critically upon aspects of the author's writing process. In Kamran Rastegar's analysis, the text overall adopts an "auto-critical" stance toward its own language that repeatedly and playfully undermines its authority to signify. Many of the chapter titles throughout the book, Rastegar points out, have "nothing in particular to do with the content" of the sections that they headline, and the pages are interspersed with typographic elements, such as ellipses and line breaks, that subjugate the flow of language to the destabilizing possibilities of the printed medium.[36] In an age when, as Geoffrey Roper notes, hand-copied manuscripts were still a common means by which literature circulated among different populations of readers,[37] the fact that *al-Sāq ʿalā al-sāq* was printed on a printing press inspired its own degree of "formal artifice," via "chapters, pages, and typefaces" whose visual presentation highlighted their printed—rather than handwritten—nature.[38] The "celebrated pointing-hand graphic element" that appeared within the table of contents of book 2 in *al-Sāq ʿalā al-sāq*'s original 1855 edition served as one such reminder for al-Shidyāq's contemporary audience of the book's machinic provenance.[39] Another was the typographic lettering used for this edition, "a special, new Arabic typeface . . . prepared and cast" explicitly for use in this book.[40]

The multiplicity of rhetorical and generic modes exhibited in *al-Sāq ʿalā al-sāq*, along with the discursive and narrative techniques and typographic devices that foreground the text's materiality as a created object, are amply remarked upon and explained in *Leg over Leg*'s paratexts, which include some 1,470 endnotes spread across the four volumes, as well as glossaries, indexes, a scholarly foreword and editorial note in volume 1, and a translator's afterword in volume 4. As Dima Ayoub has argued is often the case when paratexts are charged with facilitating the "westward movement of Arabic literature," these "evince a negotiation between translatability and untranslatability" as they seek to make culturally and stylistically distinctive elements of the source text intelligible for Davies's Anglophone audience.[41] The aesthetics of *lafẓ* in al-Shidyāq's Arabic text are conveyed to a limited extent through this method of "thick translation," as Kwame Anthony Appiah might call it, which "seeks with its annotations and its accompanying glosses to locate the text in a rich cultural and linguistic context."[42]

Yet the whole of what *lafẓ* accomplishes aesthetically in this work of Arabic literature remains out of reach to such informational apparatuses, which enframe the translation in order to comment upon the literariness of its source text, without themselves being part of how the translating language expresses this literariness in its own words. Unlike *maʿnā*, an intention to signify that transcends actualization in any single language and thus renders "la synonymie lexicale . . . un phénomène sans doute universel," *lafẓ* is particular to the specific instantiations of language that comprise this Arabic text, and which endow it linguistically and materially with its most literary qualities.[43] *Lafẓ*'s elusiveness to being translated here underscores the double bind that a translator of Arabic literature into English always faces when confronted with the formal aesthetics of the source text. *Lafẓ* is simultaneously what must be conveyed into English for the source text's literariness to be perceptible to an Anglophone audience, and that which poses a serious impediment to translation on several levels. Before examining, through a close comparative analysis of *al-Sāq ʿalā al-sāq* alongside *Leg over Leg*, how Davies accounted for *lafẓ* in his translation, the apparent untranslatability of this aspect of the Arabic text must first be reckoned with as a problematic with pragmatic but also ethical implications for how a work of Arabic literature enters the world literary system in English translation. It is to this reckoning that I turn next.

An Arabic Untranslatable

In his monumental ninth-century treatise *Kitāb al-ḥayawān*, the famed Abbasid-era intellectual and author Abī ʿUthmān ʿAmru ibn Baḥr al-Jāḥiẓ argued for the nonportability and untranslatability of *lafẓ*. Whereas *maʿnā* in the Arabic language was the common purview of "foreigners and Arabs alike, Bedouin, townspeople, and city-dwellers," al-Jāḥiẓ claimed, *lafẓ* could not be appropriated for foreign use, being an autochthonous aspect of Arabic literary language as a made craft ("*ṣināʿah*"). In particular, al-Jāḥiẓ was concerned with *lafẓ* in Arabic poetry, for he considered the selection of the correct form for poetic language ("*takhayyur al-lafẓ*") to be an essential factor in guaranteeing poetry's aesthetic value, together with a poem's execution of meter ("*iqāmat al-wazn*"), its ease of recitation ("*suhūlat al-kharaj*"), and how well it "minted" and "cast" language for its own expressive ends ("*ṣiḥḥat al-ṭabʿ wa-jawdat al-sabak*").[44]

The title *Kitāb al-ḥayawān* can be rendered in English literally as *The Book of Animals*, although James Montgomery makes a compelling case that *The Book of Living* more aptly conveys the astonishing breadth and scope of topics covered in al-Jāḥiẓ's text, which ostensibly sets out to present "a comprehensive inventory" of all God's creations and yet embeds within this quasi-encyclopedic framework a multifaceted commentary on the practices of writing, reading, and dialogic argumentation in Arabic that al-Jāḥiẓ saw as most conducive to promoting the moral and intellectual health of his contemporary society.[45] To live, for al-Jāḥiẓ, was to inhabit language as the primary medium in which one comported oneself individually and in relation to others, the principal means through which the vast compendium of human knowledge was winnowed, tested, refined, and disseminated, and the basic mediating interface between the self and the world.[46]

Elsewhere in *Kitāb al-ḥayawān*, al-Jāḥiẓ takes up directly the issue of whether Arabic poetry, dependent as it is on its choice deployment of *lafẓ*, can therefore be translated into other languages. On this theme, he writes:

> فضيلة الشعر مقصورةٌ على العرب، وعلى من تكلَّم بلسان العرب، والشعر لا يُستطاع أن يترجَم، ولا يجوز عليه النقل؛ ومتى حوِّل تقطَّع نظمُه وبطلَ وزنُه، وذهب حسنُه وسقطَ موضعُ التعجب.

> The value of poetry is limited to the Arabs, and to those who speak in the tongue of the Arabs, and so poetry is not able to be translated [*lā yustaṭāʿ an yutarjam*], and transfer [*al-naql*] does not succeed with it; for if it were converted [*ḥuwwila*], its versification [*naẓm*] would be interrupted and its meter [*wazn*] voided, its beauty [*ḥusn*] would depart and its wonder [*taʿajjub*] would be abolished.[47]

The contemporary Moroccan literary critic ʿAbd al-Fattāḥ Kīlīṭū understands al-Jāḥiẓ to be saying here that poetry tout court is the purview of Arabs alone, belonging to the Arabic language to the exclusion of all others. In his book *Lan tatakallam lughatī* (translated into English by Waïl Hassan as *Thou Shalt Not Speak My Language*), Kīlīṭū proposes that al-Jāḥiẓ is staging a Platonic dialogue in this passage between two interlocutors with divergent viewpoints as to the superiority of Arabic poetry, and that the statement quoted above should not be attributed to al-Jāḥiẓ himself but rather to one of these fictionalized figures.[48] While this may indeed be the case—as Montgomery also observes, al-Jāḥiẓ often quotes or paraphrases for rhetorical purposes the statements of others whose views differ from his own[49]—I am less interested in what these lines may be alleging about the exceptional poetic affinity of Arabs (that only they possess true poetry) than in how the passage reifies Arabic poetry, paradigmatically rooted in *lafẓ*, as something of unique value but also of unique fragility.

In the context of the role that al-Jāḥiẓ accords to the Arabic language throughout *Kitāb al-ḥayawān*, I propose that what he is invested in considering here, contra Kīlīṭū's reading, is not poetry in general, but a specific problem of translation relating to the inability of Arabic poetry's literariness to be captured fully in another language. Taken as a whole, the list that al-Jāḥiẓ gives of what is at risk in the translation of Arabic poetry encompasses its formal structure (verse and meter) and the pleasures of its reception (beauty and wonder) within a single imagined scene of loss. Siting the literariness of an Arabic poem in the intersection of what it is materially and how it registers aesthetically for an audience—the very nexus that *lafẓ* designates in al-Shidyāq's text—al-Jāḥiẓ suggests that such literariness is both untranslatable and essential to the being-in-the-world of the poem as such.

Elaborated via al-Jāḥiẓ's notion of literariness, *lafẓ* edges conceptually close to the kind of untranslatable that gives ethical cause to the work of translation in a contemporary discourse of Euro-American translation theory. For Gayatri Chakravorty Spivak, the untranslatable element of a literary text is its "rhetoricity." Obliging the translator either to choose a "safe," logical, and systematic translation strategy that is necessarily less literary, or to attempt to mediate the "rhetorical nature" of the original text into the destination language through a practice of translation whose intimacies are dangerous to both the translator and her source text, the untranslatable introduces an ethical dilemma into Spivak's theory of translation.[50] In Emily Apter's framing, the untranslatable is a "right," a sacred object, a bond of elective (rather than mandatory familial or national) kinship, the patrimony of threatened cultures, and a transcendent inscription of truth and sublimity within language. The untranslatable also stands, for Apter, largely outside of English, being equated for her with everything in the world's linguistic and literary traditions that disrupts and opposes the homogenizing aspirations of twenty-first-century Anglophone reading practices.[51] For his part, Jacques Derrida describes "the 'untranslatable'" as that which "remains—should remain, as my law tells me—the poetic economy of the idiom, the one that is important to me, for I would die even more quickly without it."[52]

There is a certain hypothetical appeal to moving between the theories of al-Jāḥiẓ (and also of ʿAbd al-Qāhir al-Jurjānī, whose own ideas about *lafẓ* were inspired by al-Jāḥiẓ's),[53] on the one hand, and those of Spivak, Apter, and Derrida, on the other, to devise an argument for *lafẓ*'s untranslatability that bridges synthetically between the ancient and the modern, between thinkers who write in Arabic and those who write in European languages. Reconceptualizing *lafẓ* along such lines, as I have argued elsewhere, would enable it to emerge through its Arabic lineage as an indigenous variant of a concept that currently enjoys widespread cachet in Euro-American literary scholarship.[54] To undertake this synthesis would be to heed the call by Mohamed-Salah Omri to reverse the "one-directional" traffic of theoretical paradigms derived from a Western context and applied to the study of Arabic literature.[55] With reference to what Hosam Aboul-Ela describes as "the wild portion of Arab thought—

made up of those trends that are markedly distinct from the obsessions of American and European thinkers and that are virtually inaccessible to the latter group," equating *lafẓ* with untranslatability would not so much add to Euro-American criticism what it currently lacks, as it would instead force this criticism to recognize that its obsessions do not belong to it alone, nor are they exclusively contemporary in their origins, rooted in the aporias and anxieties of a globalized age.[56] Such a gesture could be made to serve as the opening gambit in a bid to "occupy the canon," in Tarek El-Ariss's terms, by activating an Arabic concept to "reconstruct and decolonize" dominant precepts in Western theory.[57]

In a 2010 essay, Apter goes some way herself toward attempting to excavate an Arab-Islamic genealogy for untranslatability from Kīlīṭū's *Lan tatakallam lughatī.* According to Apter, the "lessons and anecdotes of translational travesty" that Kīlīṭū relates in this book make his work concordant with the "translational interdiction" or "duty to not translate" that pervades "recent [Euro-American] philosophy and theory." After first suggesting that Kīlīṭū has developed his own perspective on the perils of translation by extending an Islamic concern for the nontranslation of the Qur'an into a "principled opposition to facile computations of cultural equivalence" writ large, Apter zeroes in on what the Moroccan critic says about Arabic poetry, his "model untranslatable" surpassing "even . . . the Qur'an." As Apter sees it, the primary critical move that supports Kīlīṭū's transition from the sacred to the literary here—a move that jibes nicely with her own commitment to underlining the alterity of foreign literature while remaining primarily secular and humanistic, rather than ecclesiastical, in her methodologies and philosophical orientations—is his analysis of the passage from al-Jāḥiẓ on the impossibility of translating Arabic poetry that I quoted earlier, and which Apter glosses in a footnote via Kīlīṭū's citation of it.[58]

Apter's essay, while thrice removed from *lafẓ* itself and from the Arabic writings in which it emerges as an object of interest within the Arabic critical tradition—she engages with al-Jāḥiẓ only through Kīlīṭū's work, which she reads in Hassan's English translation—nonetheless offers further scaffolding for appropriating *lafẓ* as a conceptual node around which a general theory of translation ethics could be constructed, in close alignment with au courant Euro-American scholarly discourse. Extending this line of reasoning, if *lafẓ* is what ethically must not be translated, then *maʿnā* becomes its opposite, taking on its own theoretical force as that component of literature whose universality renders it endlessly translatable. Methodologically, *maʿnā* stands therefore as a summons to translate everything and always, providing a rationalization or justification for the rapacious tendencies of Anglophone world literature as a system and discipline. Yet as tempting as it is to recast the *lafẓ*/*maʿnā* pair in these terms so familiar to Western translation theory—yoking it thus to the well-worn dichotomies of untranslatability/translatability, rhetoricity/logic, foreignization/domestication, and other/self—I nonetheless hesitate to embrace such equations. When the ethical stakes in question relate to an actual practice of translating Arabic literature, figuring *lafẓ* as the untranslatable within the source text whose alterity must be preserved imposes a categorical limit on how far the translator can go in rendering the literariness of Arabic in another language, its ineluctable difference or foreignness stalling the translation act at a divide that ethically must not be crossed.

Insofar as it is irreducible to the signifying systems through which languages become calculably fungible, *lafẓ* cannot be translated (only) to the same extent that Arabic poetry, for al-Jāḥiẓ, cannot be translated. When al-Jāḥiẓ writes that this poetry "*lā yustaṭāʿ an yutarjam*," he uses the present-tense third-person passive conjugation of a verb for "to translate" that shares a morphological root with *tarjamah*, the noun designating translation in contemporary Arabic collocations like *al-tarjamah al-fawriyyah* (simultaneous translation or interpretation) and *al-tarjamah min al-ʿArabiyyah ilā al-Inglīziyyah* (Arabic-to-English translation). The phonetic similarities between *tarjamah* and the Persian *tarjomeh* and Turkish *tercüme* create ambiguity around the etymology of this Arabic word and its associated derivations. Hassan in his translator's introduction to *Thou Shalt Not Speak My Language* claims that *tarjamah* comes from the Arabic verb *rajama*, whose basic meaning refers to an act of killing with stones.[59] Yet in the authoritative thirteenth-century Arabic dictionary *Lisān al-ʿArab*, the Libyan lexicographer Ibn Manẓūr offers an entry on *turjumān* (translator)—defined as "the interpreter of a language" ("*al-mufassir li-lisān*") and "the one who translates speech" ("*huwa alladhī yutarjim al-kalām*")—separately from his discussion of *rajama*, suggesting that he does not necessarily consider *turjumān* to derive from the same root.[60]

While the etymology of the English word *translation*, which combines the Latin words for *carrying* and *across*, "suggests a transportation of meaning, a physical displacement," as Sandra Bermann notes, the Arabic *tarjamah* designates more strictly a process of semantic exchange.[61] *Tarjamah*, however, is not the only word that conveys the notion of translation for al-Jāḥiẓ. Immediately following his declaration that Arabic poetry "*lā yustaṭāʿ an yutarjam*," he restates this idea by saying first that "transfer [*al-naql*] does not succeed with it" and then that it cannot be "converted [*ḥuwwila*]." *Naql* is a noun whose root *nql* is associated with an array of words having to do with physical movement, as in *intiqāl* (transit, transport) and *mutanaqqil* (portable); *ḥuwwila* is a past-tense passive verb from the root *ḥwl* whose other derivations include terms referring to conversions between physical mediums, currencies, and molecular structures. Al-Jāḥiẓ's lexical pluralism here, I would argue, is not simply a stylistic device, but a philological exercise that reveals an unexpectedly capacious and material notion of translation permeating his thinking on this topic. Discussing the problem of translation posed by Arabic poetry, al-Jāḥiẓ uses words that imagine translation occurring via a passage through space (*naql*) or as a change in substance and medium (*ḥuwwila*). Even while they fail to provide al-Jāḥiẓ himself with a means of envisioning Arabic poetry rendered adequately into other languages, the physicality of these words nonetheless limns a method of translation that, by embracing the materiality of all languages, might enable it to proceed otherwise than merely as an exchange of semantic content between one linguistic system and another.

Taking a cue from the philological richness of al-Jāḥiẓ's statements on translation, could we not then posit that *lafẓ* in a text like *al-Sāq ʿalā al-sāq* might become translatable through a material method of translation appropriate to the materiality of *lafẓ* itself? Examining *lafẓ* in al-Shidyāq's text as a site of translational possibility, rather than as a sign of translation's inevitable failure, undesirability, or inherent violence, serves furthermore to flip the script on the theories of untranslatability outlined by Apter and others. Whereas Apter has mobilized untranslatability in her work "as a theoretical fulcrum" for thinking translation, and more specifically translation ethics, outside the intellectual frameworks of mainstream Euro-American literary criticism, I invert her logic to propose instead a theory of *translatability* in this context that is built around the Arabic concept of *lafẓ*.[62] The translatability of *lafẓ* as I describe it in the remainder of this chapter takes shape in the aftermath or on the leeward side of the sanctified notion of untranslatability that Apter advances, bolstered and buoyed by her impetus to draw out a philosophical dimension from any event of translation even as it counters impossibility with potential, and the mystification of translation with insistent and unapologetic attention to translation's praxis.

Organ Noise and Nonsense

What Davies hears as the aesthetic pleasures of al-Shidyāq's Arabic when he reads *al-Sāq ʿalā al-sāq* is the literariness of the text materialized in the sound of *lafẓ*. What he hears *with* is his body, "for sounds touch and resonate throughout . . . [a] body," so that, as Deborah Kapchan writes, "what hears" any given noise or acoustic vibration is never "just" the ears. With reference to Kapchan's idea of "sound knowledge—a nondiscursive form of affective transmission resulting from acts of listening," I propose that *lafẓ* in *al-Sāq ʿalā al-sāq* becomes translatable as this kind of affective knowledge, acquired through Davies's own reading of the text and transmitted to his Anglophone readers via his translation.[63] Such knowledge is not knowledge in the conventional sense of the word so much as it is knowledge *as* sense. What do those who read Davies's translation hear in the words of his English text? When Arabic *lafẓ* registers in their bodies as sound knowledge in English, how does this knowledge resonate within, amplify, or interfere with the repertoire of sounds that they already possess: the sounds of English phonetics, English morphology, English rhetorical style? The writing that conveys sound knowledge into the world—"sound writing," for Kapchan—does not give "a representation" of an acoustic event but "a performance in word-sound" of its affects, activating language to become "a gong resonating through bodies, sentient and non."[64] Davies's English is the gong through which the sound of al-Shidyāq's Arabic *lafẓ* re-sounds into the world.

In *Leg over Leg*, English sounds like this when it translates a passage in *al-Sāq ʿalā al-sāq* that describes the range of noises produced by a pipe organ, including

> strumming and humming, mumbling and rumbling, jangling and jingling, squeaking and creaking, chirping and cheeping, burbling and barking, clicking and clacking, gnashing and crashing, chinking and clinking, gurgling and gargling, purring, cooing, and bleating, thrumming and drumming, roaring and guffawing, glugging and gabbling, la-la-ing and lullabying, horses' neighs and the roaring of waves, blubbing of billy goats and cricking of cradles, cries of men at war, call of merlins and raven's caw, old women moaning and heavy doors groaning, snores and stertors, huffing and soughing, water boiling and grief-stricken bawling, frogs ribbiting and ears tinky-tinkling, bulls bellowing and gaming-house reprobates roaring, reverberations and crepitations, pots gently bubbling and chilly dogs whimpering, pulleys squeaking and crickets chirruping, milk flowing, chickens crowing, and cats mewing, not to mention caw-caw and hubble-bubble and wham-bam and slurp-slurp and baa-baa and tee-hee and keek-keek and buzz-buzz and schlup-flup.[65]

What Davies has translated here is a list of sixty-eight terms in the Arabic text, one that contains lengthy onomatopoetic sequences of verbal nouns from reduplicated quadriliteral roots indicating "the repetition of . . . [a] sound or movement,"[66] such as "*ṭanṭanah wa-dandanah wa-khankhanah wa-damdamah wa-ṣalṣalah wa-darbalah wa-jaljalah wa-qalqalah wa-zaqzaqah wa-waqwaqah wa-baqbaqah*," and sequences such as "*ghaṭīṭ wa-jakhīf wa-faḥīḥ wa-ḥafīf wa-nashīsh wa-ranīn wa-naqīq wa-ṭanīn wa-ʿajīj*" that repeat the same morphological pattern across multiple verbal roots to create sonic effects of assonance and rhyme.

Described in Arabic as "pleasing the senses" ("*yulidhdh al-ḥuwāss*"), the sounds of the organ are enunciated in this passage from al-Shidyāq's text to become part of the aural aesthetic pleasures of the literary work.[67] Many of the terms in the Arabic list possess no meaning independent of their onomatopoetic aspect, as, for example, *ṭanṭanah* refers to a sound of ringing, *dandanah* refers to a sound of buzzing, and *khankhanah* refers to a sound of nasal twanging.[68] Mattityahu Peled describes such lists, which are common throughout *al-Sāq ʿalā al-sāq*, as "collocat[ing] words either syntagmatically or by sense associations as long as they could be put together into some acoustic or otherwise ludic combinations."[69] Their purpose, he suggests, is less to create meaning than to produce a variety of "sound effects" within the text "achieved through the combination of . . . morphemic dissimilarity" and "the phonetic repetitiveness of . . . assonance" or other rhetorical devices that trade on language's sonic qualities.[70] Rebecca Johnson proposes along similar lines that while the lists in *al-Sāq ʿalā al-sāq* often appear to present synonyms, they in fact operate according to an accumulative logic rather than a logic of semantic equivalence and exchangeability.[71] With regard to the aesthetic function of such lists, Christian Junge maintains that they assign value to the thing that they describe not through the quality of the words that they contain but through their quantity, wherein "enumerative length becomes an indicator of importance" for the object designated.[72]

By al-Shidyāq's own account, his intention with such lists is to collect within them "synonymous articulations" ("*al-alfāẓ al-mutarādifah*") that are not "of a single meaning [*bi-maʿnā wāḥid*] or else they would be named equal, but rather . . . are synonymous in the sense that some of them could stand in the place [*yaqūm maqām*] of others."[73] The affiliation of the Arabic words in a list such as that describing the sounds of the organ, this is to say, is not through *maʿnā* but through *lafẓ* (singular of *alfāẓ*), according to a rationale that does not suppose them to have the same significance but instead to be transposable materially in space.

As Johnson writes, drawing out the etymological derivations of the Arabic word *murādif* (synonym), they are words that "pile up in layers," that "flock," "throng," or "follow one after another."[74]

When Davies translates such lists in al-Shidyāq's text, his own words accumulate and pile up in the same manner, in relation both to each other and to the Arabic words that they replace. The English words that are transposed into the positions formerly occupied by words in Arabic are not those that carry equivalent meanings to the latter, but those that take up space in the same way. How they take up space is through how they sound, how they vibrate inside Davies's own ears and then inside the ears of his readers, activating their bodies in the process of their transmission from Arabic into English. An Anglophone reader hears al-Shidyāq's organ in words that reverberate in English with rhyme ("strumming and humming, mumbling and rumbling"), alliteration and assonance ("burbling and barking"), repetition ("gurgling and gargling"), lexical strangeness ("stertors," "soughing"), and onomatopoeia ("baa-baa and tee-hee and keek-keek"). The words and phrases out of which this passage in *Leg over Leg* is composed are neither exact auditory replicas—transliterations—of the words in al-Shidyāq's list, nor do they necessarily carry identical semantic values: for instance, although Davies gives "huffing and soughing" as the translation for al-Shidyāq's "*faḥīḥ wa-ḥafīf*," this Arabic nominal couplet from the geminate verbs *faḥḥa* and *ḥaffa* would be more literally rendered in English as "hissing and rustling." What Davies translates is the fact *of* sound as a sensible aesthetic feature of the Arabic text.

Presented in "ludic" combinations, per Peled, that are organized like their Arabic antecedents for the play of their acoustics rather than according to what they signify, the English words of *Leg over Leg* transmit the formal effects (*lafẓ*) of the words in the source text rather than clarifying the single meaning (*maʿnā wāḥid*) of any of them. In so doing, they produce an aesthetic experience for an Anglophone audience that is equivalent affectively to that enjoyed by an Arabophone audience reading the same passage in the Arabic text. If in Arabic the aesthetic pleasures of this enumerative passage derive from its prolific use of words that rhyme and reiterate, both internally and relative to adjacent words in the sequence, then in English repetition remains the primary means by which the language of the text apprehends readers in an aural register, from the frequent recurrence of gerunds ending in *-ing* to the duplication of phonemes and syllables across the single long sentence that details the organ's multitude of tonal possibilities that are "capable of causing sensual pleasure."[75]

Davies's translation of the passage transmits the affects or sound knowledge of al-Shidyāq's noisy language, making the aesthetic pleasures of the organ sensible to the ears of Anglophone readers as English noise, if no longer as noise that is produced by the singular structures of Arabic grammar, phonetics, and morphology. With reference to Jean-Luc Nancy's notion of sonority, indicating sound that has been freed from the expectation that it will be understood, it is possible to identify a sonorous quality in Davies's English here, as of language that must be *listened to* for its own sake rather than *heard* for its message, and which, in being listened to, "penetrates through the ear [and] propagates throughout the entire body something of its effects."[76]

In this regard, *Leg over Leg* can be seen as translating the *lafẓ* of *al-Sāq ʿalā al-sāq* at the expense of its *maʿnā*. Yet *maʿnā* is already not a stable property of this Arabic literary work; rather, *maʿnā* is compromised throughout by the exigencies of literariness, to the extent that slippages of meaning are often exploited within the diegetic reality of the text for comic ends. In one scene, al-Fāriyāq attempts to procure a dictionary (*qāmūs*) from a group of monks but is instead led into discussions of buffaloes (*jāmūs*) and nightmares (*kābūs*);[77] in another, it is al-Fāriyāq who is ridiculed for confusing the two phonetically similar English words *health* and *hell*.[78] Johnson describes such instances of verbal miscommunication as "translation errors committed by those in a position to fix meaning." Because they require Arabophone readers of *al-Sāq ʿalā al-sāq* to "read comparatively, even within Arabic" in order to see where the error has been made, she suggests, such mistakes establish linguistic difference as a core principle of al-Shidyāq's text.[79] For these readers, the errant language of the text is an occasion for comparative readings that set multiple phonetic versions of a word or phrase adjacent to each other to determine how they differ in what they signify, but also how they are alike materially in how they sound.

The aesthetic value of *al-Sāq ʿalā al-sāq* as a work of literature in Arabic becomes appreciable to Arabophone readers through such activities of balancing difference and likeness, content and form, in which they must engage frequently as they make their way through the narrative. An episode in book 2 that recounts the misadventures of a European priest in an Arabic-speaking country who attempts to preach to his congregants in Arabic offers a case in point. The priest begins his sermon by proclaiming

أيها الكوم كد فات الوكت الآن ولكني أهتب فيكم نهار الأهد الكابل إن شاء الله

Ayyuhā al-kawm kad fāta al-wakt al-āna wa-lākinnanī ahtub fīkum nahār al-ahad al-kābil in shāʾ Allah but stops short when he realizes that his mispronunciation of certain Arabic letters—he has substituted the sound of *kāf* for that of *qāf*, *hāʾ* for *khāʾ* and *ḥāʾ*, and *tāʾ* for *ṭāʾ*—has garbled the meaning of his message. After obtaining a new sermon in Arabic written by someone more adept at the language than he, he commits it to memory and returns to the church to start again:

يا أولادي المباركين الهادرين هنا لسماء هتبتي. وكبول نسيهتي وموهزتي.

> Yā awlādī al-mubārikīn al-hādirīn hunā li-samāʾ hutbatī. Wa-kubūl nasīhatī wa-mawhizatī.[80]

That the priest's meaning is once more unclear should come as no surprise, since his error the first time was not one of grammar, syntax, or vocabulary—that is, not one that could be fixed in writing—but an error of phonic dimensions. A text composed in impeccable Arabic betrays its speaker's inability to shape his vocal apparatus to articulating many of the language's hallmark sounds, which are now shown in the priest's second attempt to include those of the letters *ḍād*, *ʿayn*, *ṣād*, and *ẓāʾ* as well.

This episode stakes out Arabic's unique phonological territory by presenting a veritable catalog of Arabic phonemes that are not present in most European languages, among them the priest's own native language (in the context of the narrative, the priest can be presumed to be either English or French). In the case of many of these phonemes, as W. Wright opined in his nineteenth-century English grammar of the Arabic language, their "correct pronunciation . . . is scarcely possible for a European to acquire."[81] Yet even while the sounds of Arabic, employed narratively here for their dramatic and comic effects, interject a reminder of the difference between Arabic and the other languages of al-Shidyāq's contemporary milieu, sound also furnishes a means by which Arabic opens outward to processes of exchange with these other languages. Precisely because the priest's mistakes are phonological rather than grammatical, his erring speech that cannot be fixed through writing is nonetheless readily comprehensible to Arabophone readers of al-Shidyāq's text. For these readers, the priest's phrases can be easily decoded as

أيها القوم قد فات الوقت الآن ولكني أخطب فيكم نهار الأحد القابل إن شاء الله

> Ayyuhā al-qawm qad fāta al-waqt al-āna wa-lākinnanī akhṭub fīkum nahār al-aḥad al-qābil in shāʾ Allah
>
> O people, our time is up now but I will address you next Sunday, God willing

and

يا أولادي المباركين الحاضرين هنا لسمع خطبتي. وقبول نصيحتي وموعظتي

Yā awlādī al-mubārikīn al-ḥāḍirīn hunā li-samʿ khuṭbatī. Wa-qubūl naṣīḥatī wa-mawʿiẓatī

O my blessed children who are present here to hear my sermon. And to accept my advice and my counsel

through the simple act of pronouncing them aloud to hear how they sound. The written misspellings of Arabic that al-Shidyāq provides to represent the auditory valences of the priest's speech must be transmuted back into an aural register in order for their errors to be corrected—not on the page, however, but through a reader's ears. The aesthetic enjoyment of this passage derives from this transformative process, wherein readers are induced to listen to *lafẓ* as they compensate for the foreign priest's errors of *maʿnā*.

As he errs, the priest utters some words that do not mean correctly in context, and others that have no meaning at all. In the first category are *kawm* ("pile" or "refuse heap"), *hādirīn* ("those who are braying" or "those who are bellowing"), and *kubūl* ("shackles" or "fetters"); in the second category are words like *wakt* and *hutbah*. The aesthetic pleasures of this section of *al-Sāq ʿalā al-sāq* for Arabophone readers arise from their identifying both kinds of mistake. Yet how could such "translation errors," as Johnson calls them, themselves be translated? The nonsense words in al-Shidyāq's Arabic could not be rendered into English except perhaps as transliterations, while the meaningful words lose their humorous quality when no longer gesturing toward their almost-identical phonetic doubles (as, for example, *hādirīn* points to the contextually much more appropriate *ḥāḍirīn*, "those who are present").

When Davies, in the second volume of *Leg over Leg*, translates these lines from the priest's two sermons as "Good yolk, my lime is up but I shall peach to you next Fun Day, God willing" and "Blessed children lathered here today to spear my peach and listen to my insides,"[82] he translates neither the meaningful nor the meaningless words of al-Shidyāq's Arabic, but rather their illocutionary force, in J. L. Austin's sense: not what they mean, but what they do, how they convey the aesthetic sensibility of the text through language that is experienced as a real-time sonic event of the reading process.[83] Just as Arabophone readers of *al-Sāq ʿalā al-sāq* are invited to recognize the errors in the priest's speech through an act of listening to Arabic, Anglophone readers are prompted to say Davies's words aloud in order to hear, rather than to read, how they violate the semantic conventions of English. What in *Leg over Leg* the priest would presumably have wished to say—"Good folk, my time is up but I shall preach to you next Sunday, God willing" and "Blessed children gathered here today to hear my speech and listen to my advice"—becomes apparent in this change of medium from written language to language that is heard. The literariness of the Arabic text is translated via this process of English's own errors becoming apparent through sound: in the absurdist humor of a sermon discussing eggs and fruit that translates the humorous insults of the original text (where the congregation is referred to as a refuse heap, as braying like donkeys), and in the substitution or metathesis of phonemes—"spear my peach" for "hear my speech"—that serves to translate the nonsense words of the Arabic. Davies translates the *lafẓ* of al-Shidyāq's text insofar as *lafẓ* operates as an aesthetic join between the discursive formations of the Arabic text and how its language registers materially as sensible sound. In so doing, he creates what one reviewer called a "tour-de-force passage" of English writing.[84] Translation succeeds *because of*, and not despite, the formal untranslatability of the source text.

Through slippages of English meaning that make it less reliable as a language to communicate information and, in so being, also more literary, the literariness of al-Shidyāq's Arabic text becomes translatable. Jeffrey Sacks has argued that, relative to other nineteenth-century works of Arabic belles-lettres that yoke language to the divine word, the coherent human subject, or the nation, so that language "is compelled to appear through a privileging of totality in relation to form and the body," in *al-Sāq ʿalā al-sāq* "language falls to pieces."[85] Yielding to instances of "*lafz* (linguistic utterance) [that] refuses to subordinate itself to *maʿna* but pluralizes it," meaning gives way to the forms that language takes to make sense to a body.[86] Deconstructed in al-Shidyāq's Arabic writing into its constituent elements of form and content, language is recomposed through acts of listening by an Arabophone reader who is also, in Davies's case, the text's translator—only to decompose again in English, into errors of meaning that engage the bodies of Anglophone readers in new sense-making activities through which language's literariness can again be heard and enjoyed. The sound of the Arabic text is "transduced" in Davies's translation, to utilize sound theorist Stefan Helmreich's term, "chang[ing] as it traverses media, as it undergoes transformations in its energetic substrate . . . as it goes through transubstantiations that modulate both its matter and meaning."[87] Throughout this all, sound retains its capacity to affect a body. As it is transformed and transduced across languages and mediating substances, *lafẓ* becomes embodied, affecting, and worldly.

Orotund English

In an afterword near the end of *Leg over Leg*'s fourth and final volume, Davies explains that he translated principally with the aim of recreating the "percussive sound" of al-Shidyāq's language, rather than to provide a "semantically accurate correspondence" in English to the Arabic text of *al-Sāq ʿalā al-sāq*. Such a method of translating, he acknowledges, "violates . . . expectations of translation as a system of (more or less) one-to-one equivalency." Indeed, Davies admits, the further he progressed in translating al-Shidyāq's text, the less literal his translation became. In the first volume of *Leg over Leg*, he attempted to provide English "equivalents conveying, in principle, the exact meaning of the Arabic word;" in the later volumes, this strategy yielded to a variety of substitute approaches: deploying "terms gleaned from the Internet" and words copied from *Roget's Thesaurus* "without regard for one-to-one correspondence between the Arabic and the English," using "Google's Latin translation facility to create nonexistent terms imitative of the orotund Arabic," and creating new word-lists in Arabic correlated only to a limited extent with the lists in al-Shidyāq's text that became the basis for the translation's lists in English.[88]

Thus, in volume 4 of *Leg over Leg*, in a chapter whose English title is "A Voyage Festinate and Language Incomprehensibly and Inscrutably Intricate," Davies has al-Fāriyāq exclaim to his wife al-Fāriyāqiyyah in English, after receiving a bit of good news,

> Rictulate, dear risible Fāriyāqiyyah, and vociferate (though not in *alarm*)! Today not even she-wolves could do me *harm*! Dunk yourself in every ounce of unguent you *possess*; dab it and daub it, and take silk brocade for your *dress*! On such a day as this, our copulatorium must be redolent of *musk*—even its limpest occupant must experience *lust*! The giddy-pate, on such a day, must run *amok* and enjoy his *luck*!

as a translation of the Arabic lines

> آلا فاهزقي يا فارياقية المِهزاق. واسلُقي فما يضرني اليوم اسلاق. ونفّجي ما اسطعت أن تنفّجي. وضرّجي وضمّجي ودبّجي. هذا يوم يعبق فيه المكتَفن. ويشبق فيه من وهن ويشمق منه ذو الددن. ويفاز بالغدن.

The Arabic text[89] here employs such an array of rhetorical devices that al-Fāriyāq's speech is made nearly unintelligible, so that another character in the story, overhearing him and al-Fāriyāqiyyah conversing, exclaims, "What is this language that you are speaking? By God I did not understand a single thing you said."[90] To convey this language whose formal artifice impedes its comprehensibility, Davies mobilizes various translational strategies. To translate the morphological parallelism of the Arabic "*fa-ahziqī . . . al-mihzāq*" (literally, "so laugh . . . laugher"), in which the root letters *hzq* are used to generate multiple words within a single phrase, Davies coins the word "rictulate" as an imperative from the Latin root *rīs-*, related to laughter, from which "risible" is also derived.[91] In the next clause, "and vociferate" rhymes with "rictulate" to recreate the rhyming effect of al-Shidyāq's "*ahziqī . . . usluqī . . . naffajī*." Two sentences later, "dab it and daub it" replicates the metathetic aspect of the Arabic "*wa-ḍarrajī wa-ḍammajī wa-dabbajī*" while also reproducing some of its phonemes (the voiced alveolar *d*, the voiced bilabial *b*).

Yet while such translations reiterate the sonic effects of the Arabic text, many of Davies's English phrasings approximate only loosely their Arabic antecedents in terms of meaning. The English "and vociferate (though not in *alarm*)! Today not even she-wolves could do me *harm*!" is a noticeably inexact rendering of the meaning of the Arabic "*wa-usluqī fa-mā yaḍurrunī al-yawm islāq*"—more literally, "berate me, for today sharp words cannot harm me." The English line is both much longer than the Arabic line that it replaces and inclusive of semantic elements not present in the latter. The wolves that appear in the English version come from a secondary, archaic meaning of *aslaqa*, the verb from which the noun *islāq* is derived,[92] while Davies furthermore interpolates additional words into the speech that al-Fāriyāq delivers in *Leg over Leg*—"musk," "lust," "amok," "luck"—in order to create a rhyme scheme in the translation (signaled with italics in the printed text) similar to that which exists in Arabic.

To recognize the extent to which Davies has translated the form of language in al-Shidyāq's Arabic text at the expense of its content in passages like this one necessarily raises questions about both the efficacy and the ethics of his approach. Indeed, some critics have faulted *Leg over Leg* for being insufficiently faithful to its source material. Robyn Creswell, calling the rhymes and other paronomastic elements of Davies's English in *Leg over Leg* "labored," suggests that the translator "would have done better to settle for a translation into lively English that got the meanings right, rather than try to reproduce the virtuosity of the original."[93] Hilary Kilpatrick, pointing to a number of mistakes in Davies's text (in how it refers to certain historic personages who appear as characters in al-Shidyāq's book and the English terms that it gives for articles of women's clothing popular in the nineteenth-century Middle East), implies that in having followed an "exploratory" approach to the translation, Davies has regrettably sacrificed a degree of lexical precision.[94]

Others who have commented on Davies's translation note his unusually active and even authorial presence as a translator. Elspeth Carruthers writes that *Leg over Leg* showcases "a duel between writer and translator, with Shidyaq's convoluted wordplay and lists of recondite synonyms spurring Davies' translation on to match him, pun for pun, in English."[95] For Tarek El-Ariss, Davies is not al-Shidyāq's rival but his reincarnation: translating through acts of mimicry and sensual reactivation, El-Ariss proposes, Davies is "re-creating the scene of writing *Saq*, its degree zero, restaging al-Shidyaq as a way of entering his text."[96] In highlighting the connection between the Arabophone author and the Anglophone translator, however, these assessments of Davies's text occlude a fundamental aspect of his translation—that although Davies may be reactivating the same writing processes that al-Shidyaq employed to create *al-Sāq ʿalā al-sāq*, he has done so for entirely different purposes, and within an entirely different linguistic context. The rhymes, coinages, and portmanteaus that define Davies's writing in *Leg over Leg*, his uses of enumeration and repetition, homophony and alliteration, are expressions of English's stylistic possibilities and not those of Arabic. The scene of writing out of which Davies's text was born is wholly and inescapably Anglophone.

Far from being a translation that "holds the agency of the translator and the demands of her imagined or actual audience at bay," in Gayatri Chakravorty Spivak's words, or one that shackles English to the goal of exerting "an ethnodeviant pressure" on hegemonic U.S. Anglophone cultural values, in Lawrence Venuti's phrasing,[97] *Leg over Leg* is replete with innovative usages of English offered up for the enjoyment of an Anglophone readership. Such usages display unapologetically both the creative prowess of the translator and the aesthetic potential of his language. Translating a text whose own objective is "to bring into relief" ("*ibrāz*," to accentuate as by embossing or making physically prominent) the "oddities and rarities" of the Arabic language ("*gharāʾib al-lughah wa-nawādirihā*") so that they can be admired and appreciated to their greatest advantage, Davies has produced a text that displays the wondrous qualities of English.[98] If, as Rana Issa puts it, "the world al-Shidyāq manufactured"—through his prolific excavation of the Arabic grammatical tradition, his compulsive participation in debates over Arabic linguistics and lexicography with other intellectuals of his time, and his Arabic translation of the Bible that sacralized not the divine word but the Arabic language in which it was conveyed—"was made to orbit around Arabic," then the world manufactured by Davies revolves around English.[99] It is English that provides the material for Davies's virtuosic act of writing, and it is English that forms the basis for *Leg over Leg*'s aesthetic enjoyment.

In other words, it is in English, and not in Arabic, that Davies's text is literary. Moreover, I propose, only by eschewing a faithful translation of al-Shidyāq's Arabic could Davies's English have taken on such literary force. If we are to assign an ethical value to Davies's translation practice, then its ethics inhere in this formula: that as it translates al-Shidyāq's Arabic, Davies's English becomes literary, and in so doing, it transmits (as an affective transmission) the literariness of this Arabic text into the twenty-first-century world literary system. Through the literariness of Davies's translation, the literariness of *al-Sāq ʿalā al-sāq* is made apparent as a function of what it does in English and does *to* English.

While presenting English as primary to a domestic practice of writing that is virtuosic in its own right, Davies's translation affirms the existence of a prior virtuosic textuality in Arabic. In this respect, *Leg over Leg* challenges assumptions about how trajectories of influence play out when Arabic encounters Western languages and literary traditions via translation. According to the standard account given by both Western and Arab scholars, Arabic literary modernity emerged in the late nineteenth and early twentieth centuries as a result of the widespread translation and imitation of European literature by Arab intellectuals and writers.[100] Davies's translation inverts this narrative of inheritance and teleological progress by showing how a work of Arabic literature makes Anglophone writing more literary in the current era while suggesting additionally that it could have done so in the past as well: *al-Sāq ʿalā al-sāq*'s publication in 1855 predates the evolution of European literary modernism as such, and yet many of its stylistic devices—its metafictional authorial interventions, mix of registers and modes of language, and self-conscious references to its own status as written discourse—are inarguably modern, or even postmodern.

Rebecca Johnson describes *al-Sāq ʿalā al-sāq* as a "masterwork and a founding text of Arabic literary modernity,"[101] while for El-Ariss, it is a text that enacts an "alternative modernity" capable of unfixing Arabic literature from Eurocentric literary standards and histories.[102] Nadia Al-Bagdadi and Raḍwā ʿĀshūr both go so far as to call *al-Sāq ʿalā al-sāq* "the first Arab novel"[103] or "*al-riwāyah al-ʿArabiyyah al-ūlā*."[104] Although other critics have maintained that al-Shidyāq's text is "too idiosyncratic to be characterized by genre categorizations,"[105] the consensus among scholars of Arabic literature is that it is an "extraordinary" literary work, key to the development of the Arabic literary corpus since the nineteenth century.[106] With *Leg over Leg*, the extraordinariness of *al-Sāq ʿalā al-sāq* in its own sociocultural and historic context becomes the basis for a text that subverts and reconfigures the expectations of an Anglophone audience for what Arabic literature is, how it comes to be literary, and how it is apprehended through its English translation.

As Davies's translation is read and reviewed within networks of literary circulation that would have remained out of reach to the Arabic text, it carries the literary and linguistic world of *al-Sāq ʿalā al-sāq* with it in an English discourse that is stretched to capacity, pushed beyond the limits of equivalence and even beyond the requirements of meaning. Far from easy to read, *Leg over Leg* disrupts an Anglophone canon of world literature predicated on English's fluent readability. Yet Davies's translation presents English as less than optimally readable not to make a political statement by foreignizing the target language, but within an aesthetic event in which English reveals its own infinite recombinatory capacities and propensity to give itself away, to fall to pieces as it couples with the other language. Even while *Leg over Leg*'s reception reconfirms the instrumental importance of English in creating world literature, Davies's text also exposes the ease with which English renounces meaningfulness and fluency for the sake of transmitting sound heard from elsewhere, from another literary corpus and another mode of aesthetic expression. To quote Talal Asad's comments on translations that require a language to "transform" itself in order to negotiate the "unusual difficulty" of a source text, *Leg over Leg* "tests the tolerance of . . . [the translator's] own language for assuming unaccustomed forms" and, in spite of what Asad characterizes as the "weaker" position of Arabic relative to English in the global language field, finds it willing and able to do so.[107]

That it is Arabic in particular that has transformed English in these ways is readily apparent to any reader of Davies's translation, because descending from right to left across the horizontal sweep of each verso page in *Leg over Leg*'s four volumes are lines of Arabic script, set in a typeface "based on an analysis of five centuries of Ottoman manuscript practice."[108] Confronted by the visual intrusion of Arabic in a book ostensibly presented as a work of English writing, Anglophone readers must wonder at the genesis of the textual object that now appears before them, within which two languages and two literatures face each other across a weave of stitching and glue that holds them eternally intimate within a three-dimensional space. By "wonder" I intend to invoke the feeling of "exalted attention" identified by Stephen Greenblatt that reaestheticizes the antique art object for the viewer in the current moment in response to its immanent materiality.[109] In this case, wonder arises as a sense among monolingual Anglophone readers of *Leg over Leg* that the Arabic alphabet as it is present in the text *is* Arabic, and that by reading this translation they are coming into contact with the language as a physical presence on the page. For these readers, Arabic is given to them in the form of letters that are never other than material, that do not signify other than as haptic impingements perceived via the "kind of seeing that uses the eye like an organ of touch," as Laura Marks would say.[110]

Reading with the ears and touching with the eyes, Davies's audience encounters Arabic synesthetically and *synaesthetically*, with a feeling for Arabic's aesthetics that is sensorially—sonically and materially—apprehended. Arabic's presence in Davies's translation is not perceived as a semiotic difference, as a trace of foreign syntax that lingers within his English as Arabic lingers within the literally translated or "relexified" language of the Francophone Lebanese novels that Michelle Hartman studies, producing "unidiomatic, antiquated, or awkward-sounding French."[111] For the majority of Davies's Anglophone readers, who cannot compare across languages to weigh each sentence in the translation against its counterpart in the original text, judging where the translator has offered an equivalent word or phrase and where he has not, Arabic resonates within the English text as an affect rather than as a cognizable linguistic quantity. If *Leg over Leg* offers what one reviewer describes as "a compelling portrait of Arabic for those without the language . . . [wherein] the Arabic language itself is almost an independent character, with its own idiosyncratic existence, a sort of tutelary genius leading us to new adventures, thoughts and experiences," then it is through the affective and affecting quality of Davies's English that the translation most powerfully achieves this outcome.[112]

Wai Chee Dimock has proposed that a literary text's transitory movements across history (and between languages) can be mapped in the acts of hearing that it has induced along its route. It is by being heard in the greatest variety of contexts that a text accrues literariness, she writes, for "the literary . . . is not an attribute resident in a text, but a relation, a form of engagement, between a changing object and a changing recipient, between a tonal presence and the way it is differently heard over time."[113] The sonics of Davies's translation are what Anglophone reviewers find remarkable about it, and what draws them to the English text *as* an English text even as they are also being impinged upon perpetually by the sound knowledge of Arabic's own literariness, which comes at them from all directions at once and enters through multiple orifices—so that in reading this work of literature in English, their bodies cannot help but resound with the aesthetics of the Arabic text.

Sonority, Nancy writes, remakes the one who listens to it into a receptacle for the vibrant acoustics and rhythms of the other, into a "sonorous, sonorized body" flourishing in the concrescence of self and world.[114] What are the possibilities that might result from such events of reading as they accumulate in the Anglophone world literary space? Might they add up even to the beginning of a new embodied orientation toward Arabic literature in general, a new "approach," as the founders of the Library of Arabic Literature hoped would be the case? Or perhaps such an approach, were it to take shape in response to reading this translation or others in the Library of Arabic Literature series, would not in fact be new; perhaps it is one that has for a long time guided the reception of Arabic literature in English, as the next chapter will suggest. And perhaps Davies's method of translating the aesthetic formations of Arabic literary language into English is not new either, but only ratified for the first time within the dominant systems of publication and circulation that determine the contours and dynamics of a literary world.

2 / Vulgarity of *Saj*ʿ: The Scandalous Pleasures of Burton's *The Book of the Thousand Nights and a Night*

A row of elegant bronze and plaster busts graces each wall of the rare books reading room at the Huntington Library in San Marino, California. Flanked by busts of Dante Alighieri and Joseph Conrad, the bust of Sir Richard Francis Burton surveys the room imperiously, a pair of walrus whiskers and the faint jag of a scar on one cheek making his face instantly recognizable to anyone with even a passing familiarity with the visage of this famous Orientalist. Burton's is an easy face to know: alive from 1821 to 1890, Burton was photographed extensively during his lifetime. He has been the subject of numerous biographies, and in recent decades he has featured as the protagonist of a series of steampunk detective novels, a prizewinning work of historical fiction, and a Hollywood film.[1]

The bust of Burton at the Huntington Library was crafted by a Wyoming-based sculptor named William Davis for a conference held at the Library in 1990 to mark the centennial of Burton's death. In the initial cast that Davis sent for review to Edwards Metcalf, a grandson of Huntington family scion Henry Edwards Huntington and an important collector of Burton-related paraphernalia, Burton's moustache appeared too bushy, his scar—the relic of an injury he received in Somalia in 1855—was too deep, and his scowl was too overbearing. "Of course, none of us living today ever knew the man personally and all we have to go by are photographs and our mental imagination," Metcalf admitted to Davis. But Burton's face was iconic, and it had to be done right—or at least, it needed to match Metcalf's idea of it. The cast was returned to Davis to correct.[2]

Today the bust stands watch over an extensive archive of Burton's personal papers and annotated volumes, all of which are available to researchers to peruse in an idyllically appointed setting amid more than a hundred acres of flowering cactus, English roses, Japanese bonsai, and hedgerows of Mediterranean olive and native California oak. In the summer of 2018, I spent a month at the Huntington Library trying to better understand Burton's relationship to a work of Arabic literature that he claimed to have translated, a work whose fame exceeds even that of Burton himself: *Alf laylah wa-laylah* (literally, "a thousand nights and a night," but best known in English as the "Arabian Nights"), a collection of stories of mixed Indian, Persian, Greek, Chinese, and Arab provenance linked together by a frame narrative about a courageous young woman named Shahrazād (Scheherazade) who defers her own death night after night by spinning a new yarn for the vengeful king who holds her prisoner. Although Burton published dozens of books of his own authorship—mostly adventure-filled ethnographic tomes chronicling his wide-ranging travels throughout Africa and the Middle East, India, South America, and the United States—it is his monumental ten-volume *The Book of the Thousand Nights and a Night: A Plain and Literal Translation of the Arabian Nights' Entertainments* and its six supplemental volumes, all published between 1885 and 1888, upon which his reputation largely rests.[3] That Burton now keeps company in the Huntington Library's reading room with the writers of the *Divine Comedy* and *Heart of Darkness*, two giants of the Western literary canon, is in no small part a credit to the enduring fame of his *Nights*.

If the worldliness of a work of literature, per David Damrosch, can be adduced from its citational and circulatory afterlife, the intertextual resonances that it has accumulated and the new audiences that it has gained far from the original sites of its production and dissemination, then Burton's *Nights* is undoubtedly world literature.[4] In addition to the copious scholarly studies of the work that have appeared over the last century-plus, Burton's *Nights* has had a rich afterlife as itself an object of literary representation. In Jorge Luis Borges's short story "El Aleph," it is after consulting Burton's *Nights* that the narrator becomes convinced that his vertiginous glimpse of the whole universe contained within a cellar in Buenos Aires is no more than an optical illusion.[5] In Salman Rushdie's novel *Shame*, a boy confined from birth within his family's dilapidated ancestral mansion teaches himself about life outside by purloining "the Burton translation of the *Alf laylah wa laylah*" from his late grandfather's forgotten library.[6] The worldliness of Burton's *Nights* rebounds onto both text and translator, securing a lasting legacy for both.

Burton's *Nights* is only one among many English-language versions of the *Alf laylah wa-laylah* stories, which were first introduced to Anglophone audiences in the early eighteenth century via "cheap chap-books" adapted from Antoine Galland's enormously popular multivolume French translation *Les mille et une nuits* (1704–1717).[7] Lengthier compilations of the tales in English followed from the translators Jonathan Scott (1800/1811), Edward Forster (1802), George Lamb (1826), Henry Torrens (1838), Edward Lane (1839–1840), John Payne (1882–1884), Edward Powys Mathers (1923), N. J. Dawood (1954), Husain Haddawy (1990), and Malcolm and Ursula Lyons (2008), in addition to Burton's translation. A translation by Yasmine Seale, the first female translator of the *Alf laylah wa-laylah* stories into English, was published in 2021. The majority of these translations, with the exception of the most recent ones, are obscure or out of print today. Why has Burton's version prevailed when these have not? What has been the draw of his *Nights* for writers like Borges and Rushdie who immortalized it in their own fiction? What is the secret of its worldliness?

This chapter proposes an answer to this constellation of questions: that in comparison to most of the other English-language editions of the *Alf laylah wa-laylah* stories published over the last three hundred years, Burton's is uniquely able to be appreciated for its literary qualities. Borges seems to have had this opinion of it—in his estimation, Burton's translation "was the best version of the *Nights*" because it opened a "gateway to the infinite *mise en abime* of story telling" characteristic of the *Alf laylah wa-laylah* tales, according to Suzanne Jill Levine.[8] In *The Written World: The Power of Stories to Shape People, History, Civilization*, Harvard literary scholar Martin Puchner's recent popular history of world literature, it is a long quotation from Burton's *Nights* that is used to exemplify the literary magic of the *Alf laylah wa-laylah* stories throughout their long circulatory history. These are stories that, Puchner writes, "it feels as if I have always known," for they are "everywhere . . . [and like] a Jinni . . . [they] change their shape and assume any number of guises . . . ready to inspire wonder and suspense, delight and horror, in new audiences yet again."[9] The worldly qualities that Puchner ascribes to the *Alf laylah wa-laylah* stories are equally—or perhaps, more truly—those of Burton's *Nights*, as it is by means of reading Burton's English text that Puchner has come to appreciate this work of Arabic literature.[10]

Unacknowledged by many admirers of Burton's *Nights*, however, is the fact that it is largely a plagiarism of another translator's work. This translator was John Payne, whose nine-volume *The Book of the Thousand Nights and One Night*, along with an accompanying three-volume supplement titled *Tales from the Arabic*, was published during the three years immediately prior to the release of Burton's own translation.[11] As early as 1906, Burton's biographer Thomas Wright alleged that he had taken "at least three-quarters" of his text from Payne.[12] Indeed, Wright claimed, Burton's *Nights* was "little more than a transcript of Payne's . . . [as] for page after page he uses Payne's identical words and phrases."[13] Wright offered in support of his assertions a meticulous ten-page parallel-column comparison of several stories that appeared in both *Nights* editions. The comparison reveals a multitude of similarities: for example, Payne's version of a story titled "The Blacksmith Who Could Handle Fire Without Hurt" begins, "A certain pious man once heard that there abode in such a town a blacksmith who could put his hand into the fire and pull out the red-hot iron without its doing him any hurt," while Burton's version of the same story begins, "It reached the ears of a certain pious man that there abode in such a town a blacksmith who could put his hand into the fire and pull out the iron red-hot, without the flames doing him aught of hurt."[14] That Burton borrowed from Payne, and not the reverse, is confirmed by the historical record: sections of Payne's translation appeared in print in 1879, whereas no evidence exists that Burton began to work seriously on his translation until as late as 1884.[15]

This chapter takes the persistent worldliness of Burton's *Nights* as an invitation to explore how Arabic literature becomes worldly in English when neither text nor translator are what they seem to be. If Burton's *Nights* is neither an original nor a faithful rendition of its supposed Arabic source text,[16] what experience of the Arabic textuality of *Alf laylah wa-laylah* does it then proffer to Anglophone readers? Given that Burton's plagiarism of Payne has been "an open secret among scholars of the *Arabian Nights* for many decades," Paulo Lemos Horta finds the continued enthusiasm for Burton's translation today among both scholars and the general public "puzzling;" in his own monograph *Marvellous Thieves: Secret Authors of the Arabian Nights*, Horta attempts to rectify this situation by devoting most of a chapter to enumerating Burton's "thefts" from Payne.[17] What puzzles Horta, however, impels me to consider more carefully the specific linguistic and aesthetic choices that Burton made in bringing these Arabic stories into English, and in particular, those that set his *Nights* apart from Payne's—for while the two translations are indistinguishable at certain points, they are in many other respects far from the same text.

An Orientalist's Body

To understand what aspect of the Arabic text of *Alf laylah wa-laylah* is translated into English via Burton's *Nights*, continuing to attract scholars, critics, and general readers over the longue durée of its circulatory afterlife, requires a shift in scope and scale from my examination of Humphrey Davies's translation of the literariness of Aḥmad Fāris al-Shidyāq's *al-Sāq ʿalā al-sāq* in chapter 1. First, whereas the events of worlding discussed in the previous chapter unfold within a comparatively rarified slice of the Anglophone literary market, the ones explored here resonate laterally across a wide swath of the English-language literary field.

To move from Davies to Burton as the Arabic-to-English translator under consideration also demands newfound attention to the particular body of the translator, whose sensory experiences of language as they inform a practice of literary translation cannot be described or theorized without reference to this body's unique affective history. Toward which poles or into which forcefields does a translator's body incline as it turns to meet the impingements of the sensible world, including those that radiate from language's material formations, and why? How did Burton, a man whose relationship to the Arabophone Middle East was "bound by his senses . . . entangled in seeing and feeling, in experiencing life [there] on the mere physical level," approach the task of translating what was—in the view of Europeans at the time—the region's most important work of literature, and for a Victorian public whose attitude toward bodies in general, and Eastern bodies in particular, was notoriously fraught?[18]

Burton's face, which confronted me daily with the irreducible physicality of this long-ago translator as I pored over his papers in the reading room at the Huntington Library that summer, is one part of the body that I seek in this chapter to retrieve, in order to understand its role in the creation of Burton's *Nights* volumes. His hands are another, their imprint tangible in the ink and pencil lead of his margin notes, which, when I pressed my own fingertips to their gossamer curves, awakened in me a version of the "archive pleasure" that Antoinette Burton has described—the "rapturous" experience of a direct physical encounter with the past that archival research makes possible.[19] Or perhaps the pleasure I felt at making contact with Burton through his annotations could be better described, in Carolyn Steedman's terms, as "feverish," delirious with the anxiety (and yet also, the hope?) that to touch what Burton had touched would be to allow myself to be contaminated by the affective remnants of this ancestral translator, to breathe his dust.[20]

Burton's body has been much described by his biographers. Particular focus has been given to the question of whether or not Burton was circumcised as an adult so that he could more easily blend in among the men of the predominantly Islamic societies where he spent a good part of his career, first as an officer in the British East India Company's private army in present-day India and Pakistan, then as an explorer and cartographer in the employ of the Royal Geographical Society in the Arabian Peninsula, and finally as British consul in Damascus. As Edward Rice puts it, although "nineteenth-century Englishmen were not normally circumcised," Burton believed the operation to be a "necessity for those who would travel in Muslim lands."[21]

Almost invariably, biographers justify their attention to Burton's genitalia on the grounds that if he were indeed circumcised (as most seem to presume that he was, though with apparently scant evidence),[22] this fact reveals the depth of his commitment to cultivating a physically mediated, experiential knowledge of the foreign sociocultural environs in which he lived and worked.[23] Although he does not discuss the state of Burton's genitals, Edward Said in *Orientalism* offers a similar appraisal of this Orientalist's approach to the East, singling Burton out as a rare nineteenth-century European who obtained his expertise about "the Orient by living there, actually seeing it firsthand, truly trying to see Oriental life from the viewpoint of a person immersed in it"—so successfully, indeed, by Said's account, that "he was able to become an Oriental."[24] For Thomas Assad, Burton's efforts to physically embody Oriental characteristics aided him in his professional and personal endeavors by allowing him to "pass" as an Arab, while for Kwame Anthony Appiah, Burton's "voracious assimilation" of all things Eastern and Islamic betokened a "rootless" cosmopolitanism.[25] Burton himself reported that while traveling in the Middle East he grew a long beard, darkened his skin with henna, and frequently wore Arab clothing.[26] According to his wife Isabel, he sometimes attended society parties in London costumed as "a Syrian shaykh" who "was supposed not to understand English."[27]

Can a connection be made between Burton the Orientalist and Burton the translator? Thomas Wright thought so, writing that Burton's "whole life" in the Middle East region, including his use of disguises, the alleged proficiency in several dialects of spoken Arabic that he acquired during his years there, and his "learning the ways and customs of the various people among whom he was thrown," "indeed was a preparation for '*The Arabian Nights*.'"[28] At the heart of the issue here, I propose, is Burton's relationship with Arabic itself. According to Said, Burton "spoke the language flawlessly."[29] Paulo Lemos Horta, on the other hand, is dubious, suggesting that Burton's supposed "fluency" in this and other Eastern languages "has been the subject of some mythmaking" by scholars, biographers, and Burton himself.[30]

At the Huntington Library, I examined three Arabic editions of *Alf laylah wa-laylah* that Burton owned, and like Horta, I found them to be sparsely annotated.[31] Horta takes this fact as evidence that Burton either did not know well or rarely read Arabic.[32] Unremarked upon by Horta, however, is that Burton's copies of a number of books containing *Nights*-related material in English—the translations by Jonathan Scott and Edward Lane, Payne's standalone volume *Alaeddin and the Enchanted Lamp*, and the volumes of his own translation and its supplements that he held in his personal library, among others—contain extensive margin notes by him both in transliterated Arabic and in Arabic script, as do many of his Arabic dictionaries and textbooks. Among these notes are vocabulary lists, translations of various English terms into Arabic, and, very often, amended spellings in Latin script of Arabic words (including many that appear in the Arabic *Nights*) that another writer has transliterated differently, the latter revealing specifically Burton's interest in the comparative phonologies of Arabic and English.[33]

A portion of Burton's annotations concern sexual and erotic terminology. Inscribed in Burton's hand in Latin script on the flyleaf of an Arabic-English dictionary authored by the well-known nineteenth-century Arabist Francis Joseph Steingass, for example, are the words *mubāsharah*, *bakāmah*, *jurdān*, *jaẓẓa*, and *zumaliq*—defined in this dictionary respectively as to "have sexual intercourse," to "abstain from sexual intercourse," "penis of hoofed animals," to "lie with a woman," and "[he] who emits his sperm before coition is completed"—along with some two-dozen other words of a similar nature.[34] Rana Kabbani has noted Burton's propensity to be "fascinated by all manifestations of sexuality" that came from the East,[35] and indeed, as many critics have observed, his *Nights* volumes are replete with pseudo-anthropological footnotes describing erotic practices and customs that he claimed to have witnessed during his travels in the Orient. Yet there is also a profoundly philological dimension to the attention that Burton gives to such terminology in his notes, reflected in his scrupulous use of diacritic markings in the Latin lettering to indicate the elongated vowels of each Arabic word and in the page references that he often provides for terms that are cited with variant spellings or definitions in multiple printed sources.

Burton's notes are simultaneously a written documentation of where and when this Orientalist found the Arabic language titillating or arousing, and a demonstration of a translator's philological enthusiasm for recording how meaning and sound move between Arabic and English. For me, as I examined Burton's notes in the Huntington Library's reading room under the watchful gaze of the man himself, they acted as a copula between this particular translator's body and the affective pleasures of language and linguistic comparison insofar as these could serve as the premise for a practice of translating Arabic literature into English. In the context of my own study of Burton's *Nights*, they furnished a link between Burton's embodied approach to the Orient and his embodiment of the role of a translator of Oriental literature. Not only were Burton's lived experiences in the Arabophone Middle East crucial to how both he and others came to conceive of him as *capable* of translating the *Alf laylah wa-laylah* stories from Arabic into English, even if the translation that he ultimately published under his name was in actuality heavily indebted to the translational labors of someone else,[36] but I propose that Burton's no less lived experiences of the Arabic language itself were equally formative in shaping the English text of the *Nights* that he produced, and which is still read and enjoyed by Anglophone audiences today.

A Vulgar Tongue

To examine closely the language of Burton's *Nights* for what it reveals about his methods of turning Arabic into English, such as they serve to differentiate his translation from Payne's, necessitates triangulating between two English texts and an Arabic literary work that is itself "palimpsestic" and ill defined, described by Saree Makdisi and Felicity Nussbaum as a "vertiginously unstable text" whose material history embraces "editions, compilations, translations, variations, and derivations" across multiple media and genres and in many languages.[37] This history confounds any attempt that a scholar might make at verifying whether a given translation or version of the *Alf laylah wa-laylah* stories is accurate to any single authoritative Arabic original. Thus, in order for a comparison to be made among Payne's and Burton's English texts and the text of *Alf laylah wa-laylah* in Arabic, this endeavor must be guided first by some understanding of what it was that Burton sought to accomplish in his version of the *Nights*. What alterations did he make to Payne's translation—which was already in print by the time Burton's own *Nights* was published—before passing it off as his own, and for what ends?

Wright proposes a purely economic motive: Payne printed only five hundred copies of his translation, and when these sold out immediately and Payne was unwilling to print more, Burton saw that there might be a profit to be made from issuing a very similar text couched as a new translation.[38] Once again, however, a return to the archives adds a further layer to the story. Burton first learned of Payne's translation in November 1881 from an advertisement in *The Athenaeum*, an influential London literary magazine of the era. Immediately thereafter, he published a notice in the same magazine in which he claimed, almost certainly speciously, to be only "a year's hard labour" away from completing a full translation of the *Alf laylah wa-laylah* stories himself.[39] Payne, perhaps wishing to avoid provoking Burton's ire, or perhaps flattered to be receiving Burton's attention and hopeful that an association with the well-known Orientalist would lead to better sales of his own forthcoming translation, invited Burton to collaborate with him in placing the final touches on his *Nights* manuscript.[40] Burton declined, but over the next several years Payne sent Burton the proofs of each volume of his *Nights* to look over before it went to print,[41] and the two men fell into a regular correspondence.

Transcripts of forty letters that Burton wrote to Payne between 1881 and 1890, copied out by hand by Thomas Wright from originals lent to him by Payne after Burton's death, are held in the Huntington Library's Burton collection. Analyzed as a paratextual frame to Burton's *Nights*, these letters reveal Burton's methodology for adapting Payne's text for his own use to hinge upon specific linguistic features of the Arabic source material. In one letter, Burton urges Payne to reproduce in his English translation the intralineal rhymes characteristic of many of the Arabic *Alf laylah wa-laylah* stories in their various published versions, writing, "I would preserve the rhymes such as 'the trees are growing and the water flowing and Allah all good bestowing' etc."[42] In another letter, he objects to Payne's manner of transliterating Arabic names into the Latin alphabet. Noting that Payne has rendered *Qamar al-Zamān* as "Kemerezzeman," with the Arabic short *a* vowel, or *fatḥah*, represented by the English *e*, Burton declares, "I should much have preferred the old 'Camaralzaman' to Kemerezzeman. All Arabs pronounce Kamar (Badawi 'Gamar') and it is hard to explain how terrible Kemer is! If you articulate the *k* (ق) properly it is impossible to pronounce a short *e* after it."[43] In a third letter, Burton suggests that the Arabic word *midfa'* (cannon) should be transliterated "madfaa" rather than "midfaa" as Payne evidently has it, because the former spelling reflects "the pronunciation all over the Moslem world."[44]

The problem with Payne's translation overall, according to Burton, is not that Payne has translated the Arabic source material inaccurately, but that he has made it unpronounceable. A translator of the *Nights* stories, Burton insists, should not "quote the dictionaries" as Payne has done, but rather "the vulgar tongue."[45] Burton returns to this idea in the foreword to his own translation, where he explains that the transliterated Arabic words that appear throughout his English text are spelled in concordance with the notion that "as words are the embodiment of ideas and writing is of words, so the word is the spoken word; and we should write it as pronounced."[46] For Burton, to translate Arabic into English requires collapsing the distance between writing and speech, a move that hangs upon the recognition that both written words and spoken words are varieties of embodied language. As words written out on a page give a physical presence to the ideas that they semiotically express, speech signifies through a voice that emerges from the body, "rising from the chest, up into the throat to shudder the vocal chords, to appear . . . in and then from out of the mouth, rippling behind the facial muscles, the nasal passage, and along the jaw," in Brandon LaBelle's description.[47]

The tongue that Burton would quote is vulgar because it speaks in a voice shaped by its passage through the body. Associated for LaBelle with "dramas and secrets of bodily pleasure" that are sensual and erotic as well as semiotic, the tongue produces both language and intensities of pleasurable feeling with a single tensile organ.[48] As a methodology put into practice in Burton's own *Nights*, vulgarity indexes the degree to which the translating language will not be held to standards of dictionary equivalence, because what it translates is not the meaning of the source language but its capacity to generate bodily pleasure. What Burton translated from *Alf laylah wa-laylah* that Payne omitted can be thought of as the source text's vocality, insofar as the voicedness of Arabic literary language could be extracted as a translatable component of the whole. If voice is the "extralinguistic" excess of language, a "material element recalcitrant to [the] meaning" that words are intended to communicate, as Mladen Dolar suggests, then by seeking to restore vocality to Payne's text Burton aimed to reinvigorate the former's English with a materiality and an extrasemantic potential that it had previously lacked.[49]

In *Leg over Leg*, discussed in chapter 1, equivalence in translation contrasts aesthetically with acoustic effect, such that the aesthetics of Davies's text derive from the sound of English rather than from how English functions to replicate the meaning of the Arabic words that it translates. Here Burton's *Nights* differs from Payne's translation aesthetically to the extent that it reproduces an embodied oral dimension of literary Arabic that Payne's does not, but which Burton quotes, activates, and ventriloquizes.

Long before they circulated in bound volumes like the ones that Payne and Burton owned in the late nineteenth century, the Arabic *Alf laylah wa-laylah* stories were recited orally in coffeehouses and private homes throughout the Arabic-speaking world. The rhymes and colloquial phrasings that abound in written Arabic versions of the tales produced after the fourteenth century CE, along with the "accordion"-like structure of the collection's frame narrative, indicate for many scholars who have studied the transmission of these stories in Arabic a work of literature designed to be performed aloud.[50] The vulgar tongue that Burton would quote is rooted in this history, and it will speak this history into Burton's English text as a plurality of vocal articulations, the record of a literary work's collective embodied past.

Without necessarily positioning his translation closer than Payne's to the meaning of the Arabic source material, Burton, I suggest, took inspiration and license from the Arabic stories' oral "popular" heritage—as it has been characterized by Muhsin al-Musawi—to deploy English in ways that highlighted its own oral qualities.[51] Many critics have commented on the particularities of the language of Burton's *Nights*. Borges wrote that Burton's "vocabulary is . . . unparalleled," noting that in his translation, "archaic words coexist with slang, the lingo of prisoners or sailors with technical terms. He does not shy away from the glorious hybridization of English. . . . Neologisms and foreignisms are in plentiful supply."[52] Lawrence Venuti takes the heterogeneity of English in Burton's *Nights* as reflective of a "foreignizing intention," showing Burton to have been making a deliberate attempt to use his translation to undermine the hegemonic norms of English literary discourse as it existed in Victorian times.[53] Tarek Shamma, on the other hand, dismisses Burton's nonstandard uses of English as an exoticizing gesture that "only facilitated the familiar process of affirming the self in contrast to the emphasized difference—or rather eccentricity—of the Other."[54]

Looking past the polarity of these interpretations, I ask instead what Burton's language adds to the aesthetic experience of reading his text. I contend that, to the extent that how Burton wrote English pushed it to and even beyond the limits of intelligibility, his *Nights* invites an Anglophone audience to embrace—and take pleasure in—a more-than-usually direct correspondence between the vocal qualities of language and its semiotic transcription. His is a text that, to borrow Haun Saussy's phrasing, reveals "alphabetic writing" as "a container inadequate to hold the burgeoning multiplicity . . . [of] orality."[55] Engaging readers with English words that emerge from the body in general as the primary vehicle of language production, but also from the individual and historically specific body of this Orientalist translator, Burton's text activates readers' bodies, too, in the event of translating a work of Arabic literature into English.

A Speaking Mouth

Among the items in the Huntington Library's Burton collection are twelve looseleaf pages of printed text that bear numerous revisions in Burton's handwriting. Listed in the Library's official collection guide as "A Plain and Literal Translation of the Arabian Nights' Entertainments, Now Entitled The Book of the Thousand Nights and a Night: corrected printed proofs of p. 159–170," they are in fact pages extracted from the third volume of Payne's *Tales from the Arabic*.[56] These so-called proofs became the basis for pages 269–277 of Burton's own second supplemental volume.[57] According to Quentin Keynes, a prominent Burton enthusiast of the twentieth century, Burton owned two complete sets of Payne's translation of the *Nights* stories, one that he kept for his personal use and one that "he had disbound . . . for the printer" and "heavily" annotated with his own comments and revisions.[58]

On one level, then, as such bald evidence of Burton's debts to Payne makes clear, the language of Burton's *Nights* cannot be examined independent of an examination of the language of Payne's text. However, as noted earlier, a survey of the marginalia in certain volumes that were in Burton's possession at the time of his death indicates that he had a philologist's interest in and knowledge of Arabic, while implying moreover that he read at least some portion of the *Alf laylah wa-laylah* stories in their original language. All of this suggests strongly that any in-depth study of the language of Burton's *Nights* must therefore seriously consider the possibility that its degree of difference from the language of Payne's text, as well as from standard Victorian English, is due to the influence of Arabic.[59] As Burton's copy of an 1835 edition of *Alf laylah wa-laylah* that was printed in Bulaq (now part of Cairo) contains the greatest number of his annotations, especially in the early pages, in what follows I take this edition as representative of the stories' Arabic text for purposes of comparing it to both Burton's and Payne's translations. It is in this comparison that the vulgarity of Burton's English becomes legible as a methodology for a practice of translating Arabic literature into English.

In Payne's *Nights*, the frame story that introduces the collection begins like this:

> It is recorded in the chronicles of the things that have been done of time past that there lived once, in the olden days and in bygone ages and times, a king of the kings of the sons of Sasan, who reigned over the Islands of India and China and was lord of armies and guards and servants and retainers. He had two sons, an elder and a younger, who were both valiant cavaliers, but the elder was a stouter horseman than the younger. When their father died, he left his empire to his elder son, whose name was Shehriyar, and he took the government and ruled his subjects justly, so that the people of the country and of the empire loved him well; whilst his brother Shahzeman became King of Samarcand of Tartary.[60]

In Burton's translation, the same lines are given thus:

> Therein it is related (but Allah is All-knowing of His hidden things and All-ruling and All-honoured and All-giving and All-gracious and All-merciful!) that, in tide of yore and in time long gone before, there was a King of the Kings of the Banu Sásán in the Islands of India and China, a Lord of armies and guards and servants and dependents. He left only two sons, one in the prime of manhood and the other yet a youth, while both were Knights and Braves, albeit the elder was a doughtier horseman than the younger. So he succeeded to the empire; when he ruled the land and lorded it over his lieges with justice so exemplary that he was beloved by all the peoples of his capital and of his kingdom. His name was King Shahryár, and he made his younger brother, Shah Zamán hight, King of Samarcand in Barbarian-land.[61]

Notable differences between the two translations include Burton's lengthy invocation of Allah, absent from Payne's version of the passage's first line; the fact that Burton's version begins and ends with rhyming phrases—"tide of yore and in time long gone before" and "King of Samarcand in Barbarian-land"—whereas Payne's version contains no rhymes; that Burton substitutes "Banu," a transliteration of the Arabic بنو, for Payne's "the sons of;" and that Burton replaces several of Payne's more everyday words ("past," "braver," "named") with archaic equivalents ("yore," "doughtier," "hight"). No scholar to my knowledge has offered a unifying explanation for why Burton altered Payne's text the way he did that locates the motivation for his approach predominantly in a single feature of Arabic literary language. This is precisely what I propose to do here, and the aspect of the Arabic of *Alf laylah wa-laylah* to which, I suggest, Burton attempts to give heed throughout his translation is its use of *saj* ʿ, a variety of unmetered, rhymed prose that is ubiquitous in the Arabic stories. Associated in the Qur'an with the declamatory orations of pagan soothsayers, during the tenth through twelfth centuries CE *saj* ʿ gained traction as a literary technique in the picaresque *maqāmah* genre most masterfully exemplified by Badīʿ al-Zamān al-Hamadhānī and Abū Muḥammad al-Qāsim ibn ʿAlī al-Ḥarīrī, becoming a defining feature of classical Arabic literature or *adab*.[62]

In the Bulaq edition of *Alf laylah wa-laylah*, the frame story begins with a passage in *saj* ʿ:[63]

> (حكي) والله أعلم أنه كان فيما مضى من قديم الزمان وسالف العصر والأوان ملك من ملوك ساسان بجزائر الهند والصين صاحب جند وأعوان وخدم وحشم له ولدان أحدهما كبير والأخر صغير وكانا فارسين بطلين وكان الكبير أفرس من الصغير وقد ملك البلاد وحكم بالعدل بين العباد وأحبه أهل بلاده ومملكته وكان اسمه الملك شهريار وكان أخوه الصغير اسمه الملك شاه زمان وكان ملك سمرقند العجم.

Displaying a variable rhyme scheme and a free-ranging rhythmic quality rather than a consistent meter, these lines are not poetry. Transliterated, the passage reads:

> Ḥukiya wa-allāhu aʿlam annahu kāna fī-mā maḍā min qadīmi al-zamāni wa-sālifi al-ʿaṣri wa-al-awāni malikun min mulūki Sāsān bi-jazāʾiri al-Hind wa-al-Ṣīn ṣāḥibu jundin wa-aʿwānin wa-khadamin wa-ḥashamin lahu waladāni aḥaduhumā kabīrun wa-al-ākharu ṣaghīrun wa-kānā fārisayni baṭalayni wa-kāna al-kabīru afrasa min al-ṣaghīri wa-qad mallaka al-bilāda wa-ḥakama bil-ʿadali bayna al-ʿibādi wa-aḥabbahu ahlu bilādihi wa-mamlakatihi wa-kāna ismuhu al-malika Shahriyār wa-kāna akhūhu al-ṣaghīru ismuhu al-malika Shāh Zamān wa-kāna malika Samarqand al-ʿajami.

*Saj*ʿ generates multiple associations in this Arabic text. It affirms the literariness of the language of *Alf laylah wa-laylah* according to traditional standards of *adab*, despite the stories' popular origins. It also links this literary quality specifically to the self-affirming give-and-take cycles of oral discourse. ʿAbdallah Ibrahim proposes that the "varied, flexible and evolving rhythm" of *saj*ʿ reflects "the needs of speech transmission and . . . the demands of reception."[64] Meanwhile, the contemporary Syrian poet Adūnīs, in his *Introduction to Arab Poetics*, describes *saj*ʿ as "a form of rhythmic speech with end rhymes . . . and a quality of evenness and regularity and sameness [as is found] in speech."[65] With respect to how *saj*ʿ functions in the Arabic *Nights* stories, Mia Gerhardt notes that it is used especially in the "standing formulas" that begin and end many of the tales, as well as "in enumerative, descriptive and sentimental passages of special interest." Distinct from its role as a "mark of stylistic artistry" in highbrow classical Arabic literature, in *Alf laylah wa-laylah*, Gerhardt suggests, *saj*ʿ is often deployed with no clear purpose other than "just for the fun of it."[66] *Saj*ʿ makes this work of literature fun, underwriting an affective payoff for both a performer and an audience. Its aleatory cadences are there to be enjoyed, differentiating the language of the *Nights* stories from nonliterary language by virtue of its aesthetic appeal.

For many nineteenth-century Anglophone translators of Arabic literature, however, *saj*ʿ was a token of what they could not or should not attempt to translate into English of a source text's literary qualities. To translate *saj*ʿ was not only "impracticable" but would produce "extremely ungraceful" and even illegible English, claimed Theodore Preston, a Cambridge University scholar whose 1850 translation of al-Ḥarīrī's *maqāmāt* converts the *saj*ʿ of the Arabic text into unrhymed English prose.[67] Payne was similarly opposed to translating the *saj ʿ* of the *Alf laylah wa-laylah* stories, explaining that although this aspect of the text "would have been by no means difficult" to translate, he had decided "that it was undesirable to do so, as it seemed to me that the *seja*-form was utterly foreign to the genius of English prose."[68]

Burton took a wholly opposite view of *saj ʿ*. In the Translator's Foreword that opens the first volume of his *Nights*, he defends *saj ʿ* as the "*sine quâ non* for a complete reproduction of the original" Arabic text.[69] In the Terminal Essay at the end of the tenth volume, he calls it "the basis of all Arabic euphony."[70] It was in such terms that Burton contested the troping of *saj ʿ* as the ultimate untranslatable. If for other translators *saj ʿ* underscored an essential incommensurability between Arabic literary language and English writing, then for Burton it was that without which a translation of the *Nights* stories would remain incomplete, as well as a principal source of what he found to like about these tales in Arabic. Lending a pleasing sound—a euphonic quality—to the language of the Arabic text, *saj ʿ* made these stories not only fun to read and hear recited aloud, but fun to translate.

Michael Cooperson has proposed that the translation of Arabic *saj ʿ* into English must begin "with the recognition that . . . [its use] in Arabic prose produces a kind of markedness" in language homologous with its "literariness." The essence of *saj ʿ* is not as a particular style of writing but as a formal instrument through which language is rendered aesthetic. Thus, Cooperson argues, a translator of *saj ʿ* does not need to make "English distinctive *in the same way* as the Arabic;" rather, it is via English that is marked as distinctively literary by the translator within English's own set of possible linguistic and discursive registers that *saj ʿ* becomes no longer "untranslatable." In Cooperson's translation of al-Ḥarīrī's *maqāmāt*, *saj ʿ* is translated into a range of ethnic and global Englishes (Scots English, Singaporean English), jargons ("legalese" and "management speak"), and slangs (including "the cowboy slang of the American West"). Justifying this approach for Cooperson is that it allows him "to show off English as al-Ḥarīrī meant to show off Arabic."[71]

Along similar lines, I suggest, Burton's version of the opening passage of the *Alf laylah wa-laylah* frame story takes license from the *saj ʿ* of the original text to do various things to English that make it distinctive as a literary language. In addition to employing rhyme and assonance in English—two central elements of *saj ʿ* in Arabic that are virtually absent from Payne's translation—Burton emphasizes archaic vocabulary and includes a transliterated Arabic word in his translation to call attention to the vocalization of English as an aesthetic problematic. How would readers of his text go about saying these words aloud? What is the correct pronunciation of "Banu Sásán"? Is the first syllable of "doughtier" homophonous with *dote* or *dot* or *doubt*? Translating the rhyming Arabic noun-adjective dual pair "*fārisayni baṭalayni*" ("two heroic knights"), Burton substitutes "Knights and Braves" for Payne's "valiant cavaliers," collocating two single-syllable English words that end with the sibilant *s* and offsetting them typographically with nonstandard capitalization to create phonetic and visual doubling in the translation commensurate with the grammatical and acoustic doubling found in the Arabic text. Burton's parenthetical interpolation into the passage's first line of six epithets for Allah, included neither in Payne's translation nor in the Arabic text, evokes the beginning of the Qur'anic sura *al-Fātiḥah* ("The Opening"): "In the name of Allah, most benevolent, ever-merciful. All praise be to Allah, Lord of all the worlds / Most beneficent, ever-merciful / King of the Day of Judgment."[72] This, of all sections in the Qur'an, is the one most frequently recited aloud by Muslims worldwide.[73]

If Burton's translation sometimes strays further than Payne's from literal equivalence to the Arabic text, then it does so for the sake of capturing what it is about these Arabic stories that makes them capable of moving the body with the rhythms of an oral aesthetic mode. At such moments, Burton's *Nights* translates rhythm as the "all" of what is carried over in the transmission act, insofar as rhythm equates with the aesthetic element of an oral text "that is least tied to words, representations, ideas or meanings," in Haun Saussy's terms.[74] To convey the literariness of *saj*ʿ in English requires a translator to appreciate for himself how this Arabic rhyming prose feels to hear and to say. It obligates him to mobilize his own vocal apparatus (tongue, lips, throat) in the process of finding English phrases that pass through the mouth in the same way, which are *sensed* rather than *known* as equivalent to their Arabic counterparts. Only in so doing can this translator convey the aesthetic effects of the source language.

Burton's translation is vulgar to the extent that its aesthetic effects depend not on fidelity to the source text but on the involvement of the body at all stages of the English text's production and reception. Linked to the translation of *saj*ʿ in the opening passage of Burton's *Nights*, such vulgarity proffers a heuristic for his practice as a whole. As Tarek Shamma notes, in addition to Burton's "prolific use" of *saj*ʿ itself in his translation—for example, in his characterization of a beautiful woman as having been "seen, white-skinned and of winsomest mien, of stature fine and thin, and bright as though a moon of the fourteenth night she had been, or the sun raining lively sheen"—his *Nights* across many sentences retains the same word order, syntactic structures, and assonant rhetorical devices as are present in the corresponding phrases of the Arabic text.[75] Contra Payne, whose goal was to provide a replica of his Arabic source material that was purified of "hiatuses, misprints, doubtful or corrupt passages, etc.,"[76] Burton aimed to provide his readers with a pleasurable experience of the language of the Arabic text equivalent to his own. Only in this way could his audience enjoy it as he had: as a work of Arabic literature composed in a language whose aesthetics are fundamentally oral and popular, given and received in the sensuality of words formed on, and transmitted by, a vulgar tongue.

Consistent with this method, the erotic aspects of Burton's *Nights* can be seen as an even more explicit means by which Burton ties an Anglophone audience's aesthetic experience of the text to the pleasures of the body. In this context, a comparison between Payne's translation of the story "The Porter and the Three Ladies of Baghdad," titled "*Ḥikāyat al-ḥammāl maʿa al-banāt*" in the Bulaq edition of *Alf laylah wa-laylah*,[77] and Burton's version of the same reveals differences that hinge upon the relative opportunities for specifically erotic enjoyment that each translation extends to its audience.

Payne translates as follows a passage in the story describing how a humble porter from the markets of Baghdad is seduced by three beautiful sisters during an evening spent feasting beside a fountain inside their opulent home:

> They ceased not to drink and carouse thus, till the wine sported in their heads and got the better of their senses. . . . Then [one of the sisters] . . . threw herself into the basin and sported in the water and swam about and dived like a duck and took water in her mouth and spurted it at the porter and washed her limbs and the inside of her thighs. Then she came up out of the water and throwing herself into the porter's lap, pointed to her *commodity* and said to him, "O my lord, O my friend, what is the name of this?" "Thy *kaze*," answered he; but she said, "Fie! art thou not ashamed?" And cuffed him on the nape of the neck. Quoth he, "Thy *catso*." And she dealt him a second cuff, saying, "Fie! what an ugly word! Art thou not ashamed?" "Thy *commodity*," said he; and she, "Fie! is there no shame in thee?" And thumped him and beat him. Then said he, "Thy *coney*."[78]

Here is Burton's version of the same passage:

> They ceased not doing after this fashion until the wine played tricks in their heads and worsted their wits. . . . [Then one of the sisters] throwing herself into the basin disported herself and dived like a duck and swam up and down, and took water in her mouth, and spurted it all over the Porter, and washed her limbs, and between her breasts, and inside her thighs and all around her navel. Then she came up out of the cistern and throwing herself on the Porter's lap said, "O my lord, O my love, what callest thou this article?" pointing to her *slit*, her solution of continuity. "I call that thy *cleft*," quoth the Porter, and she rejoined, "Wah! wah! art thou not ashamed to use such a word?" and she caught him by the collar and soundly cuffed him. Said he again, "Thy *womb*, thy *vulva*"; and she struck him a second slap crying, "O fie, O fie, this is another ugly word; is there no shame in thee?" Quoth he, "Thy *coynte*"; and she cried, "O thou! art wholly destitute of modesty?" and thumped him and bashed him. Then cried the Porter, "Thy *clitoris*."[79]

For readers of the Arabic text, this is a "scene . . . experienced . . . as a total sensual event," according to the critic Ferial Ghazoul.[80] The italicized words in the two English versions above are translations of the Arabic words "*raḥim*" (womb), "*farj*" (vulva), "*kuss*" (cunt), and "*zunbūr*" (literally a wasp or hornet).[81] These are terms with a long pedigree in Arabic erotica—*farj*, for example, has been the term of choice for referring to female genitalia in descriptions of sexual intercourse since medieval times—and they retain this association today.[82]

In Payne's translation, an antique register of English vocabulary intervenes between the audience and the ribald naughtiness of the scene, deferring or denying readers the satisfaction of recognizing the erogenous anatomy that the porter itemizes. "Commodity" and "catso" are Shakespearean in origin, the former designating a vagina and the latter being a respelling of *cazzo*, an Italian word for *penis* that was imported into English in the sixteenth century.[83] "Kaze," a variant spelling of *case*, to wit, "a container (for the penis)," is a seventeenth-century designation for the vagina, while "coney" is a "euphemistic phonetic disguise" for *cunt* that was in widest circulation among English-speakers between 1500 and 1650.[84] In Burton's translation, by contrast, "slit," "cleft," "womb," "vulva," "coynte" (an alternative for *cunt*), and "clitoris" comprise an everyday lexicon of sexual vulgarities easily comprehensible to a Victorian audience—and, I might add, readily understood by us today as well. These are words that, even without the typographic emphasis that I have given them above, project outward from Burton's text. They confront and discomfit us with their frank eroticism; they dare us to not find them as titillating now as Burton's Victorian audience did once upon a time.

Elliott Colla writes with reference to the Arabic version of this tale, whose "ludic" language for him is emblematic of that of the *Alf laylah wa-laylah* stories as a collection, that "because it takes a dirty mind to recognize a dirty pun, there are incentives for silence around this aspect of the text."[85] Yet here I have deliberately called attention to the eroticism of the stories' language, because this aspect of them has not only been central to the reception of Burton's *Nights* but has been a key element in how the Arabic stories have been received in their own linguistic context.[86] Indeed, situating the *Alf laylah wa-laylah* stories within a genealogy of Arabic-language erotica, Sahar Amer goes so far as to suggest that they constitute an "important genre that is essential to any study of sexuality in the medieval Arabic world."[87]

How our bodies respond now to reading Burton's *Nights* connects us transhistorically to the many other bodies to which these stories have given pleasures of various kinds over the centuries, in Arabic as well as in English. In its own time, Burton's *Nights* was an extraordinary commercial success: even at the hefty price of one British pound per volume, the work's initial print run of a thousand copies sold out immediately, making it the first truly profitable venture of Burton's long publishing career.[88] How can we name the constellation of embodied effects and affects that Burton's translation purveys, which are vulgar and erotic, but which are also linguistic, aesthetic, and literary? How can we explain their continued propensity to reverberate rhythmically and sensually among bodies separated by vast distances of space and time, creating a public for his text held together by the collective experience of having been moved, via an English translation, by the pleasures of Arabic?

An Unreadable Text

As a starting point for investigating how Burton's *Nights* has been received in the Anglophone literary field since its publication more than 130 years ago, I turn first to the scene of its reception that Burton himself provides in his Translator's Foreword. Here Burton imagines that, while spending the night among a tribe of Bedouin in the Arabian desert, he is called upon to entertain his hosts by reciting selections from the *Alf laylah wa-laylah* stories. As he begins to speak, a change comes over his audience: the "Shaykhs and 'white-beards' of the tribe gravely [seated] . . . around the camp-fire," along with the "women and children" who "stand motionless as silhouettes outside the ring . . . breathless with attention," suddenly

> seem to drink in the words with eyes and mouths as well as with ears. The most fantastic flights of fancy, the wildest improbabilities, the most impossible of impossibilities, appear to them utterly natural, mere matters of every-day occurrence. They enter thoroughly into each phase of feeling touched upon . . . they are touched with tenderness . . . their mouths water . . . they chuckle with delight . . . and, despite their normal solemnity and impassibility, all roar with laughter, sometimes rolling upon the ground.[89]

This is a vision replete with Orientalizing tropes: the Arabs are portrayed as congenitally superstitious, while the translator delivers an authoritative performance seemingly unsurpassed by anything the Bedouin have witnessed before. In this regard, in Tarek Shamma's appraisal, the passage operates strategically, for it "underlines Burton's mastery of the Other's environment and way of life . . . [and] confirms his qualification for the task he has taken upon himself."[90]

Yet even as this passage seeks to present Burton as a commanding figure in the genealogy of the stories' transmission, as capable of delivering on its aesthetic pleasures for an Arabophone audience as for an Anglophone one, it does so in terms that at the same time affirm the excessiveness of the text's aesthetics to what Burton alone could produce. Upon hearing the words of the *Alf laylah wa-laylah* stories recited aloud, the Bedouin react by opening their eyes and mouths, salivating, laughing uproariously, rolling on the ground, and being in all respects so overtaken by feeling that they behave entirely unlike their normal selves. In the Arabic aesthetic tradition, such a set of reactions exhibited by an audience in response to the recitation of a literary text or the performance of a piece of music is designated by the term *ṭarab*. Associated "paradigmatically" with the aesthetics of Arabic poetry, as Robyn Creswell writes, *ṭarab* identifies the ecstatic feedback loop of affect that relays between a performer and an audience.[91] The performer who facilitates the encounter between the aesthetics of language or music, on the one hand, and an audience that appreciates this language or music in an affective register, on the other, can never retain full control over the situation, as he or she acts rather as a medium for the dynamic processes of the aesthetic event. Burton's Orientalist fantasy is undone by the scene of *ṭarab* that it contains, which reveals the translator's power as subordinated within the economy of aesthetic pleasure into which he enters when he translates this Arabic text.

Musically, according to the ethnomusicologist A. J. Racy, *ṭarab* is induced especially by pieces that employ variations of melody, pitch, cadence, or lyrical syllabic length set against a regular phonic background, whose contrasting elements of "togetherness" and "individuality" and emphasis on "heterophonic interplay" and "intricate heterorhythms" serve to highlight the unusual and the unexpected within the familiar and the predictable.[92] As a modality of reception, *ṭarab* delinks the aesthetic impact of a poem or song from its discursive content, undergirding "an aesthetics of listening and delight" that responds to a dimension of the text "which can be understood without recourse to thought and requires no interpretation."[93]

Among those who experience *ṭarab*, per George Sawa's gloss on the classic account of *ṭarab* given in Abū al-Faraj al-Iṣfahānī's tenth-century treatise *Kitāb al-aghānī*, they may respond to the surfeit of feeling that a particular phrasing of text or music produces in them by standing up, clapping, stomping, swaying, dancing, and tearing or removing articles of their clothing. Such behaviors, Sawa notes, were considered in al-Iṣfahānī's time to be "proof of a good performance."[94] In the more contemporary descriptions that Jonathan Shannon gives of how Aleppans at the turn of the twenty-first century expressed their approbation while "listening to good Arab music," *ṭarab* is displayed through a variety of "linguistic, paralinguistic, and kinesthetic" actions that are largely involuntary, as listeners who "cannot help themselves" are "moved to shout, sigh, and wave their arms about."[95]

With reference to Racy's descriptions of the specific qualities of a musical performance most likely to generate *ṭarab* in an audience, *ṭarab* provides a notional fulcrum as well for identifying how the differentiated and dissonant elements of Burton's English, playing out within the familiar spaces of Anglophone literary discourse, establish ongoing and recurrent exchanges of pleasure between the *Nights* and its readers, in ways that the translator himself can only partially determine. *Ṭarab* stands here thus as a figure for a kind of literary worldliness that accumulates out of the many diverse instances during which a text has given pleasure over the course of its circulatory history, in any language. The legacy of Burton's *Nights* as world literature rests squarely upon its capacity to produce *ṭarab*, in excess of its translator's intentions and in spite of the text's Orientalist lineage, in Burton's own time and over the decades since.

To consider the pleasures of reading Burton's *Nights* as exemplary of an experience of *ṭarab* underscores the degree to which these pleasures arrive to readers accidentally or are expressed in actions and movements of their bodies that are involuntary. In Burton's era, the enjoyable aspect of his text was viewed as primarily erotic in nature. In 1886, *The Edinburgh*

Review cautioned against reading Burton's *Nights* because "it is a well-known fact that the discussion and reading of depraved literature leads infallibly to the depravation of the reader's mind. The less such things are thought and read about the less will they be enacted in real life."[96] A letter to the editor in the *Pall Mall Gazette* in 1885 dubbed Burton's text "filthy fiction" suitable only for "students . . . of pornography."[97] As Dane Kennedy observes, the publication of Burton's *Nights* occurred "at a moment in the cultural history of Britain . . . when interest in Orientalist subjects and anxiety about sexual matters had reached new heights."[98] In 1857, the Obscene Publications Act gave law enforcement agencies in Britain wide latitude to bring court cases against publishers, booksellers, and authors accused of being involved in the pornography industry—indeed, Burton's biographer Mary Lovell suggests that it was in large part to avoid running afoul of this law that a fictitious publisher was listed on the title page of Burton's *Nights* at its first printing and the volumes sold only by private subscription.[99]

Yet, such official measures had little real success in curtailing the spread of erotic works, nor did they quell the fears of those who saw this type of literature as a serious and pervasive threat to British morality. In the mid-1880s, when Burton's *Nights* was released, according to the historian Judith Walkowitz, literature with "pornographic content . . . was being hawked by young boys and girls" on the streets of London, while worried citizens responded by organizing themselves into vigilante groups to harass anyone who printed or distributed such texts.[100]

According to Ellen Bayuk Rosenman, Victorians saw the danger of erotic literature to reside in its ability to reduce a reader's body to its "'natural' state," exposing it as no more than a "hypersensitive protoplasm, trembling on the brink of dissolution because of its sexual susceptibility . . . [and] almost permeable in its responsiveness to stimulation."[101] That erotic texts were capable of producing such a result, it was believed, was because their authors had been inspired to write them by their own actual experiences of sexual pleasure, so that the fictional portrayals of the same contained within each work possessed a degree of embodied authenticity equivalent to an affective charge. Transferring erotic affects from author to reader—so that what the author had once experienced, the reader would now experience, too—the texts acted as "incantations" upon readers to "automatically effect [their own] arousal . . . need[ing] only to be uttered to call forth the same magical effect again and again."[102]

When pleasure is transmitted in this way through a literary text, reading becomes the activity of a body that has been induced to new heights of sensual feeling by what is read. Reading becomes, that is to say, an activity enmeshed in the iterative pleasurable cycles of *ṭarab*. As Karen Moukheiber notes, although *ṭarab* was considered a mark of aesthetic merit in al-Iṣfahānī's age, it also met with stringent disapproval from "pietist" critics who identified its "extreme" emotional and affective impact as causing various "harmful effects" for an audience.[103] Beyond simply the eroticism of Burton's text, might it be that what his contemporary critics found troubling about the *Nights* was more largely the extent to which its language engaged readers aesthetically and affectively at the same time? Targeting sites of "indeterminacy" in a reader's body, to borrow a term from Brian Massumi, a text like the *Nights* affirmed this body's "openness to an elsewhere and otherwise than it is, in any here and now," looping it into worldly exchanges of affect through the act of reading.[104]

Each word in the idiosyncratic language of Burton's text was a potential source of *ṭarab*: lexical oddities like *cilice, egromancy, verdurous, vergier, rondure, purfled, aidance, cucurbit, embassage, foined, Gobbo, kenned, meiny*, and *nidering*, in addition to the other rare, archaic, or foreign terms noted in preceding sections of this chapter.[105] Such words, which rendered Burton's *Nights* "unreadable" and "plac[ed it] . . . quite out of the category of English books" for one nineteenth-century reviewer,[106] are those of a language that necessitates being spoken aloud—a language that demands, in short, to be read affectively and with the body. How does this unreadable text become readable? And if it is not an English book, then what is it?

Premising its enjoyment upon nonhermeneutic modes of textual engagement that mobilize the body as the primary site of the literary encounter, Burton's *Nights* challenged an exegetic European tradition of textual interpretation and the disinterested modes of aesthetic appreciation that it incentivized. To some degree, Burton's audience in the 1880s was primed to embrace such somatic approaches to the literary. As Nicholas Dames has shown, an "influential" subfield of literary criticism in Victorian England, animated by contemporary advances in "the study of the autonomic nervous system and its interrelations with cerebral functioning," concerned itself exactly with the physiological experiences involved in reading fiction.[107] Building on Dames's work, Benjamin Morgan proposes that "Victorians read books with their bodies," welcoming "a wide range of embodied aesthetic responses" that included "the corporeal feeling of reading" and what he terms "kinaesthetic responses to the rhythms of prose."[108]

Such scholarship suggests that an analogue to *ṭarab* might be found within Victorian literary criticism itself. Yet the affective experience of reading Burton's *Nights* is also importantly different from those potentially produced by the born-Anglophone literary texts that Dames and Morgan analyze. However contingently and inchoately, Burton's text draws its aesthetics from everything that Burton himself found pleasurable in the Arabic of the *Alf laylah wa-laylah* stories: its effects and affects, its rhythms, rhymes, and vulgar and oral histories, its sensual feeling in his body and on his tongue. To explain the aesthetic impact of Burton's *Nights* through recourse to the notion of *ṭarab* underlines the particularity of its pleasures, which could only be sourced to the language of the Arabic text.

A Devilish Inheritance

How can we account for what Burton's *Nights* has done in the world? By what measurement can we quantify its pleasures, but also its ethics as an English translation of a work of Arabic literature? On the one hand, translating the Arabic *Alf laylah wa-laylah* stories so that they became "the property of the world at large," in the words of one Victorian reviewer,[109] Burton did so via an English text that entered the Anglophone literary field with what Roland Barthes might call "*brio*," trumpeting "exuberant neologisms, double entendres, transliterations," asyntactic formations and illogicality—a degree of literary jouissance and literariness "without which," as Barthes asserts, "there is no text."[110] Through such techniques, according to another nineteenth-century reviewer, "every shade of meaning, every turn of phrase, every subtle touch of literary colour in the language from which he translates" became appreciable in the vocabulary and phrasings of Burton's English.[111] Writing nearly eighty years later, Burton's biographer Byron Farwell considered the "beauty" of Burton's *Nights* to be such that it proved that "Arabic, if we can trust Burton, contains the most beautifully phrased clichés of any tongue in the world."[112] Yet on the other hand, Burton's *Nights* was also a text whose "enumeration of [the] perversions, deviations, excesses" of the Orient, presented under the guise of "*vraisemblance*," reinforced damaging stereotypes about the Arabophone Middle East and its people among Europeans readers, as Rana Kabbani has persuasively argued.[113]

The pleasures of Burton's *Nights* are a problem with which we must reckon if we are to acknowledge this foundational yet troubling text whose influence has been such that it stands in literary history as an origin point for Arabic literature's becoming worldly in English—even as Burton's own translation methods should warn us against assigning his text any true degree of originality. The worldly and the scandalous coexist inseparably in the legacy of Burton's *Nights*, their twinning evident in scholars' persistent refusal to accept the full extent of Burton's debt to Payne despite abundant proof. Norman Penzer, an early Burton scholar, argues implausibly that any translator in Burton's situation, with so many prior translations of the same literary work to consult, would inevitably have produced a translation similar to those already in existence.[114] No more convincingly, Fawn Brodie asserts in *The Devil Drives: A Life of Sir Richard Burton* that "since both translators were excellent Arabists and both were intent on translating the Nights 'word for word,' it is hardly surprising that there should be many identical passages."[115] Unwilling or unable to renounce the enjoyments of reading Burton's *Nights*, these critics instead remain in thrall to the *ṭarab* of this text; in the world literary system that should have repudiated it, it instead continues to circulate.

Tarek El-Ariss has argued that when the production of "the literary hit" is surrounded in scandal, scandal becomes recognizable as "a set of practices that unfold beyond the text in order to shape its circulation, reception, and translation." No longer tied to a single inappropriate incident, scandal in these circumstances takes on momentum and indexical purpose as it comes to constitute the afterlife of a text by means of the affects it produces, which "engulf" everyone with whom the text comes into contact.[116] Scandal consumes the bodies of author, translator, reader, critic; yet scandal also worlds. The affects of scandal are shocking, as expressed in Wright's admission that when he first compared Burton's *Nights* to Payne's, "I could scarcely believe my own eyes."[117] I was no less shocked at discovering the dual copies of Payne's translation among Burton's books at the Huntington Library, one unmarred except by water damage and the blemishes of old age and the other its mutilated, vivisected double. The events of Arabic literature's worlding, in this case, include "bindings and unbindings, becomings and un-becomings, jarring disorientations and rhythmic attunements" that are both affective in their implications, as in Gregory Seigworth and Melissa Gregg's formulation, and literal.[118] Bodies are unbound from their previous fixed states, but so are books; bodies but also languages are retuned by the rhythms of the literary into jarring new registers.

Worlding a work of Arabic literature in this way, Burton is a translator whose position in the lineage of Arabic-to-English literary translators active since the nineteenth century is complex to parse. In certain respects, he is a progenitor of the other translators who populate the pages of this book, for whom the body likewise serves to receive, inventory, and transmit into English the aesthetics of Arabic literature as a set of affective formations. From a practical standpoint, there are few if any works of Arabic literature more well-known among Anglophone readers than the so-called "Arabian Nights," and among the extant English translations of this work Burton's is surely the most famous. Is Burton's influence thus such that, to quote Harold Bloom, "we cannot get outside of him"?[119]

I take the *we* on whose behalf I pose this question to refer especially to contemporary translators of Arabic literature, who, if they feel themselves to be translating in the long shadow of this translator and his worldly text, would surely own up to their feelings only with hesitation. Among these translators I include myself, as the next chapter of this book makes clear. Our filiation to Burton is moreover one that, ethically, *must* not be admitted. His is what Jacques Derrida would call an "intolerable inheritance," one that we have "an imperative" to refuse and disavow.[120] We must not model our relationship to Arabic on his relationship to it, write our English sentences in his style, or permit his body to shed its dust upon our skin. Burton is the devilish specter of the "totally other" within the field of Arabic-to-English literary translation, and we can therefore experience the pleasure of reading his *Nights* only as a species of "unpleasure," pleasure that ethically "cannot be felt as such."[121] Yet as hard as we may try to shunt Burton aside, he haunts us. Unconsciously, involuntarily, unwillingly, whenever we translate the literariness of Arabic literature into English that registers in and as a language of the body, Burton is conjured in the aesthetics of the texts that we produce and in the practices of translation that created them.

Reading Burton's *Nights* today, as translators or scholars, we are drawn to it in spite of ourselves. In this regard we become like the caliph Hārūn al-Rashīd, who, while walking in the city one night with his vizier Jaʿfar, hears the dulcet sounds of voices and musical instruments emanating from within the house where the porter and the three sisters are entertaining each other. The caliph tells his companion in no uncertain terms, "I want to enter this house," although Jaʿfar cautions him that inside are surely "people beset with drunkenness" who may treat them poorly.[122] Just as the caliph is drawn irresistibly to want to join in the fun, we cannot resist the pull of the pleasures that Burton's text holds on offer, despite the risks that we court by indulging our desires. *Ṭarab* is a powerful motivator, acting even upon a caliph—for how else could we explain Hārūn al-Rashīd's insistence on taking part in this revelry that he hears only at a distance?—and acting as well upon us.

Ultimately the caliph begs Jaʿfar to "use artifice [*tataḥayyal*]" to gain them admission to the house.[123] The act of artifice that he requests—*tataḥayyal*, to employ an artful means of doing something, from *ḥwl*—is a verbal trick (*ḥīlah*) that etymologically is also an act of translation (*taḥwīl*). Translation is a pretext for entering into a place that was off limits to us before, for becoming proximate to that which compels us bodily, even at great potential peril both to us and to this other thing (how will the freewheeling spirit of the evening be compromised, even becoming politically dangerous for the porter and the sisters, once the caliph is among the crowd?). Rather than dwell now on the dangers of translation, however, I move next to an exploration of the modes of proximity that translation makes possible, and specifically, those that involve a translator's body in forms of relation with the other language that may even be ethical. Burton's influence plays out as well along unexpected trajectories.

3 / Ethics of the *Muthannā*: Caring for the Other in a Mother Tongue

More than twenty-five years have passed since the publication of Lawrence Venuti's seminal monograph *The Translator's Invisibility: A History of Translation*. Offering a holistic portrait of the persistently marginal status of translated literature and translation itself as a form of literary praxis in the Anglophone cultural field over a period of several hundred years, Venuti called on translators in the present to embrace an activist agenda aimed at correcting this situation. Toward this end, he urged them to take public ownership of their work through concerted acts of "self-presentation" in "prefaces, essays, lectures, interviews," and simultaneously to deploy discursive and semantic strategies when translating that would highlight the originally nonnative or "foreign" provenance of the English-language texts that they produced.[1]

The "translator-centered" approach that Venuti inaugurated with this book was vital to the emergence of a "new discipline . . . of translation studies" in the United States after the 1970s, as Susan Bassnett had already noted retrospectively in 1998.[2] Although Venuti's arguments in *The Translator's Invisibility* are so well known today that they scarcely need rehearsing, I begin with them here nonetheless because this chapter takes his hopeful prognostications for a deindividualized and disempowered translator's becoming a visible *self* as a point of departure for exploring a different transformational, and transformative, potential inhering in the figure of the Anglophone literary translator. Whereas the case studies that Venuti provides in his book—surveying the achievements of numerous Anglophone translators active between the seventeenth and twentieth centuries—marshal compelling evidence for this translator's selfhood, the single case study that I offer in this chapter aims to demonstrate not that the Anglophone literary translator has a self but that she has a body, and that it is this body that positions her to intervene ethically in her domestic literary field.

By reconceptualizing the Anglophone literary translator through her embodiment in this way, I propose in effect to flesh out the visible translator that Venuti theorized a quarter-century ago: to construct an architecture of bones and musculature inside this translator's spectral form, to endow her with proprioception and "the cumulative memory of skill, habit, posture" that such an ongoing corporeal sensibility engenders, and to wrap her in a skin constellated with nerve endings and orifices, portals for the affective incursions of the world.[3] With respect to the literary texts and languages among which she works, it is this embodied translator's "soma," her "living, sensing, dynamic, perceptive, purposive body," in Richard Shusterman's words, that provides her with a primary point of access to their aesthetic qualities.[4] Selfhood for such a translator emerges only in relation to other things, beings, and forces from outside; insofar as this translator has a self, it is of the kind designated by Brian Massumi as a "self-," articulated around an "incipient subjectivity" exceptionally receptive to linking up with the world through the free bond of its dangling hyphen.[5]

To envisage the Anglophone literary translator in these terms is to capitalize on this figure's longstanding ambiguity in Euro-American scholarship. After all, even the translator who comes into view in Venuti's volume is the source from which "the language of the translation originates . . . in a decisive way" while being also, paradoxically, "not its sole origin."[6] A lineage of thought that has hesitated to agree upon who or what translators are, or what positions they do, can, or ought to occupy in a given literary field, has left this figure available to a variety of potential appropriations and reconsiderations. Is a translator an individual innately suited to her task by "certain traits" of personality and elements of biographical history?[7] Or is she simply a function of discourse à la Michel Foucault's author?[8] Is she a writer who composes an original literary work in the target language from within a discrete subject position, or a passive vehicle through which the words of the source text pass in "quasimystical" fashion on their way to becoming intelligible in a new idiom?[9]

Amid these multiple and contradictory characterizations of a translator, the well-worn Italian pun *Traduttore, traditore* ("Translator, traitor") stands as a bit of underexamined and undertheorized wordplay.

Yet in reflecting an "underlying suspicion across many cultures that the middleman is either incompetent or up to no good," as Mark Polizzotti puts it, this adage also suggests that the question *What is a translator?* is not an idle one—not one posed, that is, merely to provoke esoteric disagreements over a translator's essential nature, but rather a query whose answer may carry ethical as well as practical implications.[10] To refrain from tying translators to any of the definitions enumerated above, but instead to examine them by giving attention to their bodies as a main site where the events of their practice occur, is to accept their intrinsic undecidability and indeed to embrace it as a precondition of an ethical translation practice. The ontological, discursive, and subjective ambiguity of translators as theorized by critics over time thus does not indicate their ethical ambivalence, per Polizzotti, but rather discloses a radical corporeal porosity: the hyphenated translator as a subject perpetually in a state of emergence relative to the surrounding world.

Among contemporary Anglophone scholars of translation, Douglas Robinson is the only one, as far as I am aware, to have proposed something like a comprehensive model for understanding how a translator's body is involved in the granular activities of her practice. In *The Translator's Turn*, Robinson charts a series of bodily events that determine a literary text's trajectory through the world, some of them socially and culturally determined ("ideosomatic") and others transpiring unpredictably on the level of an author, reader, or translator's individual corporeal response to a text ("idiosomatic"). Robinson describes this sequence as follows:

> A person writes the SL [source-language] text, charging the SL words with all the force of his or her idiosomatic experience. A second person reads the SL text, recharging the SL words with all the force of his or her own idiosomatic experience—an experience that, owing to our ideosomatic conditioning, will probably overlap in significant ways with that of the author, but never exactly. A third person (or the same person in a third capacity) reads the SL text with an ear to translating it into a TL [target language] and charges the transfer with the force of his or her idiosomatic experience: *feels* the SL and works to dredge up out of his or her TL storehouse words that feel the same, words that seem charged with something like the same force.[11]

The positivist tenor of this passage—the certainty that it projects that bodies are involved in how literature enters the world in *this* way and this way only—is characteristic of much of Robinson's scholarship. Nonetheless, I applaud his intention to foreground the role of bodies at all stages of a text's production, reception, and circulation both in its original language and in the languages into which it is translated. Even more compelling for me is Robinson's suggestion that if it is translators' "ideosomatic conditioning" within their social and cultural milieu that makes them capable first of comprehending a text in order to translate it, and second of producing a version of this text in a new language that is broadly intelligible to a target audience, then it is their idiosomatic or particularized corporeal experiences of both the source and target languages, aleatory and intimate, that permit them to translate well, with a sensibility for the overarching aesthetics of a source text no matter their distance from the aesthetic norms of the target culture. A "great translator," Robinson avers, "will not shrink from somatic confusion, somatic inconsistency, will not retreat into protective intellection, but will boldly flesh out the contradictory and conflicting body of his or her response with the overriding conviction that, if it all came from the guts, it is all of a piece."[12]

When a translator's guts furnish the unifying principle for an act of literary translation, the equivalences that allow translation to proceed become no longer only semantic but also somatic, predicated on a notion of words' "feeling the same" in one language as in another, or to one body as to another. Such a model of translation rooted in the body suggests that the differences between languages that vex a practice of semantic translation may be negotiated instead through somatic means, tying the plausibility of translation to the involvement of a translator's body. And yet in giving credence to such linguistic exchanges that occur in the guts, I do not follow Robinson in necessarily drawing a distinction between the somatic context in which translation occurs and its cultural counterpart, or in other words, between the body of a translator and the world in which this body exists. For translation flourishes as an ethical activity, I propose, precisely when the aesthetics of a literary text register more widely than in the viscera of a solitary translator, becoming rather the "somaesthetic" basis—to borrow a term from Shusterman—for an experience of a source text's literariness that resonates across a whole literary field. After all, as Shusterman writes, when the body serves "as a locus of sensory-aesthetic appreciation," the effects are salutary for both the body that is doing the appreciating and for the ambient sociocultural environment in which this body is located.[13] Accordingly, the notion of somatic translation—or perhaps, after Shusterman, somaesthetic translation—that I advance in this chapter sites the translator's body amid intersecting personal and national histories, Arabophone social, cultural, and geographic spaces and Anglophone ones, to propose that an act of translation that activates bodies inside and outside of a text for the realization, appreciation, and transmission of the aesthetics of literary language worlds both the text at hand and the bodies that make its worlding possible.

Self and (M)other

Whereas chapter 1 of this book examined how the formal aesthetics of literary Arabic are made worldly in translation, and chapter 2 investigated the worlding of the affective pleasures that such language produces in a translator and an audience, this chapter explores processes of worlding that are less unidirectional, that are reciprocal and relational rather than agential, and whose ethical potential thus depends not only upon how they promote the wellbeing of the other but also of the self. For Shusterman, the multivalent positioning of the body as an aesthetic receptor and, via its aesthetic encounters, an instrument of personal and social good makes it capable of performing ethically insofar as "ethical codes" are given tangible, perceptible heft "through incorporation into bodily dispositions and action."[14] Differently from Robinson, for whom the ethical potential of a somatic approach to translation resides ultimately in its liberalizing capacity to produce texts that convert or "turn" target-language readers away from their prior "ideosomatically [i.e., socially] programmed restrictions" and "cultural ideals" and toward a conscious embrace of the world's linguistic and cultural diversity,[15] I identify the ethical turn that a translator's body enacts along lines closer to Shusterman's: as an affective inclination of the self toward the other that is the source text, concurrent with the assumption of a disposition to care for this other that is corporeally as well as aesthetically manifested, and which involves self and other together for the betterment of both.

Abī ʿUthmān ʿAmru ibn Baḥr al-Jāḥiẓ offers a scene of a translator's turn in *al-Bayān wa-al-tabyīn*, his ninth-century treatise on Arabic oratory, rhetoric, and poetics, that illustrates the kind of bodily activity that I ascribe to the translator in this chapter. Al-Jāḥiẓ tells of a Qur'anic scholar named Mūsā bin Sayyār al-Uswārī, fluent in both Arabic and Persian, who was accustomed to hosting gatherings

> فتقعد العربُ عن يمينه، والفُرس عن يساره، فيقرأ الآية من كتاب الله ويفسّرها للعرب
> بالعربية، ثم يحوّل وجهَه إلى الفرس فيفسِّرها لهم بالفارسيَّة، فلا يُدرى بأي لسانٍ هو أبْيَنُ.

> with the Arabs seated at his right, and the Persians at his left, and he would recite a verse from God's book and interpret it for the Arabs in Arabic, then turn his face [*yuḥawwil wajhahu*] to the Persians and interpret it for them in Persian, and it was not apparent in which tongue he was more eloquent.[16]

Al-Uswārī engages his body in the process of transmitting the Qur'anic message in two languages, turning his face first to one side ("*yuḥawwil wajhahu*") and then to the other as he does so. For the philosopher Emmanuel Levinas, the face is the basic medium of an ethical interaction: when we face the other, its own face, confronting us with its utter defenselessness, "is what forbids us to kill." Possessed of "a nose, eyes, a forehead, a chin," and a "most naked" skin, this other's face is immanently embodied.[17] In Cathryn Vasseleu's explication, Levinas's other is a corporeal being that can be touched, and yet its tactility occurs ontologically "prior to any consciousness of sensation and irreducible to it." Vasseleu writes: "Levinas considers touch as the exposition of an affective involvement with others. For Levinas subjectivity is a subjection to alterity before it can be posited as the locus of its own manifestation."[18]

Not only does the other's face for Levinas summon us into an ethical relation via its bodily proximity, but in so doing it constitutes us as subjects. We are selves in the world only insofar as we exist affectively for another. Al-Jāḥiẓ's Qur'anic interpreter, pronouncing the words of the sacred book first for an audience that comprehends them in their original Arabic and then turning to translate them for an audience that does not, is immortalized for posterity at the very moment of his arrival into ethics, when translation holds two groups of bodies in relation around the singular aesthetics of an Arabic text.

This interpreter serves as an inspiration for the figure of the Arabic-to-English translator who appears in this chapter. The ethics of her translation practice inheres in the activities of being-for-another in which she is always and already participating as soon as she turns to face the Arabic text. As her body registers convergences between the material of two languages, she herself is refigured, reformed, and refrained by their passage through and across her flesh.

To show how these processes occur, and to explore the ethical interventions that a translator's turning, motile body poises her to make in the literary field within which her translations circulate, this chapter adopts a more personal approach to the topic of Arabic-to-English literary translation than that followed elsewhere in this book. The translation practice under study here is my own: that which produced an English-language work of literature titled *Limbo Beirut* (2016) out of the linguistic and literary material of the Arabic novel *Līmbū Bayrūt* (2013) by the Lebanese writer Hilāl Shūmān.[19] In placing my own body at the center of this chapter, however, I do so in full awareness that my body is only *a* body that cannot and should not be equated with any idealist notion of the body as such. As Shusterman is wise to remind us, to conceive of "the body" as though it were "only one single thing" is to verge on promoting "a dangerous essentialism or uniformity about our embodiment" that neglects the heterogeneity among actual bodies and their manifold procedures for engaging with the world and experiencing their own aliveness within it.[20]

For guidance in how to write about translation from an autobiographical vantage point, I have benefited from several exemplars of "a relatively new publishing phenomenon, the translator's memoir."[21] Like Gregory Rabassa in *If This Be Treason: Translation and Its Dyscontents* (2005), an early entrant in this genre, I assume first of all that a translator's speculations about her own practice can generate intellectually valid generalizable insights about translation at large, thus making autocritique here more than a purely narcissistic exercise. Following the model of Kate Briggs, who, when she writes about translating Roland Barthes's lectures in *This Little Art* (2017), seems frequently still to be channeling the French philosopher's voice in her own prose, my academic language in this chapter remains in ongoing conversation with Shūmān's Arabic, returning to it throughout as a repository of words to which mine continue to pay homage. From Jennifer Croft's *Homesick: A Memoir* (2019), I take license to share details about my biological history that inform who I am as a translator but also as a body that exists amid other bodies, in worlds both real and imaginary.

In my efforts in this chapter to find critically viable ways of permitting my objective distance as a scholar to be sometimes tempered or erased by the closeness of my subject matter, I have been encouraged perhaps most of all by Gayatri Chakravorty Spivak, whose writing has persistently, knowingly, perspicaciously strayed across the dividing line between criticism and autobiography throughout her academic career.[22] Of special relevance is her 1992 essay "The Politics of Translation," a pioneering piece of "metacritical reflection" on literary translation whose insights are delivered via a first-person account of her own experiences translating Bengali literature into English.[23] Yet I remain sufficiently admonished by the fact that Lawrence Venuti felt the need, in his preface to *The Translator's Invisibility*, to defend the seriousness of his study by assuring readers that although it "originates in my own work as a professional translator since the late 1970s . . . any autobiographical elements are subsumed in what is effectively a history of English-language translation from the seventeenth century to the present" to recognize that I must proceed with some caution in my approach.[24]

My body of the present day is, among the various ways that it might be described, that of a mother. I suggest in what follows that translating *Līmbū Bayrūt* prepared my body to care for that of my son, born almost exactly two years after my translation was published, by training it in certain affective modes of extension, certain ways of reaching outward and into the world in affirmation of another body's ongoing proximity to mine. Translating habituates the embodied translator to the feeling of having "someone [else] in my soma."[25] In Sara Ahmed's terms, it accustoms her to gathering the other into her "near sphere, the world that takes shape around" the body that she identifies as hers.[26] It makes a habit out of worlding but also out of being worlded, of existing affectively in relation to another. To borrow Judith Butler's phrasing, the signal processes of translating and mothering both reveal "the bodily boundary" to be no more than "the threshold of the person, the site of passage and porosity, the evidence of an openness to alterity that is definitional of the body itself."[27] So even as translators and mothers may both appear to occupy positions of superior ontological and bodily coherence relative to the other with whose care they are charged, I aim to show through my examination of myself as a translator-turned-mother that this is far from true—and that, to the contrary, to translate and to mother are both activities that radically unsettle unitary conceptions of a self, of a body, and of a natal language in which either self or body could be fully and autonomously constituted.

In *Mother Tongues: Sexuality, Trials, Motherhood, Translation*, the critic and translator Barbara Johnson links the processes of translating and mothering via their shared investment in introducing the other into language, and the common predicament in which translators and mothers alike find themselves when this task proves impossible without instigating a rupture in what was previously whole: in the other text, whose selfsame identity with its original language is violated as it is translated into the translator's tongue; and in the mother herself, who, by gifting her language to her child, renounces her claim of singular ownership over it and over the child's body whose independence from hers this provision of language all but guarantees. At the heart of Johnson's account of both processes is loss—the loss of autotelic identity, selfhood, and wholeness for the one whose language becomes differentiated from itself, othered, in these ways.

Yet for both text and mother, what has departed is offset by an accumulation of mattering—what we might call worldliness—for the ruptured self. A work of literature that has undergone translation becomes "perceptible," Johnson writes, precisely via the blockages that it throws up to resist coherence in the target language. It displays its literariness as "what is *always* lost in translation," as a remainder or untranslatable whose absence reveals, contrary to expectations, the translatability of the literary.[28] A mother for whom language has displaced "pure bodily closeness and nonverbal communication" as the essence of what she provides for her child reveals herself to be not the mute addressee of her child's inaugural utterances, a symbolic instrument of this child's autoconstitutive procedures of differentiation, but a source of signification in her own right. "However dependent on her the child may be in fact," Johnson insists, a mother's "most important lesson will be to turn 'into signifying form' everything that unites them."[29]

Translating and mothering are alike in that the marquee deployments of language in both blur the boundaries of self and other to produce gains in worldliness that exceed the subtractive outcomes of the ruptures that they also necessarily entail. I depart from Johnson, however, in where I locate the role of the body in these activities. Not at odds with signification, as it is for Johnson, the body as I see it is what maintains this suspension of additive and subtractive events, accumulation and loss, by furnishing the material medium through which self and other meet—a medium in which the energetic force of their encounters is conserved in the flesh, in affects that affirm the resonant, ongoing, and interdependent worldliness of both. Through the care of a translator or a mother, the other (a text, a child) enunciates its own, unique—although never not relational—being in the world in an embodied language that is both other and mother tongue.

Grammar of Two

Hilāl Shūmān's novel *Līmbū Bayrūt* opens with a scene of a son who takes refuge in the affective extensions of his mother's body. A young man tosses restlessly in an unfamiliar bed as violence convulses the city outside. It is May 2008, and Hezbollah militants are clashing in the streets of Beirut with fighters loyal to the progovernment Future Movement,[30] their conflict threatening to reopen the scarred-over wounds of Lebanon's massively destructive civil war (1975–1990), which killed at least 150,000 Lebanese and decimated the urban infrastructure of the capital. In the paragraphs that follow, we learn that the man is named Walīd, and that he is not alone in the bed—his boyfriend, Alfred, is sleeping beside him, oblivious to his distress. But before these additional facts can bestow purpose and specificity upon this character, we have, at the start of the novel, only an unidentified human figure who, troubled by a welter of anxieties and the warmth of the May night, "lay like a fetus in the womb of his mother" ("*iḍṭaja ʿa ka-janīn fī baṭn ummihi*").[31]

For Walīd—whose name means "newborn"—to fantasize a return to the womb in this way appears at first to betoken his incapacity to face the events unfolding outside, a desire to regress. What he does next, however, is not to give in to terror, but to look for comfort in what he has available to him right there in the bed, which is not much (Alfred only slumbers on), and which is not his mother herself but only his own body imprinted with the shape of hers:

> عانق نفسه. أغلق نفسَه على نفسِه. الركبتان مضمومتان تلمسان الصدر، ومثنيّتان حتى تكاد قدماه تلمسان مؤخّرته. يداه تجمعان رجليه أكثر، وتطويان ركبتيه أكثر.

Translated literally, these lines[32] read in English as follows:

> He hugged himself. He closed himself on himself. The knees joined touching the chest and folded until his feet almost touch his buttocks. His hands gather his legs more and bend his knees more.

When threatened, the body in search of maternal care enfolds into itself, reaffirming its ongoingness through the contingent pleasures of touch, the reassurances of skin-to-skin contact. As an enactment of what Lauren Berlant calls "lateral agency"—agency untethered from teleology—these minimal gestures offer a reprieve from the pressures of conforming to the hegemonic narratives of the modern world, whether these are tied to the good-life promises of the capitalist system that Berlant critiques, or to the toxic politics of Lebanese sectarianism. By responding to fear and uncertainty only with such movements of "floating sideways," in Berlant's phrasing, rather than with determined action—by doing a multitude of small things while *doing* nothing of consequence to help the situation—Walīd refuses to fully buy into the crisis-driven master narrative of post–civil war Beirut.[33] Instead of attempting to intervene, taking up a weapon and joining sides, or preparing to emigrate, he simply remains in bed.

Grammatically, the sentences that describe how Walīd alters his position to assume this posture of self-care contain numerous words in the Arabic dual case, or *muthannā*, a morphological category employed for subjects and objects that are two in number. Each word denoting a part of Walīd's body that is involved in this movement—knees, feet, hands, and legs—is inflected for duality, comprising in all eleven dual words in only two lines of printed type. When this character calls upon his mother's body to intercede on behalf of his survival, what the language of Shūmān's novel proffers in response is the *muthannā*. Care is provided by a grammar that, by inscribing twoness into the morphological structures of Arabic, embeds the potential for a maternal ethics into its linguistic material.

Walīd's body that finds a maternal refuge in the grammatical formations of Arabic implicates a translator in caring for its wellbeing through the grammar of how she translates such formations into her own language. To translate within the ethics of the *muthannā* is to mobilize grammar as the instrument of a translation practice that responds to the call to care for another's body as a summons to care for the other language as well, twinning mothering and translating into a single ethical praxis.

Duality in Arabic is marked for nouns and adjectives by the addition of the suffix *-āni* in the nominative and *-ayni* in the accusative and genitive, and it is marked for verbs by the addition of *-āni* in the present tense and *-ā* in the past tense.[34] As a grammatical convention, the dual carries somewhat classical associations, being all but absent from modern spoken Arabic except in certain highly circumscribed situations. In this regard, Kristen Brustad observes that the dual is no longer a productive word class in the modern dialects except in a small number of nominal constructions. She summarizes its present-day spoken usages as consisting of "frozen forms, most of which refer to body parts, a non-specific dual meaning *a couple of*, and a 'new topic' dual that has specific pragmatic functions and is limited to individuated nouns."[35] In contemporary written Arabic, on the other hand, the dual remains fully inflected, although by virtue of its comparatively more specialized function, it is rarer than either the singular or the plural.

Moreover, the *muthannā* is distinguished in Arabic by its unique acoustics. When dual endings are appended to several words in sequence, the effect is one of homophony, as in the following example from Haim Blanc's "seminal study of the dual in spoken Arabic": "*inna hādhayni al-waladayni kānā ṣadīqayni ḥamīmayni*," "these two boys were close friends."[36] In Shūmān's text, the phrases detailing Walīd's movements—"*al-rukbatāni maḍmūmatāni talmisāni al-ṣadr, wa-mathniyyatān ḥattā takād qadamāhu talmisāni muʾakhkharatahu*" ("the [two] knees [both] joined [both] touching the chest, and [both] folded until his [two] feet nearly [both] touch his buttocks"); and "*yadāhu tajmaʿāni rijlayhi . . . wa-taṭwiyāni rukbatayhi*" ("his [two] hands [both] gather his [two] legs . . . and [both] bend his [two] knees")—exhibit just such an extravagant homophonic quality. Nouns, verbs, and adjectives are inflected to create what Blanc describes as "characteristic chains of duals that go on for as long as the reference is unaltered."[37]

Modern English has no dual grammar; while prior versions of the language did contain a limited dual inflection, preserved vestigially today in the English words *twosome*, *twice*, *double*, and the word *dual* itself, these isolated contemporary remnants can hardly underpin a holistic approach to translating the Arabic *muthannā*.[38] With respect solely to the semantic content of these phrases from Shūmān's novel, a semantically accurate

English translation would be possible as long as duality were treated as a kind of meaningful redundancy or pleonasm—that is, if twoness could be assumed within the category of human knees, for example, and did not need to be indicated otherwise. Or, if the quantity of knees were ambiguous in English without additional specification, placing the word "two" before the English noun would suffice for clarification, as Roman Jakobson suggests when discussing translations of the Old Russian dual into English. Yet Jakobson's assurance that no "lack of grammatical device in the language translated into makes impossible a *literal* translation of the entire conceptual information contained in the original," on the grounds that "if some grammatical category is absent in a given language, its meaning may be translated into this language by lexical means," founders on the *nonliteral* aspects of how the Arabic dual functions in a work of literature like Shūmān's novel.[39]

Throughout Arabic literary history, the *muthannā* has often served as much an aesthetic purpose in literary language as a semantic one. What is arguably the most famous line in Arabic poetry begins with a dual-form imperative: "*Qifā nabki min dhikrā ḥabībin wa-manzili*," "Stop [both of you] and let us weep at the memory of a beloved and an encampment." This line is the first hemistich in the *mu'allaqah* or "hanging ode" of the sixth-century Arab poet Imru' al-Qays, a towering figure in the pre-Islamic poetic canon from which the entire tradition of Arabic literature is often said to have descended. Critics over time have offered various explanations for Imru' al-Qays's use of the dual address here, from speculating that the poet imagined his hero-narrator to be traveling at this stage of his journey with two companions (although the verses that follow this hemistich offer no clear evidence for this interpretation), to suggesting that Arabs in Imru' al-Qays's time were habituated by conventions of sociality to speaking with two people at once, according to Jareer Abu-Haidar.[40]

Abu-Haidar himself posits a different rationale for the presence of the *muthannā* in this line of Imru' al-Qays's *mu'allaqah*. He argues that the poet employed the dual out of "poetic exigency" in order to retain the proper arrangement of long and short syllables required by the ode's metrical form, the *ṭawīl*. Moreover, Abu-Haidar proposes, the *alif* (ا) that appears as the concluding letter of the dual imperative "*Qifā*" when it is spelled out in Arabic carries its own aesthetic force, capable of "riveting attention" in a way that the alphabetic endings of *qif* and *qifū*—the imperatives for a single or plural addressee respectively—are not. "It is no mystification to say that the *alif* in Arabic is a unique letter," Abu-Haidar observes, "in that both in the way it is written, and in its phonetic value as a letter of prolongation, it points upwards." Noting that Imru' al-Qays's first hemistich inspired countless later Arab poets to commence their poems as well with a dual-form imperative, Abu-Haidar proposes that it is the particular congruence of metrical utility and aesthetic impact contained within the utterance "*Qifā nabki*" that "has given it its abiding charm."[41] The role of the *muthannā* in this poem, it might therefore be concluded, following Abu-Haidar, is not so much grammatical in nature as it is predominantly literary.

If a first attestation of the *muthannā*'s literariness can be adduced from the pre-Islamic Arabic poetic canon, then others can be derived from the Arabic language's most famous exemplar of prose writing, the Qur'an. The sura *al-Raḥmān* ("The Compassionate"), which underscores God's supreme munificence by posing repeatedly the rhetorical question "*Fa-bi-ayyi ālā'i Rabbikumā tukadhdhibāni*" ("So which blessings of the Lord [of you both] do you [two] deny?"), is addressed to an audience of two.[42] Once again duality serves an aesthetic function more clearly than it does a semantic one. The identity of the two parties who are being reminded of God's blessings is never clarified in the sura, although some commentators have proposed that humans and jinn are its implied addressees, and others that the sura is speaking to men and women, as Michael Sells notes. In Sells's own explication of the dual's role in this sura, the "incantatory rhythmic intensity" created by the recurrence of "*Fa-bi-ayyi ālā'i Rabbikumā tukadhdhibāni*" thirty-one times in the seventy-eight-verse sura serves to draw out the sura's fundamental assertion of God's mercy and generosity into a register where it can be sensed in the form of the language in which this idea is expressed. The "Arabic refrain," Sells writes, "resounds through the sura each time as a reminder of the creative reduplication of compassion, tying that core message into the morphology and the acoustics of the language itself."[43]

The sura enumerates manifold signs of a God who is "merciful" ("*raḥmān*"): among them, that humans have been endowed with consciousness and a fertile and beautiful Earth upon which to dwell, and that the Qur'an has been revealed to them in all of its own perfection and beauty. Yet it is in the sura's repeated dual-inflected invocations to believers to acknowledge but also to *feel* God's mercy that its principal aesthetic effect resides, its power to move them toward an affirmation and an affective appreciation of their place in the world that God created.

In a different context, but operating similarly to inscribe a transcendent message into the form of Qur'anic language, the *muthannā* appears prominently as well in the sura *al-A'rāf* ("The Heights"). In the four verses of this sura that recount the story, included in Judaic and Christian scripture as well, of how Satan tricked Adam and Eve into eating fruit from a forbidden tree in God's garden, thus leading to their expulsion from paradise, twenty-eight words are inflected for duality. Transliterated into Latin script with the dual words marked in italics, the first two of these verses are as follows:

> 19. Wa-yā Adamu uskun anta wa-zawjuka al-jannata fa-*kulā* min ḥaythu *shi'tumā* wa-lā *taqrabā* hādhihi al-shajarah fa-*takūnā* min al-ẓālimīna.
>
> 20. Fa-waswasa la-*humā* al-Shayṭānu li-yubdī la-*humā* mā wūriya *'anhumā* min *saw'ātihimā* wa-qāla mā *nahākumā Rabbukumā* 'an hādhihi al-shajarati illā an *takūnā malakayni* aw *takūnā* min al-khālidīna.[44]
>
> 19. "And you, O Adam, live you and your spouse in the garden and *eat* your fill wheresoever you *like*, but do not *approach* this tree, or you will *become* iniquitous."
>
> 20. But Satan whispered to *them*, in order to reveal to *them* that which was hidden from *them* of *their* private parts and said: "*Your* Lord has forbidden *you* from this tree that you may not *become angels* or *become* immortal."[45]

The *muthannā*'s distinctive phonetic clusters cause these verses to stand out acoustically from those that precede and follow them in the sura. The pronominal suffixes *humā* and *kumā*, indicating the third-person and second-person dual respectively—in phrases like "But Satan whispered to them" ("*Fa-waswasa la-humā al-Shayṭānu*") and "Your Lord" ("*Rabbukumā*")—complemented by the repetition of the Arabic verb *to be/to become* in its second-person dual conjugation *takūnā*—as in the phrase "that you may not become angels or become immortal" ("*illā an takūnā malakayni aw takūnā min al-khālidīna*")—work together to create both assonance and rhyme. The long vowel *ā* that concludes all but one of the dual words in verses 19–20, which is the same *ā* of the *muthannā* that Abu-Haidar hails as "riveting" in the first line of Imru' al-Qays's ode, lends the verses a rhythmic quality when recited aloud that almost approaches that of metered poetry.

Every time the dual occurs in this part of the sura, it refers to Adam and Eve, the two progenitors of humankind according to Islamic doctrine. For Amina Wadud, that Adam and his wife are designated as a pair grammatically with the dual shows that Islam assigns responsibility for their infraction to both partners equally, rather than to Eve alone, as in the Judaic and Christian versions of the story. Wadud writes: "In maintaining the dual form [in these verses], the Qur'an overcomes the negative Greco-Roman and Biblical-Judaic implications that woman was the cause of evil and damnation."[46] Through its prominence in this sura, recognizable via the aesthetic effects generated by its unique morphology, the *muthannā* for Wadud encodes a feminist politics into Islam's version of a seminal episode in monotheistic scripture. Her interpretation of these verses is one of numerous pieces of evidence that she marshals in her book *Qur'an and Woman: Rereading the Sacred Text from a Woman's Perspective* to argue for an absence of gender bias in Islam's sacred text, many of which she gleans by attending to such grammatical aspects of Qur'anic language. In both Sells's and Wadud's analyses, the *muthannā* in the Qur'an elaborates an ethical dimension of the sacred text, affirming the innate largesse and egalitarianism of divine justice via the sonic and rhythmic qualities of the Arabic language.

Hoda El Shakry argues that to engage with the Qur'an as a textual object is already to accept the possibility of being made ethical by it, and of being made ethical specifically by how its language "encompasses a range of aesthetic and ethical practices that mobilize the faculties of the mind and the body" together.[47] Insofar as the *muthannā* plays a role in implementing such Qur'anic ethics, it does so as a grammar that is innately one of the body. In his study of the Arabic dual, Kees Versteegh cites an Abbasid-era grammarian named ʿAbdallāh ibn al-Ḥusayn al-ʿUkbarī, whose theory of language began from the premise that every element in a language is comprehended "either by the mind or by the senses." Within this schema, according to al-ʿUkbarī, the *muthannā* is sensibly rather than cognitively understood, since its "distinctions . . . are made with the *ʾalfāẓ* [plural of *lafẓ*]"—or that is, by altering the form of words so that they are both pronounced and heard differently, resulting only secondarily in their also coming to mean differently.[48] Recalling as well Brustad's observation that the dual in the modern Arabic dialects manifests mainly in "frozen forms, most of which refer to body parts," the *muthannā*'s association with the body can be seen as extending from describing the anatomical components out of which a body is composed, to reifying how a body situates itself in the world with respect to language's formal and affective dimensions.

As a grammatical marker of Walīd's corporeal human vitality embedded within the language of the opening scene of Shūmān's novel, the *muthannā* is heir to the history of the aesthetic and ethical effects that it has produced in Arabic texts from pre-Islamic poetry to the Qur'an. In the context of *Līmbū Bayrūt*, it reasserts the ethical mattering of anthropic life in opposition to the inhuman menaces of a militarized identitarianism that reduces people to categories of political affiliation and creed.

When I begin to translate the first paragraph of the novel, I am compelled by how the *muthannā* testifies here to the priority of human life to accept my own embodied humanity as the condition of my encounter with this Arabic text. The "animacy" of this grammar, to borrow a term from Mel Y. Chen, subtends an experience of biological aliveness for the translator as well.[49] Informed by this experience, translation takes shape as a mode of ethical and aesthetic praxis connecting the body within the text to the translator's own body that is turned toward it in a posture of care. Walīd calls out for help from his mother's body and is answered in the Arabic text by language, and in my English text by the body of a translator. Here is the first paragraph of my published translation of the novel:

> He couldn't sleep. Yet he stayed in bed. He fixed his gaze on the clothes cupboard against one wall. Its door, he saw, stood slightly ajar. Beyond it was a narrow hallway, bounded by the door's shadow on the wood floor in collaboration with the light in the corridor. Was it the bed, to which he had not yet grown accustomed? Or the May heat? He could not identify an obvious cause for his insomnia. He curled up like a fetus in his mother's belly and tried not to move. He hugged himself. He closed himself in upon himself. Knees secured against chest, doubled so that his feet nearly touched his buttocks. His hands gathered up his legs, folded in his knees, closer and closer.[50]

Throughout this paragraph, I seek methods of harnessing English's own aesthetic and affective possibilities to reproduce the effects of the Arabic dual, in the acoustics of English words and in the ways that these words encroach on human bodies both within and outside of the literary text. The brief first sentence of the novel ("*Lam yaʿrif an yanām*")[51] receives a relatively equivalent translation: "He couldn't sleep." For the second sentence of the Arabic text ("*Baqiya ṭawīlan fī al-sarīr, yanẓur ilā khazānat al-ḥāʾiṭ*"; literally, "He remained long in the bed, looking at the wall cupboard"),[52] however, I produce two sentences in English: "Yet he stayed in bed. He fixed his gaze on the clothes cupboard against one wall." The addition of "yet" suggests a tension between the pervasive anxiety of Walīd's situation and his body's tendency toward habitude that deters him from acting purposively to change his circumstances, while his "fixed" gaze underscores his physical stasis only moments before he does, in fact, begin to move.

An unsettling confluence of light and dark at the margins of the room catches Walīd's eye: "*Khallafat al-futḥah mamarran ḍayyiqan ḥaddadahu al-ẓill ʿalā al-arḍiyyah al-khashabiyyah bi-taḥāluf maʿa nūr al-mamarr*" (literally, "The opening gave way behind it to a narrow hall defined by the shadow on the wooden flooring in alliance with the hall light").[53] The verb *ḥaddada* (to define, to sharpen, to demarcate, to determine) is a word with heightened acoustic resonances in Arabic, evincing a coincidence of sound and meaning across the semantic field of terms derived from the Arabic root *ḥdd*. In the sibilance of *ḥaddada*'s pharyngeal *ḥā*ʾ is the onomatopoetics of a blade (*ḥadd*) being made sharp (*ḥādd*), while the trio of *dāl*'s that follow strike the ear with the rhythms of a blacksmith (*ḥaddād*) striking iron (*ḥadīd*). For the translation of *ḥaddada*, I select the English word "bounded." The English language does not have the phoneme *ḥ*, but the voiced bilabial *b* functions by analogy—obeying Philip Lewis's injunction to analogical and "abusive" translations characterized by double articulations of supplementarity and semantic density[54]—to also involve the human speech apparatus in an outward projection of air, here utilizing the lips rather than the throat. Like the Arabic *ḥ*, the English *b* establishes the limit point or *boundary* from which vocalization begins—after the comma, a pause, and then sound, again: "Beyond it was a narrow hallway, bounded by the door's shadow." The *b*-to-*d* sequence in "bounded" replicates that of "Beyond," creating aural parallelism between the first word of each clause in the English sentence; the parade of *d*'s echoes the hammerlike beat of *ḥaddada*'s dental consonants.

Further on, I translate the noun-adjective pair *al-arḍiyyah al-khashabiyyah* into English as "the wood floor," the rhyming *-iyyah* suffixes of the Arabic transmuting into the identical doubled *oo*'s of the two English words, which, although they do not rhyme, maintain a visual and syllabic resemblance consonant with the relationship of the paired terms in Arabic. The most common gloss for *taḥāluf* in English is *alliance*, but I translate this word as "collaboration." I do so first to retain sonically the *l* and long, stressed *ā* of *taḥāluf*, and secondarily to suggest the discomfiting nature of the physical environment in which Walīd finds himself, as the bedroom door, failing to protect the room's occupants from disturbances outside, has instead *collaborated* with the light in the hallway to produce an unsettling juxtaposition of illumination and darkness that transfixes Walīd's attention, suspending him between wakefulness and sleep.

When I reach the cluster of dual-inflected words that describe how Walīd's body shifts from pure passivity to begin enacting micro movements of self-sustenance, I focus my attention on the verbs, adverbs, and verbally derived adjectives in these lines, grammatical signifiers of motion and change. For the Arabic *aghlaqa* (closed), *maḍmūmatāni* (joined), *tajmaʿāni* (gather), and *taṭwiyāni* (bend), I select English verbs linked to prepositions that convey a sense of the body's self-protective powers: "closed himself in upon," "secured against," "gathered up," "folded in." Each preposition enacts a gesture of bringing-together, an interlinking of two or more parts in solidarity, a defensive posture. The prepositions lend their attendant verbs a Romance-language reflexive quality normally absent from English, so that, for instance, "gathered up" here shares the internally referential recursivity of the French *se rassembler* or the Spanish *juntarse*. Such semantic reduplication—such duality of meaning and morphology, content twinned with form—encompasses the human actor immanently and inseparably within the action being done.

In the same model, I translate the Arabic participle *mathniyyatān* as "doubled" to retain a countable property of twoness for the narrator's knees. Alternative possibilities would have included *folded* or *turned under*, yet "doubled" is an especially apt translation as it also alludes to *mathniyyatān*'s shared etymology with the word *muthannā* itself. The adverb *akthar* (literally, "more"), the concluding word in the first paragraph of Shūmān's novel, I translate as "closer and closer" to convey the intimacy of taking comfort in one's own flesh.

Walīd's fantasy of returning to his mother's womb is realized not in his being reabsorbed into her body but in his finding comfort in the body that she gave him, that her body formed on his behalf. Maternal ethics takes shape as an inheritance of postures and the reactivation of a shared affective history. The insights that I gained by translating this opening paragraph of the novel became a guiding principle for my translation of Shūmān's text as a whole. Recognizing the ethical capacity of the *muthannā* here enabled me to discover other elements of Arabic grammar and morphology acting similarly in later chapters to open up prosperous spaces in language where a threatened or anxious body could endure. Translation becomes an ethical practice when it mobilizes a translator's body to extend such simultaneously linguistic and literary modalities of care from the source text into the target language. In so doing, translation affirms the source text's emergence into the world literary system as an event that is at once affective, ethical, and literary.

Animate Alphabets

Līmbū Bayrūt's third chapter is narrated by a mother-to-be, Salwā. A few days before violence sweeps through Beirut in May 2008, Salwā, who is almost nine months pregnant, is struck by a car while crossing a busy street in the Lebanese capital and must be hospitalized. As she waits for her baby to be born, she passes the hours following news coverage of the conflict on TV, contemplating her relationship with her husband, who was on a business trip abroad when the accident occurred, and solving imaginary crossword puzzles in her head. The clues for the puzzles that she dreams up come from the words that she hears around her. At one point, when Salwā's mother reminds her of how angry her husband would be if he knew what had happened, Salwā uses a puzzle to neutralize the harmful impact of her mother's words:

> حوّلت كلام أمّها كلمات مبعثرة في خانات بأسهم. كلما ذكرت أمّها كلمة معتادة، "جوزك" مثلاً، حملتها بناظريها ووضعتها في الخانة المخصصة، ثم أعادت شطبها من موقعها الأول.

> She imagined transforming her mother's words into scrambled letters within squares, with arrows beside them. Whenever her mother mentioned a key word—*husband*, for example—Salwa chose the correct letters with her eyes and placed them in their proper squares, and then she went back and crossed them out in their previous positions.[55]

Deconstructing her mother's words into "scrambled letters" ("*kalimāt muba ʿtharah*"), Salwā refashions them into arrangements that signify differently. When Salwā was a child, crossword puzzles kept her entertained while she was confined to her house during Lebanon's long-running civil war. Now they again foster a comforting illusion of order as she once more waits for events outside her control to determine the trajectory of her life.

This scene offers an inaugural glimpse of a maternal ethics unfolding within this chapter of Shūmān's novel. If in the first chapter of *Līmbū Bayrūt* such an ethics is activated through the grammar of the *muthannā*, then here it is realized via the letters of the Arabic alphabet, which likewise subtend a connection between the material of language and the ongoing vitality of bodies internal and external to a literary text. Barbara Johnson, describing the upbringing of the American poet Sylvia Plath, relates that when Sylvia's mother Aurelia needed to nurse Sylvia's younger brother, she would distract her daughter with "the alphabet from the capital letters on packaged goods in the pantry shelves. . . . From then on, each time . . . [Sylvia] would get a newspaper, sit on the floor in front of me and pick out all the capital letters to 'read.'"[56] The mother who can no longer give her body to her child translates it into the material of the alphabet; out of this material, Johnson suggests, arose the language in which Plath would eventually compose her poems.

Like the letters that Aurelia Plath offers to her daughter, Salwā's letters compensate for what the maternal body itself cannot do. Salwā's own mother provides not the comfort of an embrace or a touch, but admonishments, while Salwā herself cannot assure the safety of her unborn son, now or in the future: when he is born, Lebanon's roadways will still be dangerous for pedestrians, its political situation still unstable, its history still fragmented by war. Yet for now the letters calm her, deflect the negative emotions brought on by her mother's reproaches, and help to keep her from going into early labor (a common result of experiencing physical trauma while pregnant). The puzzles furnish Salwā with a means of caring for her child and for herself, even if it is one that can only ever be minimally effective.

Interspersed throughout this chapter of Shūmān's novel, mined from the puzzles of Salwā's childhood, are clues for the novel's readers to solve. Offset from the regular printed text of the book with bolded typeface, the clues anchor reading to the same syncopated rhythms of question-and-answer that Salwā experiences as a modality of care for self and other. As a translator, I find the puzzles, for the most part, simple to replicate in English. Yet one question-and-answer pair stops me short. Approximately a quarter of the way through the chapter is the following clue: "*Kalimah min ḥarfayn murādifah lil-baḥr*."[57] The answer, given several pages later, is "*al-Yamm*."[58] Translated literally, the clue could be rendered into English as "A word of two letters, synonymous with *sea*," if *baḥr* is understood in its everyday sense as referring to a body of salt water smaller than an ocean, as in *al-Baḥr al-Abyaḍ al-Mutawassiṭ* (the Mediterranean Sea) or *al-Baḥr al-Aḥmar* (the Red Sea). How, though, could *yamm*—a highly unusual word in modern Arabic, defined in one Arabic-to-English dictionary as "open sea" and in another as "sea, ocean; large river"[59]—be translated in such a way that the logic of the puzzle would be preserved for Anglophone readers?

To translate *yamm* as *sea*, its own most ready English equivalent, would collapse the synonymy of the Arabic puzzle into identity: *sea* as the synonym for *sea*. Yet what alternative is there? *Sea* in English has no synonyms; *ocean*, *lake*, and *pond*, suggested by Thesaurus.com, all indicate a different object entirely. As Susan Bassnett observes, glossing Roman Jakobson, in no circumstances does "even apparent synonymy . . . yield equivalence," interlingually or within a single language.[60] Synonymy is a fantasy vexed by the plurality of associations, connotations, and nuances of meaning that keep words eternally at a remove from one another, each suspended amid what Mikhail Bakhtin refers to as the "thousands of living dialogic threads" that comprise the universe of human languages.[61]

Further complicating my efforts to translate this puzzle into English, I discover that *yamm* is a key word for this chapter as a whole. When the man who will eventually become Salwā's husband proposes marriage, he does so as they are sitting among the rocks that abut Beirut's seafront, close enough to the surf breaking on the shoreline for its spray to dampen their faces. The significance of this moment registers for Salwā as an awareness of *yamm*'s primordial antecedence versus the far more common *baḥr*, underlying an intuition that if she marries this man she will come to exist in a more profound and ancient way, and that this existence will be within language, and that the operative word in this language will be *yamm*:

> وهي تتابع حركاته بطرف عينها . . . استعادت كلمة "اليمّ" من شبكات كلماتها المتقاطعة. لأول مرّة، عنت لها كلمة "اليمّ" أكثر من كلمة "بحر". لم تعد كلمة معروفة تستخدم في شبكة ألعاب. خرجت. طارت. صارت أكثر من ذاك. الحرفان والشدّة على الحرف الثاني في الكلمة جعلا الشيء بأكمله يتّضح أكثر. قالتها في رأسها: "يمّ". قالت في رأسها: هذه الكلمة الأصلية، لا "بحر".

A literal translation of this passage[62] into English yields the following:

> As she followed his movements out of the corner of her eye . . . she recalled the word "*yamm*" from her crossword puzzles. For the first time, "*yamm*" meant more to her than the word "*baḥr*." It was no longer a familiar word used in crossword puzzles. It escaped. It flew. It became more than that. The two letters of the word with the *shaddah* on the second of them made the thing in its entirety clearer. She said it in her head: "*Yamm*." She said in her head: This is the original word [*al-kalimah al-aṣliyyah*], not "*baḥr*."

Later, when Salwā's water breaks at the hospital, heralding the birth of her son, she associates the bodily sensations of labor with the same elemental notion of *yamm*:

> كانت اللكزات تتعاظم وتصبح كموج اليم.
>
> اليمّ. اليمّ. اليمّ! أخذت الكلمة تتكرّر في رأسها وتكبر.
>
> . . .
>
> وضعت سلوى كما عادتها يدها اليمنى على أسفل بطنها لعلّها توقف الألم فلم تفلح. علت اللكزات فجأة، وشعرت بالسائل يخرج منها.

Literally:[63]

> The stabs of pain were increasing and becoming like the waves of *yamm*.

> *Yamm. Yamm. Yamm*! The word began to repeat and swell in her head. . . .
>
> As usual Salwā placed her right hand on her lower belly, as though to stop the pain, but she did not succeed. The stabs of pain intensified suddenly, and she felt liquid rush out of her.

The importance of the word *yamm* in this chapter comes not only from what it designates semantically within the lexicon of the novel—the Mediterranean Sea lapping at Beirut's edge, the amniotic fluid that floods from Salwā's body—but from its role in linking Salwā's past and future through language. Occurring originally in a crossword puzzle that she solved as a child, *yamm* signposts Salwā's transformation first into a wife, and then into a mother. It is a word that carries a protective affective charge: having once vouchsafed for her body's wellbeing while the civil war decimated the city around her, it now resounds in the background while her son begins his safe passage into the world from this same body. A discursive marker of important narrative events in this chapter of *Līmbū Bayrūt*, *yamm* ties plot and character development to the occurrence of a rare Arabic word.

Realizing how *yamm* functions semantically but also formally in the novel, I begin the process of translating this word by once again seeking to locate it within the aesthetic and material history of the language out of which Shūmān's text is composed. I start, that is, not with the hypothetical English words that could translate it, but with understanding *yamm*'s position in Arabic. For Salwā, who is accustomed to disassembling words into their alphabetic elements, *yamm*'s originary force derives from its letters. Although it transliterates into four letters in the Latin alphabet, the word *yamm* in Arabic is composed of only two graphemes: the Arabic letter *yā*ʾ, acting as a consonant, and two *mīm*'s collapsed into one and marked with a diacritic *shaddah* to indicate gemination (يمّ). Can the Arabic alphabet offer a means of translating this word into English? Can letters compensate for the failure of synonymy, for the untranslatability of this archaic word, for the difference between my language and the other language, for the inevitable partiality of modes of maternal care that rely on language to do what the body cannot?

The history of the Arabic *mīm* (م) begins with a letter that in several early Semitic scripts looked like this: 〰. These alphabets, whose oldest surviving inscriptions date to the second millennium BCE, were acrophonic, composed of letters that were each drawn to resemble a thing whose word in the local spoken language began with the sound that the letter was intended to represent. For example, the letter ⊏, indicating the phoneme *b*, was drawn like the outline of a house because the spoken word for *house* (*bayt* or *bētu*) started with the sound *b*; the letter 𓁹, indicating the pharyngeal voiced fricative ʿ, was drawn like an eye because the word for *eye* (*ʿayn* or *ʿēnu*) started with ʿ, and so on.[64] According to this logic, the predecessor of the Arabic *mīm* was drawn to look like a ripple of water because, as G. R. Driver explains, the "inventors" of these scripts considered their word for *water* (*mayim* or *mayyūma*) particularly well suited to "reproducing the *m*-sound . . . and therewith, of course, the picture of water [was chosen] to be its symbol."[65]

As W. J. T. Mitchell notes, the history of the development of modern writing systems has been marked in many cases by letters' surrendering such material connections between image and meaning to better facilitate the efficient transport of ideas into text. Yet he suggests nonetheless that modern writing, whose "first form . . . [was] the pictogram," can still be recuperated as "visible language" insofar as many contemporary alphabets retain within their letters traces of the icons and pictures that inspired them. To attend to the image within the text elevates writing from an abstracted sign system and reactivates its potential to become "the medium in which the interaction of image and text, pictorial and verbal expression . . . seems to be a literal possibility."[66] In a similar vein, Sybille Krämer proposes that modern writing can be rehabilitated as more than "a mere discursive construct" for semiotically rendering human speech by "resurrecting a fundamentally visual-iconographic dimension" or "iconicity" within it that inheres in its technological, numerical, and cultural usages.[67]

When I delve into the alphabetic history of the Arabic word *yamm*, I do so in a bid to restore this word's iconicity, its capacity to conjoin synthetically between visual and discursive modes of language, between the form of language and the things in the world that language signifies. Aiding me in this endeavor is that the things within the letters of the modern Arabic alphabet are more accessible to an Anglophone translator than they might at first seem. The modern Arabic letter *bāʾ*, representing the phoneme *b*, is not only the first letter in the standard contemporary Arabic word for *house* (*bayt*), but the shape of the grapheme ب still evokes, however subtly, the floorplan of a house. The modern Arabic letter representing the phoneme ʿ is *ʿayn*, whose name is homophonous with the word for *eye*, and which especially in its initial form عـ still resembles an eye.[68]

Moreover, further research into the origins of the Arabic letter *mīm* reveals that it shares a common lineage with the letter *m* in the Latin alphabet, the alphabet in which English and most other European languages are written today. By around 1050 BCE, a standardized alphabetic lettering system adapted from the early Semitic scripts had come into use in the Phoenician cities of the coastal Levant, and from there it spread throughout the Mediterranean and across the Near East and Mesopotamian regions, eventually giving rise to both the Nabatean alphabet (probably the most immediate ancestor of the modern Arabic alphabet) and the Greek alphabet (the progenitor of the Latin alphabet).[69] In the course of these developments, the early Semitic letter 〰 that looked like water transformed first into the Phoenician 𐤌, and then its genealogy branched in one direction to create the Arabic م and in another to create the Greek μ and, eventually, the *m*.

Within the Arabic *mīm* and the Latin *m* alike, then, is water. So it is in water that I look for a translation for *yamm* in the English language. According to the authoritative thirteenth-century Arabic dictionary *Lisān al-ʿArab*, *yamm* is a sea whose depth and boundaries are unknown.[70] It is also the word used in the Qur'an's version of the Moses story to refer to the water to which his mother entrusts the safety of her infant son. According to the Qur'an, God tells this long-ago mother: "Suckle him, and if you are afraid for him then throw him in the river [*al-yamm*] and do not fear or be sad, for We shall restore him to you and make him one of the apostles."[71] Among the peoples of the ancient Near East before the arrival of Islam, Yamm was the name of the sea god whose cyclical defeat each winter brought the return of calm seas and life-giving rains in the spring.[72] The word *yamm* encompasses both a history of water as that which maintains and sustains life—saving the infant Moses, bringing fertility to the land—and water itself.

For Salwā, *yamm* is linked to both her father and her mother. It is a reminder of her father, now deceased, who came home each day during the civil war with a new book of crossword puzzles for his young daughter to solve. It is also a word differentiated in spelling by only a single letter from the Arabic أم / *umm* (mother) and its English near-homophone *mom*. What ethics of care does this word reveal, entextualize, and make translatable within Shūmān's novel?

Laying bare *yamm*'s alphabetic genesis, I locate a connection between its signifying content and its material form. The meaning of يمّ is mirrored graphically in the shapes of the letters that compose it. To account for this linkage in my English translation of Shūmān's novel, I offer simply: "Yamm." Not so much a word equivalent in meaning to its Arabic predecessor as it is a translation of the Arabic word's form into a different alphabet (and yet, an alphabet whose DNA it shares), "Yamm" introduces the worldliness of an Arabic letter into my English text. For the clue to

Salwā's puzzle that could be translated literally as "A word of two letters, synonymous with *sea*," my translation offers instead, "The four-letter name of an ancient Canaanite god of the sea," and several pages later, the answer that it gives is "Yamm."[73]

Following a similar approach, I translate the passage that relates Salwā's seaside conversation with her future husband like this:

> As she followed his movements out of the corner of her eye, she remembered her father. She recalled the name of the sea god from the crossword puzzle. Yamm. For the first time, *Yamm* meant more to her than *sea*. It was no longer just a word in a puzzle. It had escaped. Flown. Become more than that. The four letters, sealed at the end with the doubled *m*, made the whole thing come into focus. She pronounced it in her head, *Yamm*. She said to herself, This was the original word, not *sea*.[74]

Finally, when Salwā goes into labor in *Limbo Beirut*, it is the repetition of "Yamm" in English that provides a rhythmic accompaniment to her contractions.[75]

To the extent that "Yamm" in English translates the Arabic word يمّ, it does so by returning letters to their embodiment: the م and the *m*, two graphemes whose shared genetic code reveals the worldly thingness of water contained within them both. This water, which Salwā experiences as an affective condition of becoming a wife and mother, and which I recover to compensate for the lack of synonyms between Arabic and English and even within English itself, entangles my own embodied future with that of this fictional character. Salwā becomes a mother; I become a mother. Translation activates a common history and affective structure, an entwined genealogy of care linking translator and text, English and Arabic. يمّ and "Yamm" are not synonyms, nor are they the same word, for each exists within a different alphabet; rather, they are words with the same ethical potential inscribed in and upon their own bodies.

Johnson writes that having been "fed the letters of the alphabet in place of the mother's body" when she was a child, Sylvia Plath was later in life "unusually struck by the strangeness of other alphabets." That this is so is evident for Johnson in Plath's fiction: when the semi-autobiographical protagonist of Plath's *The Bell Jar* attempts to write a thesis on James Joyce's novel *Finnegans Wake*, she is thwarted by the visual incomprehensibility of Joyce's writing, which appears to her "like Arabic, or Chinese," animated by a foreignness that defies her academic efforts at interpretation. Joyce's version of the Latin alphabet purveys an otherness that cannot be intellectually comprehended but only experienced sensorially, in the "fantastic, untranslatable shapes" of letters that seem to "separate, each from the other, and jiggle up and down" within the literary text.[76]

If I have emulated the mothers Aurelia and Salwā in my method of translation, activating a compensatory ethical potential in language by deconstructing words into their constituent alphabetic parts, then my readers will be like Sylvia, struck by the strangeness of Arabic that is translated into English letters yet not fully, offered in tangible proximity without being assimilated completely to English discourse. When they solve Salwā's puzzle in English, readers of *Limbo Beirut* will experience the otherness of Shūmān's Arabic in familiar letters repurposed to embody a word in another tongue—and yet this tongue is also and already English's own.

Scenes of Survival

Over the course of five chapters narrated by seven principal characters, *Līmbū Bayrūt* presents a collective portrait of a generation of young men and women raised during the tumultuous years of Lebanon's civil war who are confronted anew in May 2008 with urban violence of a magnitude that they had hoped never again to experience. As bitter skirmishes between the opposing factions fill Beirut's downtown with gunfire and frightened citizens barricade themselves in their homes, the repressed traumas of the war threaten to resurface. Yet, however unwelcome such a return of trauma may be, Shūmān's novel suggests, it also elicits new modes of self-care from the people of Beirut or prompts them to reclaim old ones, affective routines that seek to maintain or reconstruct the ordinariness of everyday life amid the upheaval of current events.

Thus, throughout the novel, we find Shūmān's characters keeping up with their mundane daily habits in spite of the violence in the streets. They continue to walk through the city in defiance of the blockades that have sprung up to cordon off one neighborhood from the next, as though to stake their claim on its urban space by resignifying it through their embodied practice, enacting "a process of appropriation," in Michel de Certeau's terms, that is intended to keep Beirut for themselves.[77] They eat, sleep, take showers, and talk on their mobile phones, sustaining themselves and one another. Through these simple actions, they attempt to save their city and its inhabitants from the catastrophe taking shape around them. By turning inward into their own bodies, they resist the narratives within which their national past has always already inscribed them.

Rejecting the political as monumentally determinative of their relationships with others, they embrace instead a shared human embodiment that cuts across the fatalistic discourses of sectarianism and the interminability of strife.[78] The novel's concluding paragraphs offer a glimpse of how such affective ties might unfurl into something like a scene of collective optimism for Beirut. Narrated in the future tense, these paragraphs feature the final chapter's anonymous protagonist setting out on foot into the city during a break in the violence to witness the reestablishment of a kind of postconflict normalcy:

> أخرج إلى شارع الحمراء الرئيسي . . . [و]سأمشي على رصيف الشارع بعكس اتجاه السير. وأجد الحياة عادت لطبيعتها، ويكون بعض الباعة قد بدأوا بإزالة آثار الرصاص عن محلاتهم، وبتغيير الواجهات الزجاجية المحطّمة. سأقف للحظات . . . ثم أتابع طريقي. سيكون الشارع مزدحماً كما قبل، وعمال النظافة يعملون بشكل عادي. سأتوقف لأشتري جريدة من كيوسك . . .

> I will go out to Hamra Street . . . [and] I will walk down the sidewalk in the opposite direction of the traffic. And I will find that life has returned to normal, and that some of the store owners are beginning to patch the bullet holes in their shops and to replace the shattered glass façades. I will stand for a few moments . . . and then I will continue on my way. The street will be crowded just as before, and the cleaning crews working in their usual fashion. I will stop to buy a newspaper from a kiosk.[79]

This passage depicts what Lauren Berlant might call a "scene of survival," a bid to fashion a future enunciated around "new idioms of the political, and of belonging itself," even if these idioms can be expressed only haltingly, and even if this future is one that must be scavenged from the detritus of "a waning fantasy" of the goodness of the present.[80] It is unclear from the way the episode is framed in the novel whether the first-person narrator is actually seeing what he describes here, or only imagining it. Is it a real future, or only a future that might be? As the people of Beirut prepare to return to their routines, they do so not with any certainty that their actions will improve their country's inefficient and dissolute system of governance, nor with the assurance that by patching the bullet holes now they will not have to patch them again next year, or next week, or tomorrow. Yet they carry on anyway.

The final pages of the novel depict a "new ordinary," in Berlant's phrasing, that "has emerged in the displacement of the political from a state-citizen relation to a something else that is always being encountered and invented among people inventing life together, when they can."[81] By walking through the city in order to observe this process taking place, and observing in order to put words to what he sees, the anonymous narrator binds into a fragile communion these disparate activities of remaking for the future. "*Rubbamā ʿalayya an usāhim bi-jaʿl al-qiṣṣah, alātī kuntu juzʾan minhā, taqtarib qadr al-imkān min al-kamāl. Rubbamā*," he muses.[82] In my translation: "Perhaps I must help, as much as possible, to bring the story of which I was a part to a close. Perhaps."[83] With these words, the novel does, in fact, come to an end. The narrator's "perhaps" ("*rubbamā*") is a gesture toward the potentiality for something better that is really only a return to what came before, the future recycling the past. It is a futurity that invites only a bare minimum of optimism. Yet it is enough, if barely, for *Līmbū Bayrūt* to conclude with a modicum of hope.

The shared structures of feeling within which the novel entangles its characters are echoed by its interwoven plotlines, which culminate in one principal character's being struck and killed by a car driven by the protagonist of another chapter, as the former is attempting to detain Walīd for spray-painting a wall in a militia-controlled area; the dead man is then brought to the hospital where the final chapter's narrator works as a doctor, and where he is seen not only by this character but also by Salwā as she is about to go into labor. The modes of interrelation that Beirut enables for its residents are life-affirming but also fraught with dangers both psychic and corporeal. To belong to a society, a city, a nation is to be reliant upon that entity's well-being for one's own flourishing and the flourishing of those who come after. Civil strife, deficient urban planning, and a traumatized population render existence in Beirut precarious for this generation and the next.

Interdependency furnishes opportunities for affective survival alongside and with the aid of others, but it also imposes affective risks upon the self. Yet as Judith Butler reminds us, interdependency is not a choice. Our bodies at the moment of birth are "given over to others" to care for, and as we grow up we persist in needing favorable social, economic, and material conditions in order to thrive, as "forms of support" proffered by the collective structures that we dwell within and without which "life itself falters or fails." For to a profound degree, Butler maintains, "no body can sustain itself on its own."[84]

Butler's primary figure of interdependency is the child, but it could as easily be the mother. In her memoir of early motherhood, Rachel Cusk writes that only when she became willing to trade in the privileges of an autonomous self for the minimum of an interdependent relationship with her infant daughter were they finally able to "get on with the business of living together." "All that is required is for me to be there," Cusk discovers, "an 'all' that is of course everything, because being there involves not being anywhere else, being ready to drop everything. Being myself is no compensation for not being there." Motherhood is embodied for Cusk as a "mere sufficiency" of presence, a positioning of the self in proximity to the other that is necessary for the survival of both.[85] For Julia Kristeva, a mother's own body exists perpetually in relation to the body of the child that "had been its inside." "What connection is there," Kristeva wonders, "between myself, or even more unassumingly between my body and this internal graft and fold, which, once the umbilical cord has been severed, is an inaccessible other?"[86]

In this chapter, I have proposed an answer to Kristeva's question that applies to mothers and translators alike, two figures whom Barbara Johnson brings together via their common propensity to having their relationship to the other construed via language, and whom I have linked furthermore through their analogous positions of affective relationality vis-à-vis this other. The connection that remains is in the linguistic material of the mother tongue, shaped by and offered up from a mother's or a translator's body that has facilitated the other's emergence into the world.

Language retains the imprint of the other as a change in form, a new discursive and aesthetic arrangement, a worlding. Kristeva's essay from which I have just quoted, ostensibly a study of the symbolism of the Virgin Mary, cannot retain its formal coherence but splits into parallel columns at irregular intervals to accommodate a second text in which Kristeva ruminates on the dynamic fleshly interchanges that link her body to that of her newborn son. In the first chapter of playwright Sarah Ruhl's essay collection *100 Essays I Don't Have Time to Write: On Umbrellas and Sword Fights, Parades and Dogs, Fire Alarms, Children, and Theater*, several sentences are halted in midclause by interruptions from Ruhl's young son; one concludes abruptly with a numeral 7 that he has typed on her keyboard.[87] The multitude of section breaks in writer Jessica Friedmann's memoir about postpartum depression reveal a text composed "in the Notes app on my phone . . . sometimes at parks, pushing the swing one-handed; sometimes at the supermarket."[88] My translation of Shūmān's novel exposes its ongoing dependence on the Arabic text in language that maintains the affects of an Arabic grammar and the alphabetic genealogy of an Arabic word within the literarý formations of English.

The portrait that I have given in this chapter of a somatic and somaesthetic practice of translating Arabic literature into English has sought to show how engaging the body of the translator as a locus of theoretical significance opens up new perspectives on the dynamic interrelations of self and other that translation always already entails. In so doing, this chapter has registered my own body as a site of critical exploration. And yet my body has hardly been made legible as a singular or stable object of inquiry; per Butler, it "is not, and never was," nor will it be, "a self-subsisting kind of being."[89] Al-Jāḥiẓ tells us that so long as al-Uswārī was engrossed in the activity of translating the Arabic text of the Qur'an into Persian, bystanders were unable to tell "in which tongue he was more eloquent" ("*bi-ayy lisān huwa abyan*").[90] Translating for and in relation to the other obscures the distinction between languages when they meet on the tongue of a single translator. It also obscures the translator, regarded in the midst of turning his or her body from one side to the other, so that when this translator becomes visible it is in a blur of motion. My translating body, to the extent that it has become visible over the preceding pages of this chapter via its interactions with Shūmān's text, yields its visibility not as a static image but as a record of "the sum total of the relative perspectives in which the body has been implicated, as object or subject, plus the passages between them," as Brian Massumi would say.[91] A translator who is no longer invisible, I am seeable not for who I am but because of what my body has done.

4 / ʿ*Ajamī* Politics and Aesthetic Experience: Translating the Body in Pain

During the winter of 2019–2020, a major exhibition titled *Theater of Operations: The Gulf Wars 1991–2011* ran for several months at the MoMA PS1 museum in Queens, New York. Conceived as an artistic retrospective on "the legacies of American-led military engagement in Iraq" in the contemporary era, the show brought together paintings, videos, photographs, and mixed-media installations "by more than 80 artists based in Iraq and its diasporas, as well as those responding to the war[s] from the West."[1] In many of the artworks, Iraqi bodies featured prominently: in Jamal Penjweny's photographs of ordinary Iraqis concealing their faces behind portraits of the former Iraqi president Saddam Hussein, leaving only their bodies visible; in Susan Meiselas's documentary images of mass graves in Iraqi Kurdistan; in Thomas Hirschhorn's video of a manicured finger scrolling through pictures of mutilated corpses on a digital tablet; and in Hanaa Malallah's fifty pencil portraits of Iraqi civilians killed in a U.S. airstrike on a shelter in Baghdad in 1991.[2]

Within the "sensorium of war" evoked by these images, Iraqi bodies provided American audiences who saw *Theater of Operations* with a perceptual and affective focal point enabling them to engage both realistically and nonrealistically with the effects on the Iraqi populace of the events surrounding the two Gulf Wars of 1990–1991 and 2003–2011.[3] I begin this chapter with a brief discussion of this exhibition because it underlines a historical and cultural-political dimension to the questions posed throughout this book about how an Anglophone public comes to apprehend the embodiment of an Arab or Arabophone other via this other's aesthetic mediation. While such interactions, as I have argued, are never wholly determined by the external circumstances within which they occur, the ethical possibilities of such meetings are nonetheless inevitably entangled in the circumstances of their own sociality, historicity, and cultural locatedness.

This chapter examines the aesthetic experience for an American audience of reading a work of translated Iraqi literature in the United States at the height of the second Gulf War (the so-called Iraq War) as an affective, ethical, and political event. *I'jaam: An Iraqi Rhapsody*—an English translation by Iraqi novelist and poet Sinān Anṭūn, with the American academic Rebecca C. Johnson, of Anṭūn's own Arabic-language novel *Iʿjām* (2004)—was published in the United States in 2007, a year in which at least 18,000 (and by some estimates, as many as 26,000) Iraqi civilians died as a result of U.S. military actions in Iraq.[4] As in *Theater of Operations*, the Iraqi body figures in this work of translated literature as both an object of representation and an aesthetic node. Through the practices of reading that it delineates, it implicates American readers in the history of their country's violence against Iraqis, so that to consume Arabic literature in English translation becomes in this case an explicitly political act. And yet the text's political intervention is mobilized through and not in spite of its aesthetic aspect. Its capacity to have a political and an ethical impact emerges out of the irreducibly literary encounters that it stages between a textual body that exists within language, and a reading body hailed by language to share in the affective situation of this embodied other.

Whereas previous chapters addressed the affective and embodied histories of translators themselves as these inform the activity of translating a work of Arabic literature into English, in this chapter the bodies that are most intimately involved in the pragmatics and ethics of the translation act are those of two populations—American and Iraqi—defined by their political affiliations and collective social histories rather than by their personal identities. Beginning with *Theater of Operations* allows me to bring these populations into focus as actors in the multifarious processes of interchange between Arabic and English texts and publics that this book as a whole examines. Doing so moreover enables me to situate this chapter's study of the reception of *I'jaam: An Iraqi Rhapsody* in the United States vis-à-vis an ongoing critical discourse attentive to the ethics of how and for what purpose Iraqi bodies are made perceptible to Euro-American audiences via their aesthetic representation, to the extent that this discourse also informed the reception of the MoMA PS1 show in 2019–2020.

Among the first to be concerned explicitly with these questions was the French philosopher Jean Baudrillard. As coverage of the first Gulf War dominated TV networks globally in 1990–1991, Baudrillard claimed that the war was "not taking place" because the pervasiveness of images of the conflict impeded the possibility of its mattering in any way other than as a visual performance. Under such conditions, he maintained, the Iraqis who were killed in the war were reduced to "blanks," a numberless mass of "sacrificed extras" whose deaths were relevant only to the extent that they helped to shore up the spectacular simulacrum of the war's false reality.[5] More recently, the widespread dissemination in international news outlets from 2004 onward of photographs of Iraqis being abused by American soldiers at the Abu Ghraib prison near Baghdad cast doubt on "the 'ethical' use of the imagery of torture and other atrocities" even for ostensibly salutary purposes, as Elizabeth Dauphinée has contended.[6]

Insofar as critics pondered the effects upon American viewers of seeing *Theater of Operations*, this was framed likewise in largely ethical terms. Confronted with images of "Iraqi pain, and our complicity" in causing it, as one critic put it, American audiences were obligated ethically to "think about their own responsibility for what happened."[7] Yet another critic wondered whether seeing Iraqi bodies in pain might not only further "desensitize" spectators to the suffering that Iraqis had endured during the two wars, thus reifying "art's worldly futility" in achieving any measurable ethical impact.[8] For so long as ethics depends upon the conscious recognition of one's own obligation toward the other, it is attenuated by the semiotics of the aesthetic image that always requires interpretation to become legible. As Dauphinée notes, "there is no single way" to understand the Abu Ghraib photographs: if for one person they offered a strong rationale for ending the war in Iraq, then for another they provided confirmation of the inhumanity of Iraqis that had made the war acceptable in the first place.[9]

However, when the body serves as the site where the self apprehends the pain of the other, alternative modes of ethical engagement emerge. Leaving aside the vexed question of whether bearing witness to others' suffering will "necessarily strengthen conscience and the ability to be compassionate," or whether, on the contrary, such acts of witnessing only "transfix" and "anaesthetize," as Susan Sontag once argued that they do, attending to how pain registers in affects shared among bodies frees ethics from being assessed principally by what is comprehended in or learned from an aesthetic image by an individual interpreter.[10]

In *I'jaam: An Iraqi Rhapsody*, the pain of Iraqi bodies becomes legible as part of the novel's "aesthetic regime," in Jacques Rancière's terms—as one aspect of its irreducibly literary capacity to be both political and ethical.[11] To the extent that reading this translation of a work of Iraqi literature in the midst of the Iraq War could be an act with ethical ramifications for the American public, this result would come about by means of an aesthetic experience that repositioned American bodies within the same sensible world also inhabited by Iraqi bodies. Under such conditions, the pain suffered by the protagonist of Anṭūn's novel—a young Iraqi man imprisoned and tortured under the Saddam Hussein regime for writing antigovernment poetry—would signify not as that of a victim whose need for salvation justified the U.S. invasion of Iraq in 2003 on human rights grounds, but as pain that was also the readers' own. If readers of the novel had once moved in lockstep with the consensus of a national discourse that supported the war as justly waged against the evil of the Ba'athist state, then the aesthetic experience of reading this text would unpin their bodies from their former places in the American social collective and orient them dissensually relative to its hegemonic structures of feeling and normative behaviors.

And yet for Iraqi pain to come to matter affectively for the American readers of Anṭūn's novel would not entail their necessarily responding to it consciously in any particular way. Bodies subscribe to their own responsive logic of cause and effect and are altered by the impingements of the sensible environment in ways independent of and sometimes undetected by the conscious self. Following Pierre Bourdieu, the body as this chapter conceives of it is a malleable entity defined by its "(biological) property of being open to the world, and therefore exposed to the world, and so capable of being conditioned by the world, shaped by the material and cultural conditions of existence in which it is placed." Possessed of "the capacity to be present to what is outside itself, in the world, and to be impressed and durably modified by it," the body acquires its own "*corporeal knowledge* . . . of the world quite different from [that gained by] the intentional act of conscious decoding."[12] Bourdieu's notion of a corporeal knowledge distinct from what is grasped through conscious awareness is mirrored in Brian Massumi's differentiation between reactions to a stimulus that are knowingly perceived, and affective reactions that play out viscerally as preconscious frissons of bodily intensity. "Visceral sensibility," Massumi explains, "immediately registers excitations gathered by the five 'exteroceptive' senses even before they are fully processed by the brain."[13]

Whereas for Bourdieu bodily knowledge is inculcated among individuals in a group to comprise the basis of a corporeally habituated sociality, for Massumi what the body knows is irreducible to any social function, for affect always exceeds the self-referential systems that society constructs to maintain its own coherence. The ethical potential that I locate in the act of reading the English translation of Anṭūn's novel is both social in the sense that reading it is capable of constituting a new collective "habitus, a particular but constant way of entering into a relationship with the world" via a set of bodily dispositions, thereby engendering a new overall orientation for the society to which the readers belong; and radically antisocial insofar as the habitus that reading produces in this case is disruptive to this society's prior self-sustaining mechanisms.[14] What is critically important is that the ethical event takes shape in the moments before readers have time to consider the import of the representations of Iraqi pain that the text contains, and thus before an intellectual attitude toward the suffering that it portrays can be acknowledged or articulated.

Within the process of aesthetic reception, I understand these moments in which affects are still the sole reaction that a literary text has produced in a reader to be capable of structuring the whole aesthetic experience of that text. When a work of art compels our senses to distribute across our own viscera affects of pain that originated in the other's suffering body, this is already an ethical outcome, even before we recognize it as such, and indeed, even if we never admit it to be so. No longer limited to an atomized sensation of "the integral human body as the locus of moral sovereignty," as Talal Asad has characterized the body of the autonomous subject-agent idealized by post-Enlightenment Western thought, pain becomes "a social relationship" creating "the conditions of action and experience" for self and other alike.[15]

While mindful of the important distinctions between how literature is received and the reception of works of visual artistry,[16] I nonetheless propose that a final example from the MoMA PS1 show helps to clarify these ideas. One of the artworks included in *Theater of Operations* was an installation by the American artist Tony Cokes titled *Evil.16: (Torture. Musik)*. The installation consisted of two parts: a digital screen displaying excerpts from a 2005 news article by the Egyptian American academic Moustafa Bayoumi describing how the U.S. military had utilized music as an instrument of torture against Iraqi prisoners during the early period of the Iraq War, and an audio soundtrack of some of the same Western pop songs that were used for this purpose piped at high volume through the surrounding gallery space. Intended like many of Cokes's artworks to induce an audience to take part in "reading as a physical activity" or reading "experienced via the body" by juxtaposing textual and sonic elements in defamiliarizing and disturbing configurations, *Evil.16: (Torture.Musik)* employed "the affective resonances" of music to make the political and ethical relevance of the information conveyed by the words on the screen apprehensible to its viewers on a physiological level.[17]

When visitors to the MoMA PS1 show stepped inside the gallery containing Cokes's installation and read about Iraqi bodies in pain, their own bodies were simultaneously shaken and violated by the same sensory input that had inflicted this pain on these other bodies. As Bayoumi reported, U.S. military personnel considered their music-based torture method to be a kind of "torture lite" because it could "unravel [victims] . . . without laying so much as a feather on their bodies."[18] Yet, as Bayoumi's interviews with multiple former detainees who were subjected to this kind of torture illustrate clearly, pain that leaves no apparent marks on the body still affects it. Such pain is still *painful*, in the sense that it alters, for the worse, a body's lived sense of the world. The embodied experience of American museumgoers who paused before Cokes's installation long enough to both read and listen differed from that of the Iraqi prisoners in degree rather than in kind. An aesthetic encounter that does not visibly scar a body with its incursions is still capable of causing it pain.

Like Cokes's artwork, the English translation of Anṭūn's novel induces a bodily apprehension in the self of injuries inflicted upon another via the affective responses that it provokes. Differently from a work of visual art, however, *I'jaam: An Iraqi Rhapsody* achieves this result through language. Faced with the violent events of history, literary language becomes itself an instrument of violence: in Tarek El-Ariss's phrasing, it "embodies . . . [this] violence, writing violence against violence, confronting it in a spectacle of cruelty."[19] Through such tactics, a work of Arabic literature in translation strikes back against the dominant social structures of the American literary field into which it arrives, in order to cleave open by force, from within the very material of the bodies that inhabit this field, the possibility of a more ethical configuration.

As it does so, it figures its effects as a foreign and a foreignizing intervention into the collective practices of reading Arabic literature in English in the United States that is simultaneously an affective contestation of a longstanding American politics of aggression toward the Iraqi populace. This quality of foreignness I designate in this chapter as "*ʿajamī*," both to underscore its notional relation to Lawrence Venuti's idea of foreignization in translation and to differentiate it etymologically from Venuti's natively Anglophone concept.[20] Meaning literally "foreign" or "barbaric," often in reference to a non-Arabic-speaking other, *ʿajamī* connotes a range of valences relevant to situating Arabic as one language amid the many languages of the world. For Annette Damayanti Lienau, *ʿajamī* designates an element of "literary and linguistic self-consciousness" that has attached itself to "the transnational legacy of Arabic—as both language and cultural symbol" as it has mingled with, changed, and been changed by its interactions with other languages and cultures over time. At certain moments and in certain places, Lienau proposes, these encounters were freighted with the violent interlingual politics of Arabic's own imperialist tendencies toward the secular vernaculars of the broader Islamic ummah; at others, they allowed Arabic to mount an "egalitarian challenge" to European colonial idioms.[21]

Arabic today retains material traces of this worldly history. The vocabulary of modern Arabic, especially its colloquial dialects, abounds in *ʿajamī* borrowings from the languages of northern and western Africa and western Asia, acquired as Arabic spread beyond the Arabian Peninsula to become the lingua franca of the emergent ummah. The convention of using dots to distinguish among identically shaped letters in the Arabic alphabet (for example, differentiating ب from ث, or ح from خ) was an *ʿajamī* innovation adopted from Nabatean or Syriac in the seventh century CE, and for this reason the act of dotting letters is known in Arabic as *iʿjām*—literally, "making foreign," from the same lexical root *ʿjm* from which the word *ʿajamī* is also derived.[22] In the first case (the interpolation of foreign words into the Arabic lexicon), the addition of *ʿajamī* elements was seen initially as corrupting the sacred tongue of Islam with alien content;[23] in the second case (the addition of dots), the *ʿajamī* intervention served to elucidate existing Arabic orthography. To the extent that an introduction of *ʿajamī* material from one language into the material of another is capable of transacting a more equitable relation between the two idioms, this process is never not potentially cruel, never ethically unambiguous.

In Anṭūn's novel, it is the overturning of the convention of *iʿjām* that furnishes the principal literary conceit of the text in Arabic, while also being that which allows its English translation to pose its most forceful challenge to dominant American epistemological and affective paradigms around the war in Iraq. The *ʿajamī* is at the heart of the text's aesthetics in both languages. In what follows, I begin by examining the *ʿajamī* aesthetics of the novel in Arabic as a first step toward understanding the aesthetic experience produced by its English translation. If in the Arabic novel *Iʿjām*, the pain of the Iraqi body remains recursively inside the text, then in *I'jaam: An Iraqi Rhapsody* it escapes to enact a transgressive affective event in the American public sphere. The complementarity of how Iraqi pain works in these two versions of the text restages, in a literary and linguistic register, the dilemma of representational ethics posed by the artworks in the MoMA PS1 show: of what (if anything) can be accomplished in the world by the aesthetics of this pain, and at what cost to the other whose pain it is and to the self whose pain it is not. As the Iraqi artist Hanaa Malallah noted in the wall placard accompanying her installation in *Theater of Operations*, any "ethical appeal to our common humanity and vulnerability" that an artwork might make is necessarily "fleeting and does not, cannot, restore" the lives lost and bodies damaged in acts of war.[24] What art can do, however, is move viewers or readers to experience their own embodiment differently, and in so doing, to experience that of the other differently as well.

Striking Blows

The Arabic novel *Iʿjām* is presented to readers as though it were not in fact a novel but rather the autobiographical account of an Iraqi university student named Furāt, composed during his captivity in a Baghdad prison in the mid-1980s.[25] Ikram Masmoudi describes the character of the prisoner in Iraqi fiction set during the Baʿathist era with reference to Giorgio Agamben's notion of "bare life"—a "modality of existence where . . . natural or biological life . . . is politicised through abandonment and exposure to sovereign violence," in her gloss—as a figure whose political circumstances are concomitant with the embodied state of living in anticipation of death.[26] To the extent that literature can give an account of those who were "coerced, silenced, marginalised, abandoned and tortured" by the Baʿathist regime, and who existed socially, legally, and politically within the state "as the living dead," Masmoudi argues, it does so by recuperating their "perspectives" as "a strategic critique of the dominant discourses" of this regime.[27]

In the context of Masmoudi's remarks, I begin here by examining Anṭūn's novel *Iʿjām* as a work of literature that demonstrates the ethical and political insufficiency of art in accounting for the bare life of an Iraqi imprisoned by the Baʿathist state. To recover only the "perspective" of one who lives as though dead is a gesture inadequate to compensating for the material loss of the body subjected to sovereign violence. Yet what else can art do?

The novel begins with a memorandum, attributed to an employee at the Iraqi Interior Ministry, explaining that when Furāt's manuscript was discovered in his cell after his death, it was found to have been written in an Arabic script without dots. This government worker has taken it upon himself to restore the missing dots on the letters so that the manuscript can be read. Yet as soon becomes apparent, during this belated process of *iʿjām* (dotting) a multitude of errors have been introduced into the text, each one serving to recast parodically the official terminology of the Baʿathist regime. *Wizārat al-thaqāfah wa-al-iʿlām* (the Ministry of Culture and Information) has become "*wizārat al-sakhāfah wa-al-īhām*" ("the ministry of foolishness and deception"), *al-ḥirṣ al-dīmūqrāṭī* (the democratic endeavor) has become "*al-hars al-dīmūqrāṭī*" ("the democratic crushing"), *īdiyūlūjīyā al-Baʿth* (Baʿathist ideology) has become "*īdiyūlūjīyā al-ʿabath*" ("ideology of nonsense"), *al-majlis al-waṭanī* (national council) has become "*al-malḥas al-waṭanī*" ("national wasteland"), and so on.[28]

The mistakes are subtle. In some cases, they have been generated by the addition or subtraction of a dot from a single letter in a word; in other instances, letters have been transposed metathetically or an emphatic letter exchanged for its nonemphatic counterpart. Containing twenty-eight letters "only six [of which] would be unambiguous if the device of dotting had not been adopted," the Arabic alphabet presents many opportunities for such slippages to occur.[29] Arabic's phonological repertoire, for its part, contains multiple pairs of contrasting emphatic and nonemphatic versions of the same phoneme, such as the pharyngealized *ṣ* (represented by the letter *ṣād*) and the alveolar sibilant *s* (represented by the letter *sīn*), which when they are exchanged produce words that sound almost but not quite alike. Why the Interior Ministry employee has allowed these mistakes to enter into the text remains unexplained in the novel's conceit. Perhaps Furāt's orthographically fluid manuscript has afforded this government flunky an opportunity to carry out his own covert gesture of protest while attributing it to a dead dissident. Perhaps, more mystically, Furāt has somehow encoded these errors into his writing, so that when it is subjected to a process of *iʿjām*, they appear as though by magic from the pen of its transcriber.

In the context of the novel's setting in Baʿathist Iraq, the respellings serve as a means of turning state discourse against itself. As Ofra Bengio has observed, the Baʿath Party's strategic use of language was key in enabling it to consolidate and reinforce its control over every aspect of Iraqi society after it ascended to power in 1968, and especially under the leadership of Saddam Hussein, Iraq's president from 1979 until his removal by the United States in 2003. By appropriating keywords from the lexicons of political, military, and religious vocabulary in Arabic and assigning them with fixed meanings consonant with Baʿathist aims and principles, Bengio explains, the regime was able to cultivate its own unique repository of "slogans and clichés," "codewords," and "jargon." Through the incessant repetition of such terms and phrases over a series of decades, according to Bengio, Arabic itself became, under Baʿathist rule, "a 'value-loaded' language in which every word is either 'good' or 'bad,' an idiom in which words are not meant to reflect a given reality but rather to pass them through a filter of value significance."[30]

Anṭūn's novel introduces mobility into this static language, as the incorrect implementation of *iʿjām* upends the orthographic system that anchors Baʿathist discourse to the promotion of an authoritarian ideology. At the furthest extent of the text's disruptive rewriting of official terminology, the word *Baʿth* (Baʿath) itself is refigured as *ʿabath*: nonsense, frivolity, futility. Through such methods, the text engages in what might be thought of in Jacques Derrida's terms as a type of "play," activating the instabilities of the sign to counter the centering, centripetal force of the regime's use of Arabic.[31] Dislodging words from their ossified positions, the novel disputes their attachments to origin points in the official discourse and reveals their potential to reverse the systemization and cooptation of language for totalizing ends.

Along these lines, Friederike Pannewick proposes that *Iʿjām*'s "playfulness" is calculated to "render . . . inoperative" "the ruling sign systems" of the police state that has oppressed and imprisoned its protagonist. Yet in Pannewick's reading of the novel, the "act of protest" that it undertakes remains, in her estimation, aesthetic rather than overtly political. Instead of articulating an explicit critique of the Iraqi state under Saddam Hussein—indeed, the Iraqi president's name is never mentioned in the novel—*Iʿjām* relies on "a tactic of camouflage that once in position reverses power relations."[32] The text, Pannewick writes, is "political and critical, but only at a second glance."[33]

The principal target of the novel's subversive energies is not the regime as such, but the forms taken by the regime's language: orthographic and phonetic, morphological and visual. Repurposing linguistic form rather than reappropriating political content, the oppositional writing staged by this text is one whose politics are camouflaged, requiring a second glance to become legible, fundamentally aesthetic in character. The Saudi critic Saad Albazei suggests that insofar as the sarcasm and "linguistic ironies" of Anṭūn's Arabic text enable it to strike a series of "blows" against the Baʿathist regime, this attack is staged self-reflexively through "the writing process" itself, so that in order to recognize the novel's resistant thrust, "Arab readers are expected to pay special . . . attention to the style and form of the work."[34] To notice and appreciate the politics of Anṭūn's novel in Arabic necessitates a sustained engagement with its ways of being literary.

Backgrounded to the formal play of signs through which *Iʿjām* contests the hegemony of the Baʿathist regime is the fate of the dissident himself whose undotted writing has emancipated language to take on this role. Play opens language to the Derridean "adventure of the trace," unleashing its revelatory "monstrosity" against the corralling structures of slogans, jargon, and terminology, but throughout it all Furāt remains in prison.[35] Without chapters or clear section divisions, the novel shuttles feverishly between passages detailing Furāt's abuse by his captors and ones describing events in his past life, recalled out of order and in fragments: soccer matches, political rallies, dates with his girlfriend Arīj, classes at the university, conversations with his grandmother. The more pain Furāt suffers in prison, the further removed the novel's narrative becomes from anything that might be considered a plot, and the less obviously do its representations of places and situations refer to any version of an Iraqi reality outside the walls of the building where Furāt is held captive.

Elaine Scarry calls pain "resistant" to being expressed in language because, unlike other "emotional, perceptual, and somatic states" that a person experiences that possess "referential content" outside themselves, pain "takes no object."[36] Pain reduces language to nonsignifying form, and the form of language in this novel about a body in pain is also the principal source of both its aesthetics and its politics. Bringing together Pannewick's and Albazei's readings of *Iʿjām* with Scarry's account of pain's fundamentally extralinguistic nature, I propose that Anṭūn's text in Arabic dramatizes the politics of the body in pain as a problematic of linguistic content versus literary form. In so doing, it exemplifies and calls attention to the inability of a work of art to address materially or in any way make up for pain's effects on the body that experiences it, or to alter the political realities that caused this body to suffer—for it is the same loss of narrative coherence and mimetic truth that reveals the extent of Furāt's pain that also allows the language of Anṭūn's text to take on a heightened aesthetic quality.

In the novel's final section, in contrast to what happens to Furāt when the material integrity of his body is compromised by forces outside his control, the letters of the Arabic alphabet are liberated by their lack of dots to travel along "lines of flight" previously blocked to them by their need to signify. Letters become animate, "bodies without organs," as Gilles Deleuze and Félix Guattari might put it: embodied on their own terms, if with entirely different ethical implications than those associated with the terms of Furāt's human embodiment.[37] When Furāt's cell door finally opens late in the novel, it is not to let him out, but to let the letters in:

> انسلّ الألف من الباب متبختراً وكان يشعّ بضوءٍ بنفسجيٍ ساحر أضاء ليلي. وقف أمامي وخلع الهمزة التي كان يرتديها على رأسه كقبّعة. رماها خلفه فارتطمت بالجدار الذي تحوّل فجأةً إلى مرآة كبيرة. انحنى أمامي باحترام ثمّ أشار إلى الباء، الذي كان قد أطل برأسه، بالدخول. دخل الباء ووراءه التاء والثاء. تخلّصت من نقاطها بعد أن انحنت أمامي هي الأخرى. كان كلّ حرف ينظر بعدها إلى نفسه في المرايا ويضحك، ثمّ يبدأ بالرقص والقفز والدوران. دخلت الحروف تباعاً. الجيم والحاء والخاء ثمّ الدال والذال والراء والزاي والسين والشين. تصاعدت الضحكات وتساقطت النقاط تباعاً. وبدأت الحروف التي لم تكن تحمل نقاطاً بحمل النقاط من الأرض ووضعها في عروتها أو على رأسها... . سرق السين نقاط الشين وضحك بصوت عال ثمّ وضع سبابته على فمه وهو يقول: "ششششششش". ... الميم نام على بطنه ورفع رأسه واعتمر نقطتين التقطهما من الأرض. ... تراقصت الحروف في كلّ مكان، تواقع بعضها بعضاً بأوضاع مختلفة ومحظورة.
>
> The *alif* slipped through the doorway like vapor, radiating a bewitching violet light that illuminated the night. It stopped before me and removed the *hamza* that it was wearing on its head like a cap. It flung it over its shoulder, where it crashed against the wall, which had transformed suddenly into a large mirror. Then it bowed graciously to me and signaled to the *bā*ʾ, which was poking its head through the doorway, to enter. The *bā*ʾ came in, and behind it the *tā*ʾ and the *thā*ʾ. They all stripped off their dots, after bowing to me one after the other. Each letter looked at itself in the mirror and laughed; then each began to dance and leap into the air and spin in circles. The rest of the letters entered the room in sequence: the *jīm* and the *ḥā*ʾ and the *khā*ʾ, and then the *dāl* and the *dhāl* and the *rā*ʾ and the *zayy* and the *sīn* and the *shīn*. They laughed aloud and their dots fell off one by one. The letters that lacked dots began to pick up the others' from the floor and put them in their buttonholes, or place them on their heads. . . . The *sīn* stole the *shīn*'s dots and, laughing, raised its finger to its mouth and said, "Shhhhhh." . . . The *mīm* lay down on its stomach and raised its head to ingest a pair of dots that it had plucked from the floor. . . . Everywhere there were letters dancing together or copulating in assorted forbidden positions. [38]

Leaping, spinning, laughing, dancing, and having kinky sex, the Arabic letters *alif*, *bā*ʾ, *tā*ʾ, *thā*ʾ, *jīm*, *ḥā*ʾ, *khā*ʾ, *dāl*, *dhāl*, *rā*ʾ, *zayy*, *sīn*, *shīn*, and *mīm* mock Furāt with their bacchanalian tableaux. They taunt him with the physical freedom of their bodies—heads, fingers, mouths, and stomachs that are their own to do with what they will. They look in the mirror and see themselves as subjects of their own narratives, agents of their own bodily destinies, no longer objectified by the propagandist language of the state nor by the exigencies of Furāt's narration. In contrast to Furāt, who since being thrown in prison has wanted only to "escape from my body [*ahrub min jasadī*] and be done with it forever," their coming-to-embodiment is celebratory, self-indulgent, profligate with possibility.[39]

As the scriptorial form of language attains a degree of embodied selfhood exceeding that of the human language user, the positions of writer and written invert. Letters mobilize their own disorganized and rhizomatic routes of movement, entrance, and egress unavailable to the human prisoner, while the writer remains trapped inside the carceral system of the regime. "Do I write or am I written? [*Aktub am uktab?*]" Furāt wonders. "Did they put me here because someone wrote about me [*kataba ʿannī*]? I'll gouge an eye/ *ʿayn* [*sa-afqaʾ ʿayn*], or even a *ghayn*, from anyone who tries to read me!"[40] Deprived even of grammatical agency, no longer able even to claim "the linguistic status of [a] 'person'" who speaks as *I*,[41] Furāt can only mount his defense from inside the autotelic semiotics of the regime within whose structures he is both physically and discursively inscribed. Punning on the Arabic phrase *faqaʾa ʿaynahu* (he took out his eye, he dealt him a blow), Furāt threatens those who would read him with a violent attack against their *ʿayn* or their *ghayn*: respectively, the eighteenth and nineteenth letters of the Arabic alphabet in the common modern sequence. Resistance can only be simulated as an act of violence against letters. This alphabetic attack is the sole recourse left to Furāt; to the extent that his "blows" are capable of avenging the violation of his body, they can never exceed the play of language. It is not really an eye for an eye that he threatens, but an *ʿayn* for an *ʿayn*.

If such an attack serves to subvert, then its subversive potential is as simulacral as everything else in the Baʿathist state's version of reality. As Achille Mbembe argues, the regime that rules through a "system of signs, images, and traces" incentivizes no less symbolic methods of resistance that exploit "the potential for play, improvisation, and amusement, within the very limits set by officialdom." Marshalling its energies not into direct confrontation with the regime but into forcing the regime to contemplate reflexively the "vulgarity and the baroque [within itself] that the official order tries hard to hide," such resistance remains within the semiotic and aesthetic conditions predetermined by the state.[42] If the play of writing in Anṭūn's novel frees signification from the stranglehold of official discourse, then what is signified instead is not the reality beneath or outside the simulacrum, but a fiction of a different order: language as a "play of signifying references," as Derrida would call it, an aesthetic supplementarity, a literature.[43]

Embracing Pannewick's and Albazei's observations about the essentially literary nature of *Iʿjām*'s subversive politics entails recognizing that in this novel, literary language alone is tasked with compensating for what is done to the body of its protagonist, and that ethically, language fails in this task. Wordplay reverses the values of signs, but it cannot save Furāt himself, whose body disappears into the prison of the regime. The novel's literariness is offered in exchange for this body, art given for a pound of flesh. Aesthetically, linguistically, the human is instrumentalized to art, defying or transgressing the precept of Kantian ethics that to be a "person" is to be immanently affirmed as an end in oneself, "as something that may not be used merely as means."[44] Yet how could it be otherwise, when personhood was already compromised historically and affectively before the novel was written, compromised not just grammatically—for the *I* who can no longer speak as *I*—but in the form of bodies battered, beaten, raped, mutilated, dismembered, or accosted with unbearably loud sounds? How can art be held responsible for this body?

Faced with the real conditions of the body imprisoned by the Ba'athist regime, to represent the viewpoints and situations of those who were reduced by it to the barest kind of life, in Masmoudi's terms, while being the only means of resistance or critique that literature by itself can muster, is ethically never enough. As Anṭūn put it in a 2010 interview, *Iʿjām* portrays the "plight and suffering" of Iraqis as a way of reckoning with "the impossibility of fully knowing what became of the victims." The loss of the victims' bodies, for Anṭūn, is terminal; it is one from which "we can never fully recover," and with which "we can never come to terms, fully."[45] Such a loss stands mournfully as an unassimilable externality to Kantian ethics, and within the aesthetic elaborations of a single Arabic literary text, it can only be conveyed as such.

Body Counts

In translation, however, the ethical potential of the text's literariness changes. No longer striking blows against the all-encompassing semiotic systems of the Ba'athist state, the English novel instead pitches its attack against the sensibilities of the American public sphere into which it arrived in 2007. This was the same year in which the American president George W. Bush deployed an additional twenty thousand U.S. troops to Iraq in a strategic move known as the "surge," and not coincidentally, it was the second deadliest year for Iraqi civilians of the nine-year war (surpassed only by 2006), according to figures compiled by the Iraq Body Count project from media reports, hospital and morgue records, and Iraqi government data.[46]

Many Americans at the time would not have been aware of these statistics, however, given that the U.S. military since the war's outset had refused to count the Iraqi dead. "American officials say numbering the enemy dead in the midst of battle is dangerous and ultimately fruitless. They say it is not a statistic that interests them. They speak in lifeless terms of 'degrading' or 'attriting' enemy military formations," the *New York Times* reported in 2003. In the summation of General Tommy R. Franks, commander of U.S. military operations in the Middle East when the war began: "we don't do body counts."[47] And yet the Iraqi body at the center of *I'jaam: An Iraqi Rhapsody* was one that could not but count for an American audience that read the novel in its English translation in 2007. The injuries suffered by Anṭūn's protagonist Furat (as the character's name is spelled in English) are described for readers in exacting detail, as in these passages:

> I feel an intense pain in the back of my head from the blow I received when I tried to resist. It becomes aggravated when he pulls my hair or pushes my head, rubbing my nose in that gray cloth that has been colonized by a foul smell—a mixture of sweat, blood, and layers of dirt. The pain surges to my wrists and joints when I try to pry open the wires that cut into my skin. I can feel his sticky fingers on my right thigh as he holds me down. His dirty fingernails dig into my skin. . . .
>
> My hands were tied in the position of eternal applause. His hot breath burned my neck and inflamed my disgust. He would talk and laugh at first, but he'd soon give over to a soft panting as he was about to ejaculate. . . . Many small things shattered inside of me every time, things I can't name or identify. . . .
>
> Perhaps they have won, with all this filth they've smeared on the walls of my memory and subconscious—their slogans that reek of piss, the shit that piles up in the abandoned streets of my body. How can I be rid of it without dying myself, or going mad? Their chants penetrate my ears and eyes and seep out of my anus, only to invade again through my mouth, and I have no choice but to swallow them, while they mock me.[48]

Following Suzanne Keen, such accounts of what Furat endures could be seen as inducing a "vicarious, spontaneous" process of intersubjective empathic identification between readers and this literary character: as Furat's suffering is itemized in precise terms, readers imagine themselves to be suffering as well.[49] Yet the images of Iraqi pain contained in Anṭūn's novel register not only imaginatively but affectively for an American audience constitutively implicated in inflicting pain on other Iraqi bodies in the present. For Tarek El-Ariss, affects in literature provide "a counterpart to the question of representation . . . [by] identifying new crossings between the literary and the political, experience and writing. These links are inscribed in the body, a site of literary and cultural narratives and histories."[50] Affects alter how and why literary representations come to matter, rendering them far more than scenarios that play out in the "safe zone" of a "fictional world" as they are for Keen.[51] Insofar as the depictions of Furat's suffering body in *I'jaam: An Iraqi Rhapsody* served to counteract the U.S. military's official position that Iraqi pain had no importance for the American public, they did so by means of this pain's literary affects, its worlding in and through the medium of a literary text.

When they register a response within the communal structure of feelings that defines a public as a gathering-together of bodies for common political and social ends, literary affects have the potential to realign this structure into new and more ethical formations. In Raymond Williams's definition, a structure of feelings unites a population within a set of "meanings and values as they are actively lived and felt." The processes through which such collectivization occurs, Williams asserts, are not epiphenomenal to the dominant institutions and ideologies that distinguish a society at a certain historical moment, but co-constitutive with their operations. Insofar as a structure of feelings works to "exert palpable pressures and set effective limits on experience and on action" for everyone in a society, its influence infiltrates arenas of affective life not overtly managed by the state, while also reifying and reinforcing many of the state's official mechanisms as themselves at least partly affectively constituted.[52] To the extent that Furat's pain was capable of provoking a social rather than an individual response from American readers, it did so by mobilizing affects of a literary and an aesthetic nature against a structure of feelings whose own affects were produced and experienced socially. The affects of Anṭūn's novel would reverberate in the collective American body as an attack on the constitutive values and institutional and ideological frameworks that made this body cohere as a social formation. It was on this level that Furat's pain would come to "count" for an American public.

In the prevailing rhetoric of the Bush administration during the early months of the Iraq War, the violation of Iraq's territorial sovereignty and the forcible removal of its president were branded as democratizing activities carried out for the good of the Iraqi people. When President Bush himself hailed the success so far of American military operations in Iraq in his January 2004 State of the Union Address, he noted that thanks to the actions of the United States, "the people of Iraq are free."[53] The rhetorical function of Iraqis in this statement echoes their function in statements made by U.S. Secretary of Defense Donald Rumsfeld and U.S. Vice President Dick Cheney at around the same time.[54] In such formulations, Iraqis serve as what Alain Badiou calls the "universal human Subject," providing justification for U.S. military actions in Iraq on ethical grounds.[55] When the rights of this subject are violated by an evil of the magnitude of the Baʿathist regime, according to this logic, ethics can be acceptably recast as the "imperative to intervene," and going to war becomes the right thing to do.[56]

In this context, ordinary Americans could watch scenes of the war playing out on television, and listen to the speeches of their leaders, and identify themselves as belonging to a nation whose actions were ethical. This process of identification carried its own affective dimension. Badiou aligns the "general feeling provoked [in Western audiences] by the sight of atrocities" that are inflicted upon others far away with a sensation located "halfway between fear and enjoyment." Such a "pathos," he writes, comes of knowing that evil is proximate, "almost knocking on the protected gates" of the Western metropole, but knowing also that it cannot reach the Western self, because the one who suffers is always an "Other," a "complex" and "enigmatic" victim of third-world miseries from which the West is ontologically immune.[57] For Badiou, this feeling was central to the sensible experience of being "Western" in the late twentieth century, and it was no less core, I suggest, to the affective sensibility of being American in the first decade of the twenty-first century. Even in the wake of the "welter of emotion" and "affect-flooding" that overwhelmed Americans after the attacks of September 11, 2001, delivered misery directly onto U.S. soil, the kind of everyday evil that Iraqis were understood to have suffered under the Baʿathist regime remained a condition external to the American structure of feelings at this moment in history.[58]

If, by reading Anṭūn's English novel, Americans came to apprehend the suffering of Iraqis within a different structure of feelings, this outcome could arrive only and always as an effect of the aesthetic experience that the text provided. A structure of feelings is an emergent and unstable formation, perpetually evolving to accommodate changes in the material conditions of the lives that are lived within it. As such, writes Williams, it hovers at "the very edge of semantic availability," impossible to describe fully or pin down to a single significance or set of outcomes. To the extent that a structure of feelings can be expressed or invoked in a signifying medium, this medium must be "art and literature," whose "specific feelings, specific rhythms" communicate meaning in the contingency of an aesthetic experience rather than as a definitive fact.[59]

As in Anṭūn's Arabic text, the aesthetics of the English novel are rooted in the transgressive wordplay with which Furat's manuscript resignifies and literally re-forms the official discourse of the Baʿathist regime.

In *I'jaam: An Iraqi Rhapsody*, however, each misspelling or pun is accompanied by a footnote on the same page in which the "correct" word or phrase is given. The presence of these footnotes implies that, in the diegetic reality of the English novel far more than in that of its Arabic counterpart, Furat's efforts to resist even the discursive hegemony of the state—let alone its biopolitical power—have ultimately been futile. If the persistence of the orthographic mistakes in the Arabic novel is mystifying, then in the English translation it seems to confirm that the state always has the final word on how and for what purposes language is permitted to signify, as though the errors have been allowed to remain only so that the government can make a public show of refuting them.

Moreover, by rendering the linguistic ironies in the English novel unmissable for an audience, the footnotes alter the hermeneutic payoff of the reading process. Whereas readers in Arabic must skillfully extract the parodic elements from the text by utilizing all their knowledge of, and instinct for, the ways in which Arabic letters come together to produce words, there is no comparable task given to readers of the translation. An Anglophone reader learns immediately that "the Ministry of Rupture and Inflammation" should be "the Ministry of Culture and Information," that the "simulation" of Democracy should be its "celebration," that the Eighth of February "revulsion" should be the Eighth of February "revolution" (referring to the military coup that brought the Ba'ath Party to power in 1963), and that a lecture on "National Hemorrhage" should be a lecture on "National Heritage."[60]

Unlike their Arabophone counterparts, Anglophone readers do not have to *do* anything to get the satire of the text. Each malapropism holds out a promise of the satisfaction that would come with discovering the twist, the rub, the join within language where an anticipated meaning has unraveled to articulate something funny, sarcastic, slyly derogatory. Yet in each case, this gratification is blocked by a footnote, which beats readers to the punch, giving away the punchline before they can think of it themselves. In comparison to the Arabophone audience of *I ʿjām*, the audience of *I'jaam: An Iraqi Rhapsody* is left passive and unable to participate fully in what reception theory calls "the production of the signified" that actualizes the text's semantic and aesthetic potential through the act of reading.[61]

Just as Arabic turns against Furat, English turns against the readers of *I'jaam: An Iraqi Rhapsody*. Their encounter with the text is a disagreeable one: there is no enjoyment to be derived from the formal artifice of words that point to several meanings at once, but only the frustration of finding that the text's literariness always and already surpasses their capacity as readers to grasp it. In his preface to *I'jaam: An Iraqi Rhapsody*, Anṭūn explains the ambiguity of an Arabic manuscript in which *iʿjām* or alphabetic dotting has not been utilized by way of a comparison between Arabic and English, suggesting that just as one Arabic letter without its dots might be easily mistaken for another, in English "an uncrossed t might be misread as an l." Yet the similarity only goes so far, he notes, for "in Arabic, the richness of the root system and the high number of variations and combinations . . . produces a much more complex situation [than] if one does not cross his or her t's."[62] Just as the sophisticated linguistic conceit of the Arabic novel exceeds the more limited capacities of English orthography, so, too, do the hermeneutic pleasures of the text remain out of reach to Anglophone readers.

Readers of the translation are instead held captive within a discursive environment in which, as for the citizens of Ba'athist Iraq, "clarity of meaning" must be categorically preserved, "vaguery or ambiguity" is prohibited, and "individual interpretation" is a crime.[63] They are, that is to say, trapped within the same linguistic environment in which Furat himself is imprisoned—this character with whom they were first led to identify intersubjectively, but whose subject position they have now assumed as their own. And because Furat is not a subject but an object reduced to bare life by the regime's carceral system, they, too, become only bodies as they read this text, interpellated within the painful affective conditions that the literary text has created for them.

Intrinsic to the aesthetic regime of the English text, pain is a *literary* affect to the extent that it is produced and disseminated as an aspect of the literariness of this work of translated Arabic literature. For Jacques Rancière, the "literariness" of a text indexes its "availability" or potential capacity to demarcate "a partition of the perceptible in which one can no longer contrast those who speak and those who only make noise," or those who speak as *I* and those whose vocal expressions are heard only as the din of the suffering other.[64] To read Anṭūn's novel in English effects an alteration in the sensibilities of those who read it, insofar as to possess or inhabit a sensibility is to live affectively within the political and social structures of a given community—to exhibit a certain "affective habitus," in Elspeth Probyn's terms.[65]

Reading this work of translated literature would produce a disruption in how American exceptionalism was embodied in the early twenty-first century as a feeling of physical safety from the pain of others. The ethical implications of the affective sharing brought about by reading Anṭūn's novel in English arise not from how reading it collapses self and other into a single universal type of human subject, but from how doing so affirms the universal objective embodiment of both Iraqis and Americans. The affects of pain could be experienced by a fictional Iraqi prisoner or by an American reader—if *never* in equal measure, then with the equally reductive outcome of ratifying both Iraqi and American bodies as composed only of a fragile and borderless material. As Teresa Brennan writes, affects that have an "origin . . . independent of the individual experiencing them" reveal the body's innate porosity.[66] An American body that reads is no more intrinsically self-contained or cohesive than an Iraqi one degraded by torture. Neither body belongs to an "individual whose desire and ability to act are taken as unproblematic,"[67] and for neither can pain be overcome or managed through conscious will, subjective agency, or the imposition of historical certitude on the habits of feeling conditioned by the violence of the present.

Political by Default

When literary affects provide a join between an American self and an Iraqi other, reading a work of Arabic literature in English translation, even as it remains irreducibly an aesthetic activity, becomes at the same time rife with political possibility. The politics of Anṭūn's novel in English depends, on the one hand, on how this literary text could introduce what Rancière calls "a new configuration of the sensible" into the collective embodied experience of being American within the neo-imperial world order ushered in by global U.S. military hegemony beginning in the second half of the twentieth century.[68] Anṭūn's Arabic text, opposing itself to the political force of the Ba'athist regime, remains within the simulacrum, within the sign system that official discourse has imposed on reality. The English text, by contrast, does not counter politics with art, but opposes one set of collective practices of feeling with another. Its politics are activated not as an attempt to change the "real world" that exists "as the outside of art," but in the reconfigured sensory experiences of "what is given as our real, as the object of our perceptions and the field of our interventions" that the literariness of the text generates for its readers.[69]

To attend to the politics of *I'jaam: An Iraqi Rhapsody* in the American literary field also necessitates recognizing that just as in Anṭūn's Arabic text, the political here emerges from the aesthetic, but that the import of the co-implication of aesthetics and politics in the English novel is entirely different. Indeed, the very fact that the politics of Anṭūn's text in English cannot be dissociated from its aesthetics constitutes its own kind of political and ethical effect vis-à-vis the norms of the English-language market for Arabic literature in translation. That these two aspects of a literary work in Arabic should operate in concert, as they do here, countermands a core assumption about Arabic literature that has informed American views of it at least since Fredric Jameson claimed in the mid-1980s that, in contradistinction to the aesthetically focused novels of the Western canon, all "third-world texts . . . necessarily project a political dimension."[70] This notion persists today in what Kuwaiti scholar and author Mai Al-Nakib has described as the "general expectation in the West" that "all Arab literature is . . . by default, political," and that in so being, it stands "in contrast with" Western literature, which is "defined by its opposite (nonpolitical or more than *merely* political)."[71]

In light of the longstanding ubiquity of such perspectives among both Euro-American literary scholars and the Anglophone general public, the reviews of *I'jaam: An Iraqi Rhapsody* that appeared in the American press following its publication suggest a text not readily assimilated to the preexisting knowledge systems of the American literary field, any more than it could be accommodated to the affective structures shaping this field on the collective level of American social experience. A review of the novel in the *Los Angeles Times* deemed it "eerily beautiful," while the *Village Voice* called it "strange, and beautiful;" in the literary journal *Counterpoise*, Anṭūn's novel was described as "stunningly lyrical."[72] These appraisals call attention not to how *I'jaam: An Iraqi Rhapsody* might help American readers "comprehend the unknown, fear-inducing, politically overwhelming Middle East," in Al-Nakib's words, but instead to the text's aesthetic qualities.[73]

Although published at a time when, by Ikram Masmoudi's assessment, interest "in Iraq in general and Iraqi society, culture and literature in particular" was on the rise in the United States and other Western countries due to the Iraq War, *I'jaam: An Iraqi Rhapsody* vexed reviewers' attempts to extract data about these topics from their readings of the novel.[74] As one reviewer complained in the *San Francisco Chronicle*, "there is very little to place the narrative in Iraq."[75] What the novel offered instead to "an informationally eager Western readership" (as the audience for Arabic literature in English translation has been characterized by the translator Marilyn Booth) was concatenating scenes of linguistic play, a plot deranged by the fragmenting force of pain, and a portrait of Iraq mediated solely through the hazy lens of Furat's memory.[76]

Not only did such features of Anṭūn's novel obviate its anthropological value, but for some reviewers the text's overt literariness appeared moreover ill suited to its content. In the view of American literary critic Claudia Roth Pierpont, the "self-consciously literary" presentation and "formally focussed, internally preoccupied tone" of the novel distinguished it unfavorably from other Iraqi prison narratives that adopted a more documentary approach, such as Maḥmūd Saʿīd's *Saddam City* (2004; *Anā alladhī raʾā*, 1981), the style of which, Pierpont wrote, was "plain and direct, without literary pretensions," and which provided a "density of detail" about prison life that *I'jaam: An Iraqi Rhapsody* did not.[77]

The difference between the two novels, Pierpont suggested, was surely due in no small part to the divergent personal histories of their authors: whereas Saʿīd was jailed multiple times under the Ba'athist regime, Anṭūn had "never been in prison."[78] Not political in Jameson's sense of being primarily a "national allegory,"[79] Anṭūn's novel also defied another assumption common among Euro-American critics—namely, that a work of Arabic literature should perform what Booth refers to as "Orientalist ethnographicism," "a way of seeing and writing the Other that grounds authority in a written narrative of personal experience."[80]

Anṭūn was born in Baghdad in 1967 to an Iraqi father and an American mother; after the first Gulf War, he immigrated to the United States, earning a master's degree from Georgetown University and a doctorate from Harvard University and eventually joining the faculty of the Gallatin School at New York University, where he continues to teach today.[81] When the United States invaded Iraq in 2003, Anṭūn became a frequent spokesperson for the Iraqi perspective in the American public sphere. And yet in this role, despite having spent much of his adult life in the United States, and despite being by familial ancestry a member of Iraq's Chaldean Christian minority (a population persecuted by the Ba'athist regime), he was fiercely and unrelentingly critical of the war.[82] In *About Baghdad*, a feature-length documentary filmed in the Iraqi capital shortly after it was first occupied by U.S.-led coalition troops that Anṭūn codirected along with several other U.S.-based Arab academics, Anṭūn presents himself as an "exiled Iraqi writer and poet" returning to "see what has become of his city after wars, sanctions, decades of oppression and violence, and now occupation."[83] Released in U.S. theaters in 2004, the film follows Anṭūn through an urban landscape decimated by coalition bombs as he interviews various members of the Iraqi populace about their views of the invasion, which are overwhelmingly negative, offering a far different portrait of how Iraqis were responding to their so-called liberation from that propagated by the U.S. government at the time. Consistent with what Anṭūn later described as his commitment to "being doubly critical and being oppositional always and everywhere" when it came to taking a position on U.S. policy in the Middle East, other public statements that he made about the war during its early years were similarly polemical, whether he was denouncing President Bush as the "new emperor" of Iraq (in an article in *The Nation* in May 2003) or calling on Americans to recognize the war as a "crime committed against Iraqis" (in a March 2008 guest appearance on *The Charlie Rose Show*).[84]

As an "Arab immigrant writer" in the United States per Waïl Hassan's definition, Anṭūn should have been ideally suited to merging "the two classic stances of the native informant and the foreign expert" to render the events unfolding in Iraq legible to an American audience.[85] Yet he refused to play this role, and in so doing, simultaneously denied this same audience the opportunity to bring a biographical framework to bear in reading his novel, whose damning portrayal of Iraq under Saddam Hussein's rulership appeared irreconcilable with its author's staunch and vociferous objections to the war that had toppled this very regime.

Further impeding any facile rapprochement between the figures of Anṭūn-the-biographical-subject and Anṭūn-the-author, insofar as these two personae had the potential to work in tandem to situate *I'jaam: An Iraqi Rhapsody* in the American literary field, was the fact that Anṭūn is also the novel's co-translator.[86] For an author who translates his or her own work, Susan Bassnett suggests, the original text functions only as "a draft" whose "signs are not necessarily fixed." In "self-translation," the "boundary lines between 'original' and 'translation,' between draft and finished work," and even between languages "dissolve."[87] These categories are ones that are fundamental to conventional understandings of the translation process and of translators themselves, and in the case of *I'jaam: An Iraqi Rhapsody*, the presence of Anṭūn's name beside Rebecca Johnson's on the title page collapses these distinctions, creating uncertainty over the provenance of this English text, and over the relationship between it and the Arabic text that preceded it.

In other roughly contemporaneous instances in which a work of Arabic literature was translated into English partly or solely by its author, scholars comparing the translation to its Arabic source text have usually shown the author to have removed or modulated cultural, religious, or linguistic elements of the original work during the translation process in order to ease its reception in English.[88] Within a critical discourse that has tended to view such authorial interventions as lamentable or outright wrong, the political stakes of self-translating Arabic literature into English are often framed as analogous to those of self-translating from "minor" into "major" languages more generally—a situation in which, as Michael Boyden and Liesbeth De Bleeker propose, the "inherently asymmetrical" relationship of the two languages involved puts the "strangeness" of the original text perpetually at risk of being erased or in some way diminished by the translation act.[89]

Neither Anṭūn nor Johnson has, to date, commented publicly on the nature of their collaboration, making it impossible to parse what each might have contributed to the text. What becomes clear, however, when *I'jaam: An Iraqi Rhapsody* is examined alongside *Iʿjām*, is that this English text is in no way less strange than its Arabic predecessor. The relative strangeness of the translation is not so much a function of which information or which forms of alterity native to the source text it either preserves or suppresses, but of how it circulates in the American literary field as a text that is resistant on multiple levels to being read within the "horizon of expectations" that has long framed the reception of Arabic literature in translation in the American market.[90] Readable as aesthetic rather than ethnographic, and as a text whose degree of documentary authority and real-world political commitments cannot be divined from its author's biography, this text refuses to be political in the terms that Arabic literature in English translation is supposed to be. Instead, it asserts an *ʿajamī* politics that inscribes the strange and the other as an inescapable fact of the reading experience, as a foreign intervention into the normative domestic paradigms of the American reading self.

Monstrous Literature

Haytham Bahoora proposes that as "literary and artistic representations of the body's violent dismemberment and mutilation" have established themselves as "a recurring feature of . . . Iraqi cultural production" over the past several decades, violence has become a constitutive aspect as well of the Iraqi creative process.[91] Examining a selection of contemporary Iraqi novels that engage mimetically with the events of recent Iraqi history, Bahoora identifies a common "literary strategy" among them that "does not simply seek to represent experiences of terror, but to produce it in the reader," leaving this reader "disoriented" or overwhelmed with "a sense of fear and repulsion," "terror," or "horror."[92] Relatedly, Yasmeen Hanoosh has argued that the aesthetic devices of defamiliarization, formal experimentalism, and "narrative strangeness" to which contemporary Iraqi literary texts—among which she includes *Iʿjām*—often resort in an effort to portray an Iraqi reality that "defies the prerequisites of realism" generate experiences of reading that "at once rivet" and "disorient" their audience.[93]

The history of Iraqi pain over the last half-century—a period that also encompasses the Iran-Iraq War of 1980–1988 and the economic devastation wrought by more than a decade of international sanctions imposed on Iraq following its invasion of Kuwait in 1990—cannot be conveyed via mimetic verisimilitude. Transmitting this pain into the world literary system through texts that circulate beyond Iraq, whether in Arabic or in translation, Iraqi literature requisitions affects that turn this pain back against its readers. Through this aesthetic method, and if in no other way, Iraqi pain becomes apprehensible as a worldly condition of the body.

Anṭūn has said that he wrote *I ʿjām*, his first novel, for "those who think they know the burden [*fadāḥah*] of what we lived through in Iraq [but] do not have the patience to listen to our pain [*laysa ladayhim ṣabr lil-inṣāt ilā alaminā*]."[94] His second novel, *Waḥdahā shajarat al-rummān* (2010), centers on a young man in Baghdad who is tasked with washing and preparing for burial the bodies of Iraqis killed during the first months of the Iraq War. As in *I ʿjām*, the "burden" of Iraqi pain registers in this text via descriptions that accost readers with their graphic accounts of what can happen to a body in Iraq. A taxi driver drags a burning passenger from his taxi after it is struck by an American missile, although the man is "already charred and I could smell his burned flesh and hair;" when the corpse is transported to the washing house, it must be carried in "a thick bag of nylon . . . with its sides stapled" to prevent it from disintegrating.[95] A severed human head that the narrator washes is described as having a surface "like thick plastic," with "yellowish" edges and "tattered skin tissue and flesh and the dried pink and gray ends of blood vessels" trailing from the stump of its neck.[96]

Waḥdahā shajarat al-rummān was published in English as *The Corpse Washer* in 2013. Unlike *I'jaam: An Iraqi Rhapsody*, *The Corpse Washer* is solely Anṭūn's translation. To date, this is the only of his novels that he has translated into English all on his own; indeed, for the translations of his next two books, Anṭūn played almost no part in the translation process.[97] By his own account, his decision to not self-translate these subsequent works was because he himself feared to read them. Unleashed into a literary text, the monstrous affects of the Iraqi body in pain turn against even their author. Translating *Waḥdahā shajarat al-rummān* "is something I would not do again," Anṭūn admitted afterward, "because since I happen to write about very traumatic and tragic situations, translating the novel in a way forced me to relive all of the events."[98]

Insofar as the body in pain possesses a social and political history, its historicity makes it always excessive to any origin point in the creative imaginary of an individual author. The violence that Anṭūn's writing inflicts on its readers and on Anṭūn himself is ultimately that of the Baʿathist state, now reincorporated into the affective material of literary language. The "beast [*waḥsh*] that Saddam's regime created" lurks inside Iraqis to this day as an ongoing embodiment of their violent past,

Anṭūn has said, "hiding in their cultural and social marrow."[99] A beast in Tarek El-Ariss's sense as well, its beastliness or "*waḥshiyyah*" reemerges into the world in the "violent confrontation with violence" that Anṭūn's writing stages, and which is tantamount to an act of "aesthetic and ethical interrogation"[100]—of structures of self and other, and of literature as a mimetic medium wherein pain must be accommodated to the requirements of its own representability. The monster has been let loose into the world literary system because the writer could not write otherwise; representations of pain concatenate to produce an unbearable reading experience that is borne nonetheless upon a reader's body.

In her book *Ugly Feelings*, Sianne Ngai explores the "semantically" and "syntactically" negative feelings of "pain or displeasure" that certain works of literature produce in their audience (including anxiety, paranoia, disgust, boredom, and envy, among others). Such feelings are "weak," according to Ngai, because they lack moral intentionality and cathartic potential; their affective impact on a reader is associated not with the recognition of or solution to a real-world problem that the text has revealed, but with the metareflexive negativity that a reader feels toward himself or herself for having had this affective response in the first place.[101] In other words, these feelings are recursively more concerned with the suffering of the self than with the suffering of the other. Being inwardly oriented in this way rather than "object- or goal-directed," they are therefore "politically ambiguous" and "obviously not as strategic as the emotions classically associated with political action."[102] Yet precisely by reason of their lateral (rather than purposive or forward-looking) motion, Ngai argues, ugly feelings are imbued with an underrecognized political potential. They do not serve to motivate or inspire, but instead to critique and diagnose, confronting us with the fact of our own affects, our own sensing, embodied selves.

Like Ngai's ugly feelings, the affects produced by reading *I'jaam: An Iraqi Rhapsody* enter the American literary field laden with political possibility not because they necessarily incentivize new behaviors among an American public, but because they transmute the other's pain into the self's own experience of suffering that is never more nor less than an aesthetic event. The ugly feelings that this Iraqi novel generates run a diagnostic on the bodies of American readers, and in so doing, expose them as unexpectedly vulnerable to a plethora of affective impingements from the world, and unacceptably complicit in the world's historic structures of violence.

To examine the aesthetic experience of reading Anṭūn's English text as a political event with ethical implications in the American public sphere, as I have done in this chapter, offers an avenue for considering how objectless forces that act proprioceptively on the body—forces that are not headed anywhere and that do not seem to *do* anything—can reposition us in relation to the body of the other who suffers. Pain wends its way across the elastic surfaces of the body or the networks of a literary system, becoming sharable as it rises to the depth level of an intensity, a transmissible energetic charge. At this level, the proprioceptive zones of proximate bodies converge within co-implicated and worldly structures of feeling that are also zones of translation. Each time this Arabic novel in translation was read by a member of the American public in 2007, this occurrence was one that could be described as an ethical event in Alain Badiou's sense, as enabling "a new way of being and acting": in this case, constituting a new American subject who was, to an embodied extent, no longer a subject as before but an object of affects and experiences that originated in an Arabic writing and an Iraqi body.[103]

In aggregate, reading serves to gather a new public out of those who have read and those who, by reading, have been made to feel, or for whom the literariness of a text has been felt as an affective contagion and a collective experience. Addressed by a text such as Anṭūn's, American readers could no longer retreat into the affective dead zone of a "long history of indifference" to Arabic literature and to the contemporary geopolitics of the Arabophone Middle East.[104] Nor could they remain at a safe distance from an other held at bay as a figure of absolute alterity, to be pitied or even intervened on behalf of, but always and irremediably other. To encounter Iraqi pain as an aesthetic experience transforms this pain from a conceptual premise into a truth, as Badiou would call it—but one that is *true* always and only to the degree that it is literary.

Conclusion: Beyond Untranslatability

In the early 1980s, the Cairo-based comparative literature journal *Alif* published a multipage interview with the pioneering Arabic-to-English translator Denys Johnson-Davies. Renowned for having brought Sudanese writer al-Ṭayyib Ṣāliḥ's much-admired novel *Mawsim al-hijrah ilā al-shamāl* (*Season of Migration to the North*) into English for the Heinemann African Writers Series in 1969, Johnson-Davies was already considered at the time—in fellow translator Roger Allen's admiring description—"the doyen of translators of modern Arabic literature into English."[1] Yet in the interview, Johnson-Davies is reticent to discuss his many achievements as a translator and an outspoken advocate for Arabic literature in the Anglophone cultural sphere, work that he would pursue tirelessly until his death in 2017 at the age of ninety-four. To the contrary, he instead expounds at length upon the difficulties of translating Arabic literature into English. On a "purely linguistical" level, he explains to Ferial Ghazoul, the *Alif* editor and literary critic whose questions frame the majority of the interview, "Arabic grammar and syntax differ widely from that of English," demanding "thought processes" from a translator that are exponentially "more complicated than those demanded of someone translating from a Romance language." More fundamentally, he suggests, because translators of Arabic literature into English must reckon with "two languages whose cultural backgrounds, ways of thought, etc. have so little in common," misunderstandings, mistranslations, and even a degree of translation failure are unavoidable.[2]

In this book, I have sought to provide an alternative portrait of Arabic-to-English literary translation to that offered by Johnson-Davies. Each Arabic text examined over the preceding four chapters contains at least one distinct linguistic feature (morphological, phonetic, grammatical, or orthographic) that confronts an Anglophone translator with the irreducibly singular materiality of the source language's aesthetics. Yet in each case, as I have shown, an affective register of language enables the literariness of the Arabic text to resonate anew in the material formations of English. If it is too much to posit from this modest clutch of examples, contra Johnson-Davies, that Arabic and English as a rule thus tend toward commensurability rather than divergence—to claim, in other words, that for every problem of Arabic-to-English translation there is always a solution—then at least these case studies provide a different heuristic platform from which to begin theorizing translation as an operative condition of Arabic literature's existence in a multilingual world.

As Johnson-Davies's comments illustrate, Arabic literature's own translators have not always believed (and still do not always believe) that it is translatable into the linguistic and aesthetic idioms that would make it readable outside its native context. To give due credence to Arabic literature's translatability is to see its potential as world literature with fresh eyes. In conversation with notions of world literature, notably that proposed by David Damrosch, that identify it with certain modes of reading and circulation, I have argued in this book that not only can works of Arabic literature be "read *as* literature" when they begin "circulating out into a broader world," but even more crucially, that it is possible for them to be read as *Arabic* literature.[3] What makes a given work of Arabic literature in English translation readable in this way—as both world literature *and* Arabic literature—is not that it possesses an intrinsic quality of universal literariness shared with all literatures in all languages. Rather, it becomes readable according to both metrics simultaneously when it has been translated so as to impinge upon readers of the translation with the resonant material of Arabic literary language itself, involving them in encounters with the text's literariness that are at once contextually specific and aesthetically relatable.

Put another way, the studies in this book have sought to demonstrate that when Arabic literature becomes world literature, its literariness is affirmed in ways that reveal it to be both like and unlike that of other literatures. To the degree that Arabic literature's "literariness" is indicated linguistically "as a differential concept correlated with ordinary language," in Haun Saussy's formulation, it has this quality in common with other literary traditions in which texts' essentially literary nature can be divined by juxtaposing their rhetorically extraordinary instantiations of language alongside banal versions of the same. Yet as Saussy notes, to stop here at defining literariness "does not adequately mark the fact that literariness *emerges from* contexts and methods of reading," insofar as literariness is constituted also through the "kind of reading that discovers," in the material of the artistic medium, a "dense, specific habitat" within which the literary resides. By reason of the association of literariness with reading practices and reading contexts, Saussy proposes, it is never an entirely comparable quantity across texts from disparate national, linguistic, and historical backgrounds, vexing the most ardent ambitions of comparative literature scholars to render it equivalent.[4]

The literariness of Arabic literature, such as it has been brought into focus over this book's preceding chapters, is neither a token nor symptom of this literature's radical distinctness from the world's multiplicity of other literary traditions. Not untranslatable, Arabic literature cannot furthermore be held up totemically as proof of the alterity of the Arabic language or Arab culture. As it emerges into worldliness via its translation into English, Arabic literature's literariness compels habits of reading that unearth the aesthetics of the Arabic text blooming within the habitats (the bloom spaces) that English writing furnishes. This trading in of alterity for bloom spaces that the translations examined in this book enact, in concert with the recent improvements in the actual market conditions for English translations of Arabic literature noted in this book's introduction, should give us hope for the future of Arabic literature in the Anglophone literary field. Hope that each work of Arabic literature that arrives into English will be read first for the pleasure of the text itself. Hope that whenever Arabic literature is translated into English, this process will be carried out by a translator who responds to the foreignness of the source text not by politicizing it but by subordinating politics to ethics, and politics to aesthetics—or, that is, by drawing political potential only from what is already ethical and aesthetic in the text itself. For Arabic literature today, it just may be that, to quote Kathleen Stewart, "all the world is a bloom space now."[5]

Other than the brief account of the evolving dimensions of the market for Arabic literature in English translation given in the introduction, I have until now deliberately shied away from dwelling on the economic and commercial factors that contribute to making Arabic literature world literature. I have done so in favor of considering formations of worldliness that are produced and consecrated within the texts themselves, taking to heart Pheng Cheah's plea in his monograph *What Is a World?* for scholars to cease yoking literature's worldliness to that of the world that "globalization creates," and to instead "rethink . . . world literature as literature that is an active power in the making of worlds, that is, both a site of processes of worlding and an agent that participates and intervenes in these processes."[6] Yet the situation of Arabic literature as a commodity in the global literary marketplace is also relevant to the story that this book has sought to tell of how Arabic literature becomes worldly in translation—and, I would argue, it is a part of this story that should, if unexpectedly, also provide due cause for optimism.

Early in the present century, Roger Allen, whose long and illustrious career as a translator and scholar of Arabic literature in the United States surely qualifies him for doyen status in his own right, observed that "the general situation regarding the translation of Arabic literary works into English is probably the least satisfactory of all the European languages," in terms of "the possibilities of publication, the amount and variety of Arabic literature available in the target language, and the receptivity among the readership for translated works."[7] Two decades later, literature in Arabic is not only being translated into English at a far greater rate than it once was, but the resulting translations, along with their Arabic source texts, could increasingly be thought of as comprising a single transnational field for Arabic literature, in which it is now possible for a given work of Arabic literature to circulate among Arabophone and Anglophone audiences simultaneously and be read within symmetrical cultural contexts. If consuming the same textual content at the same time across disparate geographic locations affirms readers as belonging to a single shared imaginative community, as Benedict Anderson once proposed, then the commercial successes of Arabic literature in the global literary system establish a capacious geography for these texts: not a nation, as for Anderson, but a world.[8]

Critics of the changes that globalization has wrought in the world literary system have tended to identify the global commercial success of any non-Euro-American literary corpus with a range of deleterious effects on the texts themselves and on the typologies of reading that they invite. As Sarah Brouillette explains, this critique is rooted in a "basic narrative" of world literature "as an elite, homogenizing, complacent commodity . . . a cultural accompaniment to an encompassing process of global market expansion."[9] What is at stake is the nature of the worldliness that literary texts attain when they circulate at international scale. In the terms of an unsigned opinion piece titled "World Lite" that appeared in the American culture magazine *n+1* in 2013, non-Western literary works that do well under such conditions manifest a "spurious worldliness" premised on their ability to enthrall audiences with touristic glimpses of exotic peoples and locales, while being utterly divested of political urgency and cultural authenticity.[10] In a similar vein, Emily Apter has lamented the "oneworldedness" evinced by texts whose circulation is ensured principally by their participation in the global "literary monoculture" of the present age.[11]

Postcolonial, non-Western, and Global South writers have long been seen as complicit in creating this situation. In an early iteration of this view, Timothy Brennan suggested in 1997 that "authors ranging from Brazil to South Asia," eager to capitalize on the recent international achievements of a handful of non-Western authors, had begun producing "a genre of third-world metropolitan fiction whose conventions have given their novels the unfortunate feel of ready-mades."[12] Arab writers were not immune to this trend, as Jenine Abboushi Dallal argued in a 1998 essay titled "The Perils of Occidentalism: How Arab Novelists Are Driven to Write for Western Readers." In an era when "the new transnationalism" of literary tastes in the West had made it at least minimally plausible that Arabic literature might attract a readership outside the Arabophone region, Arab writers were increasingly "writing for translation," or in other words, not for their own local publics but for a "target audience . . . which is primarily Western," Dallal contended. She noted in this regard that many works of Arabic literature newly published at the time seemed explicitly to foreground topics (such as Islamic fundamentalism or the oppression of Arab women) that were known to be of interest to Western audiences, and she observed moreover a steady rise in the number of novels published in Arabic each year, although this literary form, in her estimation, had "not really caught on" yet in the Arabophone region except among "a small audience of Arab (bourgeois, Western-educated) intellectuals."[13]

Notwithstanding Brennan's assertion that "Arabic fiction," because it seemed to have found "its way accidentally into translation," frequently confounded the expectations of Western readers in the 1990s, Dallal's appraisal of Arabic literary production in an era broadly recognized as one of ascendant cultural globalization (according to anthropologist Arjun Appadurai's assessment, for example) offers a starting point for examining how debates over the globality of literature in general in modern times intersect with specific questions concerning the evolution of the form and content of Arabic literature during this same period.[14] To envisage a future for Arabic literature as world literature in which its achieving something like international market success could be seen as salutary rather than regrettable necessitates weighing the same contradictory factors that have fueled a vigorous academic conversation about world literature since at least the end of the last century. The homogenizing pressures exerted on Arabophone authors and Arabic-language texts by the imperative to succeed globally are real and cannot be discounted; and yet the world-making and worlding potential of Arabic literature when it is read transnationally in its original language and in translation must also be recognized.

In what follows, I propose that the case of international literary prizes as they have lately functioned to reshape the trajectory for Arabic literature in the world offers a lens through which to consider these alternate possibilities for what happens to Arabic literature when it scales upward and outward to become as extensive as the world that contains it.

Prizes and New Publics

Since 2000, new literary prizes have proliferated across the Arabophone region, honoring novels, short stories, and book-length translations into and out of Arabic. Among these have been the Abu Dhabi-based Sheikh Zayed Book Award (Jāʾizat al-Shaykh Zāyid lil-Kitāb), whose prize in the literature category was first given in 2007 and is worth 750,000 AED (around $200,000 USD); Saudi Arabia's King Abdullah Bin Abdulaziz International Award for Translation (Jāʾizat al-Malik ʿAbd Allāh bin ʿAbd al-ʿAzīz al-ʿĀlamiyyah lil-Tarjamah), first awarded in 2008 for translations to and from Arabic of works in multiple humanities disciplines and worth $200,000; the Doha-based Katara Prize (Jāʾizat Katārā lil-Riwāyah al-ʿArabiyyah), first awarded in 2015 and worth $300,000 divided equally among five published novels, with an additional $150,000 in prize money split among five unpublished novels; and Kuwait's AlMultaqa Prize for the Arabic Short Story (Jāʾizat al-Multaqā lil-Qiṣṣah al-Qaṣīrah al-ʿArabiyyah), awarded annually since 2016 to a single collection of short stories and worth $20,000.

The best-known of these new awards, in the Arabophone region and abroad, is the International Prize for Arabic Fiction or "IPAF" (al-Jāʾizah al-ʿĀlamiyyah lil-Riwāyah al-ʿArabiyyah; the prize is also known by the popular moniker "Arabic Booker" thanks to its structural similarities to the UK's Booker Prize and the involvement of several members of the Booker Prize Foundation in organizing the IPAF's launch in 2007).[15] Funded by the cultural arm of the government of Abu Dhabi in the United Arab Emirates, the IPAF awards $50,000 annually to the novel that its five-member panel of judges considers to have been the best published in Arabic during the preceding year, along with $10,000 to each of six finalists (including the ultimate winner); separately, the prize provides financial and logistical support for the translation of the winning novel into other languages, especially English.

The infusion of money that these literary prizes as a group have introduced into what was previously a poorly funded area of Arab cultural production, and the prestige that the IPAF in particular has bestowed upon certain works of Arabic literature and their authors since its inception, have reconfigured the contemporary Arabic literary field in multiple ways.[16] Meanwhile, the practices of reading and writing that the prizes appear to motivate, and the critical discourse that has arisen in the Arabophone public sphere to respond to and account for these practices, raise pertinent questions about the readability, translatability, and literariness of Arabic literature when it becomes world literature. Yet despite their wide-ranging implications for "the very production and circulation of Arabic literature" in the current era, the impact of these prizes, as Mohamed-Salah Omri observes, has rarely "been discussed, let alone theorized."[17]

One effect of the prizes, according to Muhsin al-Musawi, has been the "prodigious growth of the novel" in the Arabic literary sphere today ("*al-namūw al-ṭāfiḥ fī al-fann al-riwāʾī*").[18] Indeed, if the Arabic novel was a marginal genre twenty-five years ago, as Dallal claimed, then it has now in the twenty-first century far eclipsed poetry—once the favored mode of Arabic literary production—as the chief form in which new Arabic writing is published. In the guise of this "most international genre," as Rebecca Walkowitz has called the novel in the era of world literature, Arabic literature can be more readily accommodated to the requirements of the global publishing industry.[19] During the year (2009–2010) that I served as the cultural program manager for the Abu Dhabi International Book Fair, a major annual trade and bookselling event in the UAE capital that hosts the IPAF's gala prize ceremony each spring, I frequently heard Western publishers complain that they did not know where to start when it came to acquiring works of Arabic fiction for translation into the languages of their domestic markets. Few publishing houses in Europe and the United States employ Arabic-literate editors, and the arena of Arabic-language literary production is vast and not well indexed in comparison to that of other languages (it is often difficult, for example, to obtain comprehensive data on the regionwide sales of a particular novel or author's work). A prize like the IPAF ameliorates these problems somewhat by providing, in each year's roster of shortlisted and longlisted nominees, what serves in effect as a curated catalog of apparently translation-worthy works of new Arabic fiction. Indeed, to date the vast majority of novels that have won the IPAF since it was first awarded in 2008 have been translated into English, as have many of those nominated for the prize.[20]

One way of interpreting the proliferation of Arabic novels spawned by the IPAF and other contemporary prizes is to see this as the culmination of a process whereby indigenous Arabic forms of writing are gradually eclipsed by this paradigmatically Western literary genre—a process begun two centuries ago with the first appearance of Arabic literary texts self-consciously fashioned after European novels, or presenting themselves as translations of European novels, whose publication laid the groundwork for the emergence of the modern Arabic novel in the early to middle decades of the twentieth century. By this reasoning, the preeminence of the novel in the Arabic literary field today marks a final rupture vis-à-vis a prior heritage of premodern Arabic writing. Underlying this view, and fundamental to standard accounts of the evolution of the Arabic novel, is an assumption that the novel as a genre lacks autochthonous roots in Arabic literary history, having been imported wholesale from the West during the period of accelerated cultural exchange between Arabophone societies and Europe known as the Nahda (*Nahḍah*).[21] Yet as Rebecca Johnson has argued, this assumption overlooks the degree to which nineteenth-century Arab authors and translators conceived of their texts not as derivative of European prototypes but rather as "merely the latest" entries "in a long-standing and bidirectional history of literary contact" between Arabic writing and the writing of the greater world, for they saw the European literary works upon which their own texts were modeled as themselves indebted to a worldly array of other novelistic traditions, including those from the Arabophone region.[22]

As Johnson writes, anyone who turns to these early Arabic novels "looking for the location of the form's 'origins' will instead find a history of infinite regress."[23] The story of the Arabic novel is not a teleological narrative of progress from native literary genres to imitative protonovels to the literary modernity epitomized by the mature mid-twentieth-century texts of the Egyptian Nobel laureate Nagīb Maḥfūẓ and others of his generation, but is instead characterized by the recursive movements of novelistic tropes and styles, content and form, into and out of the Arabic language. Multiple and transnational in its orientations since long before the present era, flexible and reactive in its contours, the Arabic novel, as Johnson writes, "takes translation and cultural transfer as its foundation."[24] Adding to this the persuasive arguments made by some scholars that the fundaments of the Arabic novel owe as much to classical Arabic literary forms like the *maqāmah* as they do to the literature of nineteenth-century Europe,[25] the novels that have overtaken the Arabic literary field in the twenty-first century should thus be seen, I would contend, not as an aberration in the history of Arabic literature but as yet another confirmation of Arabic literature's ongoing embeddedness in the world.

The new literary prizes have also brought about shifts in where and by whom Arabic literature today is read. Notably, the reception patterns that the prizes seem to have inaugurated call for reexamining the notion that "Arabs simply do not read much . . . despite having achieved near-universal literacy since the 1960s," an idea that has been often accepted uncritically by Anglophone and Arabophone critics alike.[26] Frequently cited in support of this view is the ubiquitous data point—attributed sometimes to a 2011 report by the Arab Thought Foundation, and sometimes to UNESCO—that Arab readers on average read for only around six minutes per year.[27] If there was ever any truth to this dubious statistic, whose origins remain exceptionally obscure,[28] a very different portrait of reading practices among the literate public of the Arabophone region has emerged in recent years. In a 2007 survey of approximately six thousand self-identified readers in nine majority-Arabophone countries (Algeria, Egypt, Jordan, Lebanon, Morocco, Palestine, Saudi Arabia, Syria, and Tunisia), between one-quarter and one-third of respondents in each country reported regularly reading contemporary Arabic fiction.[29] Although no comparable figures (as far as I am aware) exist for today, the time that has elapsed since this survey was conducted—a period exactly coincident with the spread of literary prizes across the region—has witnessed substantial growth in the readership of Arabic literature as assessed by several metrics.

First, whereas inadequate distribution networks across national borders once made it difficult for consumers in one Arabophone country to access books published in another, vastly improved internet penetration across the region now allows works of Arabic literature to circulate with facility among dispersed populations of readers as e-books or in PDF format, whether legally or in pirated editions. A second factor of note is that attendance at the region's most popular annual book fairs now regularly numbers in the millions: in early 2020, for example, the Cairo International Book Fair hosted 3.5 million visitors over fourteen days.[30]

Finally, anecdotal accounts suggest that novels honored by the IPAF in particular often attract special interest today at bookstores throughout the urban centers of the Arabophone Middle East, with customers regularly stopping by "to inquire about buying the novels whose titles have appeared on the lists" of this prize's nominees and winners.[31] During my own visits to bookstores in Cairo, Abu Dhabi, Dubai, and Beirut between 2008 and 2017, I frequently observed displays of such novels conspicuously located near the store's entrance, each volume encased in a wraparound band or emblazoned with a cover medallion bearing the prize's name. Such care taken to ensure that these novels are maximally visible to potential book buyers signals at least the expectation that there exists a real and robust market for modern Arabic fiction among the Arabophone populace of the contemporary Middle East.

As contemporary Arabic literature has increasingly achieved a degree of popular success among the literate public of the region, however, critics have tended to be skeptical that this development has worked to the advantage of the texts themselves on an aesthetic level. If Arab writers were once faulted for writing for Western readers, they now stand accused of writing to appeal to the tastes of prize committees and members of a general populace that lacks the discernment to differentiate between good books and bad ones. According to a critique that has been prominently articulated in Arabic-language media outlets since the mid-2000s, the works recognized by the IPAF and the other awards comprise a class of "prize novel" ("*riwāyat al-jawāʾiz*") characterized by its formulaic adherence to a "recipe" ("*waṣfah*") of themes, plots elements, and stylistic devices.[32] Along the same lines, Roger Allen has noted the emergence in recent years of a category of Arabic "best-sellers" identifiable by the dual qualities that they avoid "the ambiguity, uncertainty, and stylistic and generic complexity that is characteristic of much recent novelistic production in Arabic" and that they "have sold unusually large numbers of copies."[33]

At base, this critique of the so-called prize novel rests upon a perception that Arabic literature that succeeds at being readable—whether among prize judges or regular readers—is also therefore less literary. To the extent that the new prizes are seen as functioning to "bring about an ever closer alignment between the works recognized as 'best' or 'most important' and those which are simply the bestselling or the most popular," to quote James English, "aesthetic value" is understood to have been traded in for "commercial value" as the primary determinant of worth for literature in the contemporary Arabophone cultural field.[34]

And yet, in a "world economy of prestige" whose metrics of "symbolic capital" are "less and less tightly bound to national markets," literary prizes also create opportunities for readability to emerge as an augur of success on a global scale.[35] Anne-Marie McManus calls for theorizing the IPAF as an award that produces "a contingent intersection between national and world literary fields" by creating patterns of circulation for winning novels that encompass simultaneously micro (local) and macro (international) scales of reading and reception.[36] When the readable Arabic novels that are a hallmark of contemporary Arabic literary production are translated, their readability refracts across the world literary system to open up avenues for other works of Arabic literature to prosper as well.

Assessed by how widely and with what results it is *read*, whether in Arabic or in English, Arabic literature takes on expansive new aesthetic possibilities in the world. Paradoxically, while the readability of contemporary Arabic literature jeopardizes its perceived aesthetic standing regionally, on another level this same quality has propelled it toward a new degree and kind of worldliness. Arabic literature's worldliness today is dependent upon such catachrestic arrangements of the regional and the global, the aesthetic and the readable, that can only be theorized via critical paradigms that do not seek to impose binary distinctions between what is authentically Arabic literature and what is not. Arabic literature, as this book has sought to show, cannot be so simplistically assessed, insofar as Arabic literary texts that are read nationally or regionally become those that are read globally as well, and insofar as a work of Arabic literature in translation can still contain within it remnant formations of Arabic's own linguistic material. To borrow Brennan's formulation, Arabic literature is now, and to an unprecedented extent, "at home in the world" that globalization has created.[37]

One exemplary illustration of McManus's point about the intersecting or overlapping routes that Arabic literary prizes help to create for Arabic literature to reach world audiences is that Arabic novels in English translation have lately begun appearing in significant numbers on Anglophone literary prize lists as well. In 2019, Marilyn Booth's translation of *Sayyidāt al-qamar* (2010) by the Omani writer Jūkhah al-Ḥārithī, titled in English *Celestial Bodies* (2018), became the first novel translated from Arabic to win the Man Booker International Prize.[38] The same year, Jonathan Wright's translation of Māzin Maʿrūf's *Nukāt lil-musallaḥīn* was longlisted for this prize (and his translation of Aḥmad Saʿdāwī's *Frānkishtāyn fī Baghdād* was previously shortlisted in 2018); two years later, the longlist included Elisabeth Jaquette's translation of ʿAdaniyyah Shiblī's *Tafṣīl thānawī*. In the United States, a novel translated from Arabic has been a finalist or been longlisted for the National Book Award for Translated Literature every year since its establishment in 2018: Max Weiss's translation of Dunyā Mīkhāʾīl's *Fī sūq al-sabāyā* in 2018, Leri Price's translation of Khālid Khalīfah's *al-Mawt ʿamal shāqq* in 2019, Jaquette's translation of Shiblī's *Tafṣīl thānawī* in 2020, Price's translation of Samar Yazbik's *al-Mashshāʾah* in 2021, and William Hutchins's translation of Muḥammad Ḥasan ʿAlwān's *Mawt saghīr* in 2022. Works of Arabic literature, and more particularly Arabic novels, have become the kind of literature that can win prizes; this is increasingly as true in the Anglophone slice of the transnational Arabic literary field as in its Arabophone counterpart.

As soon as *Celestial Bodies* won the Man Booker International Prize, reviews of the work began appearing in prominent U.S. media outlets. Across these venues, reviewers described al-Ḥārithī's polyphonic family saga about three sisters growing up in an Omani village as a work of "taut character studies" and narrative arcs "lightly tethered to what the French call *récit*—the moment in which the story is being told," and pondered the relationship between "form and idea" in a text that purported to be a novel even while it stretched the "novelistic form" in unconventional ways "to suit . . . [the] specific mimetic requirements" of its story.[39] Although there may not seem to be anything especially extraordinary about such statements, the standard-issue blend of plot summary and expert analysis that these reviews employ to introduce Booth's translation of al-Ḥārithī's novel to an Anglophone readership marks a significant departure from how works of translated Arabic literature were once reviewed in the U.S. media (when they were reviewed at all).[40]

In the words of Marcia Lynx Qualey, a blogger and critic who has been closely tracking Arabic literature's position in the Anglophone literary field for more than a decade on her website ArabLit.org, the critical reception of al-Ḥārithī's novel in its English translation showed that it "has been read widely as *literature*."[41] Perhaps even more unusually, some reviewers of *Celestial Bodies* took care to discuss aspects of Booth's translation separately from their treatment of al-Ḥārithī's novel. One praised Booth for crafting "exquisite English descriptions from Alharthi's original Arabic," while another cited specific lines from the English text where Booth had "done a wonderful job of conveying a lyricism I can only assume is present in Alharthi's original."[42] In their acceptance of the basic literariness of al-Ḥārithī's text, coupled with their acknowledgment of the translator's role in conveying this literariness into English, these reviews demonstrate how the consecration of Arabic literature in the international Anglophone prize circuit leads to greater recognition of Arabic literature's aesthetic qualities in Arabic *and* in English simultaneously, even (or especially) among critics who cannot read it in its native language.

The fact that al-Ḥārithī's novel had won a major European award via Booth's English translation did not go unnoticed by Arabophone readers. Within "two or three days" of the announcement in May 2019 that *Celestial Bodies* had been selected as the winner of the Man Booker International Prize, the Arabic-language media was abuzz with discussions of the text, as "a large number [of people] read the novel"—which had not received much attention at the time of its publication in Arabic almost a decade earlier—"whether as a pirated e-book or by buying it" in a bookstore. Vigorous debates ensued on Arabic-language websites and social media platforms over the quality of al-Ḥārithī's writing and the accuracy of her portrait of twentieth-century Omani village life.[43]

The reception of this work of literature in translation among Anglophone readers informed how it came to be read in Arabic. If al-Ḥārithī's novel was able "to gain entry into the corpus of World Literature" only via its "translation into English," then in following this path to worldliness it has not at all become the "deracinated" expatriate text that "migrates forever to another cultural world" which Harish Trivedi describes in his chapter in the recent volume *Translation and World Literature*.[44] Although it remains to be seen whether al-Ḥārithī's novel, now that it has been deemed to have literary value in English, will assist Omani literature as a whole in achieving greater recognition within its own regional milieu, the movements of this text have already traced recursive, reiterative routes into and out of several linguistic spaces, as it traveled into the Anglophone literary field only to return again to Arabophone readers.[45]

The conditions for Arabic literature's being read in Arabic and the conditions for its being read in English converge at the point where an Arabic novel is read as literature or read *at all*. Literary prizes, as they help to establish a transnational field for Arabic literature, collapse the literariness of Arabic literature with its readability. In so doing, they instigate a shift away from an earlier model in which Arabic texts that were little read in their native environments were translated for international audiences who were even less likely to read them. Within the parameters of the contemporary world literary system, what is literature is what is read as such, and the confluence of regional and Western prizes acting to thrust Arabic literary works into circulation in this system in ever greater numbers inscribe this logic onto the Arabic literary field as well. Far from figuring the literariness of Arabic literature as an incommensurability that poses obstacles to its translatability, as Denys Johnson-Davies saw it, these prizes recalibrate its literariness according to the definitions of the international literary market. They index the emergence of a worldliness for Arabic literature configured around all the sites globally at which it is read, and of a practice of translating these works into English that assumes from the outset their capacity to move an audience, in Arabic and in translation equally.

The Extent of a World

In early 2020, Marilyn Booth offered a translator's perspective on the globalization of Arabic literature during a panel at the Emirates Airline Festival of Literature in Dubai. On the panel with her were *Sayyidāt al-*

qamar author Jūkhah al-Ḥārithī and the Lebanese writer Hudā Barakāt, whose novel *Barīd al-layl*—winner of the 2019 International Prize for Arabic Fiction—Booth was then in the final stages of translating into English. Discussing the optimal circumstances for an Arabic novel in English translation's being read as literature rather than sociologically by its target audience, Booth suggested that this outcome depended jointly on which texts translators chose to translate and the commitments that they brought to bear in doing so. Specifically, she proposed, Anglophone readers are most likely to read a work of translated Arabic literature "first as a novel, as a work of art" if the translator, too, has approached it in that spirit. To that end, she explained, she herself endeavored to translate primarily "novels that to me speak as works of art" and to "emphasize the artistic" in the English texts that she produced.[46]

Booth's comments here reveal something of a shift in her own sensibilities as a translator. In essays written earlier in her career, Booth—who has held academic positions at the University of Illinois Urbana-Champaign, the University of Edinburgh, and Oxford University—extolled the importance of translating Arabic literature so as to deliberately shore up the "foreignness" of the source text against the global market forces compelling its homogenization and domestication.[47] By the same token, she portrayed herself, in her role as a translator, as an "ethical political agent" for whom following "a foreignizing approach" to translating Arabic literature into English "constitute[d] [a] responsible political intervention."[48] When and why did the "resistant strategies" that Booth freely acknowledged employing in her translation of a modern Arabic novel published in 2002 cede to the more avowedly artful methods of translating manifested in *Celestial Bodies*?[49]

If Booth's approach has changed, then it has done so in tandem with the larger-scale evolution of the transnational field for Arabic literature described in the preceding section of this conclusion. As the readability of Arabic literature becomes determinant of its worldliness, the predominant practices of translating Arabic literature into English transform concurrently to keep pace with this development. In this regard, Booth noted in her remarks at the Emirates Airline Festival of Literature the emergence of a younger generation of Arabic-to-English translators—who are "not only enthusiastic but extremely good"—for whom translation is primarily an artistic endeavor, pursued with the support of publishers alert to the aesthetic appeal that Arabic fiction in translation holds for Anglophone audiences.[50] Among this new cohort of translators, Kareem James Abu-Zeid and Elisabeth Jaquette perhaps deserve particular mention. Both have situated themselves deliberately outside of the academy.

Abu-Zeid earned a PhD in comparative literature from the University of California Berkeley in 2016 but had decided even before completing his degree that academia was not for him.[51] In interviews, he has been critical of the efforts at border policing between languages that have sometimes preoccupied scholar-translators of Arabic literature and dismissive of the intellectual orthodoxies of mainstream Euro-American translation theory.[52] For her part, Jaquette has described herself as part of "a younger generation of translators mov[ing] away from more academic, literal translations."[53]

Moreover, both of these translators have professed to see a correlation between the literariness of a text in Arabic and English alike and its capacity to succeed with a broad spectrum of Anglophone readers. Jaquette has stated that she "selects fiction [to translate] based on its literary merit as opposed to its anthropological value," and that when she translates, her goal is "to strive not for the literal but the literary," for she is "more interested" in creating translations that will be received as "literature" than she is in producing texts suitable for publication "by university presses."[54] For Abu-Zeid, the objective is to produce English-language texts that do not "sound translated," so that, for example, a collection of Arabic poetry in translation will "read like *poetry* in English."[55]

Distinct from translators of an earlier era, Abu-Zeid and Jaquette disavow the notion that Arabic literature's being accommodated to the preferences of Anglophone readers and the commercial exigencies of the Anglophone literary market should be viewed categorically as a negative. Their translations, following from this logic, are seamlessly and fluidly Anglophone, making it easy to forget—while, for example, reading Jaquette's *Minor Detail*, or Abu-Zeid's translation of Lebanese writer Rabīʿ Jābir's novel *Taqrīr Mīhlīs* (2005), published in English as *The Mehlis Report* (2013)—that these are works of *translated* literature. And yet they are indisputably not inaccurate to their source texts. Their own literariness reveals these translators' radical openness to the aesthetics of English as well as of Arabic, uninflected by the philosophical and political pieties that shaped the work of their predecessors.

Rather than regret the absence of the recognizably foreign in the translations that these two much-laureled and, in Jaquette's case especially, prolific translators have produced to date, we ought to view their texts instead as paradigmatically demonstrative of Arabic literature's capacity to be literary in English in the current global age of world literature. For both Abu-Zeid and Jaquette, there may be biographical reasons for their turn away from foreignizing translation methods. Both were born in the 1980s and studied Arabic in the United States and abroad in the years following the attacks of September 11, 2001. (Abu-Zeid, whose parents are Egyptian and American, was raised in Kuwait and the UAE but did not begin learning Arabic in earnest until he was in college).[56] In the early years of the so-called War on Terror that the United States launched in response to these attacks, Arabic-to-English translators became a vital asset to American military and intelligence operations in the Arabophone Middle East and domestically. As Elliott Colla has noted, during the first decade after 9/11 the U.S. government invested "a total of more than $10 billion" in cultivating translators for these purposes.[57] Not unrelatedly, according to data collected by the Modern Language Association, enrollment in Arabic-language classes at U.S. colleges and universities increased to record levels during this same period, peaking at around 35,000 students nationwide between 2009 and 2013.[58] Could it be that, having witnessed firsthand how the otherness of all things pertaining to Arabic and the Arabophone region could be conscripted rhetorically to justify occupation abroad and Islamophobia and other forms of anti-Arab racism at home, these translators have been hesitant to accentuate the alterity of their Arabic source texts in their translations?

What ethical commitments inhere in the refusal of a rising cohort of Arabic-to-English translators to see Arabic literature as ontologically different, or to see Arabic literary language as incommensurable to the demands of English syntax, phonetics, or morphology? If Humphrey Davies's translation of *al-Sāq ʿalā al-sāq* examined in chapter 1 converts the irreducible aesthetics of Arabic *lafẓ* into a virtuosic English most readable in a sonic register, while Richard Francis Burton's translation of *Alf laylah wa-laylah* explored in chapter 2 transmutes Arabic *sajʿ* into English words that are appreciated vulgarly in the body rather than understood; and if *Limbo Beirut* and *I'jaam: An Iraqi Rhapsody*, investigated in chapters 3 and 4 respectively, recast reading Arabic literature in English as an ethical and a political event that provides audiences with routes of affective contact to the other-within-language that is the *muthannā* and the foreign-within-language that is the *ʿajamī*; then in Abu-Zeid's and Jaquette's texts the genealogy of Arabic literature in English translation that this book has charted, however loosely, over its four earlier case studies culminates in works that are simply enjoyable to read.

Let me conclude by suggesting that such readability should leave us, as Booth professes herself to be, "optimistic" about the situation of Arabic literature in the global literary system today.[59] For a translator to produce a work of literature in the target language that is read and valued for the literary pleasures that it purveys is an act with profound ramifications for determining how, where, and why Arabic literature matters in the contemporary world. Affect blooms into affection, enabling works of Arabic literature in translation to be measured not against a horizon of expectations for what Arabic literature is or should be, but within a "bodily horizon" reconfigured as a "horizon of likes," in Sara Ahmed's terms.[60] As readers extend their affections across a shrinking world to encompass an Arabic novel within the orbit of what they like to read, Arabic literature becomes integral to who they are as bodies in and citizens of this world. The "objects that give us pleasure," Ahmed writes, "might even establish *what we are like*."[61] We are what we like; we are made and remade by it as it constitutes us in relation to its own worldliness (even as it itself is simultaneously inclining to us, recalibrating itself in order to please us, *wanting* to be liked). When Arabic literature is translated into English texts that are likeable, a global public of Anglophone readers worlds and is worlded in return.

Acknowledgments

Since I initially began thinking about the translation of Arabic literature into English well over a decade ago, I have benefited from the guidance and support of numerous others. My thanks go first to my advisers at the University of Texas at Austin: to Kristen Brustad, for her infectious enthusiasm for the Arabic language in all of its guises; to Karen Grumberg and Hannah Wojciehowski, who read carefully and munificently and proffered counsel and encouragement in equal measure; and above all to Tarek El-Ariss, interlocutor, critic, role model, and confidant. I owe you all a debt of gratitude.

The number of scholars in the Anglophone academy who write about Arabic literature is small enough that there are few, if any, whose work has not been in some way formative to this book's development. At countless annual meetings of the American Comparative Literature Association (ACLA), the Middle East Studies Association (MESA), and the Modern Language Association (MLA) over the years; at the thematic conferences on Arabic literature hosted by Columbia University in New York and Paris in 2013, 2017, and 2019; and throughout my tenure as an editor at the *Journal of Arabic Literature*, I have been enlightened and inspired time and again by the scholarship of my peers. Nonetheless, I am particularly grateful to Michael Allan and Rana Issa for their wise and generous comments on the first complete manuscript of this book at a workshop in the summer of 2020: you have both helped immeasurably. Conversations with Kareem James Abu-Zeid, Hanan Al-Alawi, Dima Ayoub, Hoda Barakat, Michael Cooperson, Humphrey Davies, Anthony (Antoine) Edwards,

Rachel Green, Elisabeth Jaquette, Samantha Landmesser, Annette Damayanti Lienau, Katie Logan, Dina Mahmoud, Marcia Lynx Qualey, Johanna Sellman, and Shaden Tageldin were illuminating at successive stages of my thinking about this book and the arguments that it would ultimately make. The graduate students in my pair of seminars on Arabic literature and literature of the body at the Pennsylvania State University in 2019 and 2020 reminded me always that no idea is above interrogating and showed me by their own example how to do so with intelligence and grace.

I thank Jonathan Abel, Magalí Armillas-Tiseyra, Dima Ayoub, Krista Brune, Anthony (Antoine) Edwards, Hoda El Shakry, and Katie Logan for providing feedback on various portions of this book along the way. I remain profoundly indebted to Hilal Chouman for entrusting me to translate his novel. My book would not exist without yours. To my fellow editors at the *Journal of Arabic Literature* since 2014—especially Muhsin J. al-Musawi, Elizabeth Holt, and Rebecca C. Johnson—I am grateful for all that you have taught me about Arabic literature and for making the praxis of an academic life feel at least occasionally like a collaborative enterprise. My colleagues and mentors at the American University in Cairo Press and the Abu Dhabi International Book Fair, especially R. Neil Hewison and Nadia Naqib: thank you for starting me on the path to writing this book long before I had any inkling that I would end up studying and translating Arabic literature myself (rather than editing the scholarship and translations of others). The Department of Comparative Literature at Penn State has been nothing short of magnanimous in supporting me both pragmatically and personally since I arrived here in 2016; my deepest gratitude to Bob Edwards and Charlotte Eubanks in particular for making this so.

Many thanks to Tom Lay and the editorial and production staff at Fordham University Press for their essential contributions to making this book a reality, and to the two anonymous reviewers commissioned by the Press to read my initial submitted manuscript in early 2021, without whose exceptionally insightful commentary and suggestions this book would be only a shadow of its current self. The research and writing of this book were supported by a Mayers Fellowship at the Huntington Library in San Marino, California, in 2018; a Humanities Institute Residential Fellowship at Penn State in 2019; a Center for Humanities & Information Faculty Fellowship at Penn State in 2021; and the Caroline D. Eckhardt Early Career Professorship in Comparative Literature at Penn State. The publication of this book was funded in part by a Helen Tartar First Book Subvention Award from the American Comparative Literature Association. An open access edition of the book was made possible through sponsorship from the Penn State TOME Initiative. I am grateful to Nja Mahdaoui for allowing me to feature his gorgeous artwork on this book's cover.

A portion of chapter 2, since modified, was published as "Vulgar Pleasures: The Scandalous Worldliness of Burton's 'Arabian Nights,'" *Journal of World Literature* 6, no. 1 (2021): 45–64; and a version of part of chapter 3 was published as "Feeling the Grammar: Literary Translations of the Dual Inflection in Arabic," *Philological Encounters* 4 (2019): 26–54. I thank these journals for permission to reprint these articles in revised form in the present volume, and for the constructive feedback of their editors and anonymous reviewers along the way.

Last but by no means least, thank you to my parents for raising me in a home where reading literature was understood to be the precondition of a pleasurable life, and to Te-Ping Chen for over two decades of the most sustaining friendship possible. Chris, Miles, and Ilias: as long as I exist in proximity to you, I, too, am worlded.

Notes

Introduction. From Embargo to Boom: The Changing World of Arabic Literature in English

1. Edward W. Said, "Embargoed Literature," *The Nation*, September 17, 1990, 278.

2. See, for example, the citations of Said's essay in Hosam Aboul-Ela, "Challenging the Embargo: Arabic Literature in the US Market," *Middle East Report* 219 (2001): 42; Waïl S. Hassan, "Agency and Translational Literature: Ahdaf Soueif's *The Map of Love*," *PMLA* 121, no. 3 (2006): 759, 765n1; Marilyn Booth, "Translator v. Author (2007): *Girls of Riyadh* Go to New York," *Translation Studies* 1, no. 2 (2008): 197; Shaden Tageldin, "The Returns of Theory," *International Journal of Middle East Studies* 43 (2011): 729; Mohammed Abdullah Hussein Muharram, "The Marginalization of Arabic Fiction in the Postcolonial and World English Curriculum: Slips? Or Orientalism and Racism?," *the minnesota review* 78 (2012): 138; and Ruth Abou Rached, "Pathways of Solidarity in Transit: Iraqi Women Writers' Story-Making in English Translation," in *The Routledge Handbook of Translation, Feminism and Gender*, ed. Luise von Flotow and Hala Kamal (New York: Routledge, 2020), 48.

3. Waïl S. Hassan, "Arabic and the Paradigms of Comparison," in *Futures of Comparative Literature: ACLA State of the Discipline Report*, ed. Ursula K. Heise (New York: Routledge, 2017), 189.

4. This was the current number as of October 2022. The database is hosted at https://www.publishersweekly.com/pw/translation/home/index.html.

5. See, for example, Humphrey Davies's translation of ʿAlāʾ al-Aswānī's *ʿImārat Yaʿqūbiyān*, published as *The Yacoubian Building* by Harper Perennial in 2006, and of Ilyās Khūrī's *Bāb al-shams*, published as *Gate of the Sun* by Picador in 2007; Marilyn Booth's co-translation (with the author) of Rajāʾ al-Ṣāniʿ's *Banāt al-Riyāḍ*, published as *Girls of Riyadh* by Penguin in 2007; Roger Allen's translation of Ḥanān al-Shaykh's *Ḥikāyatī sharḥun yaṭūl*, published as *The Locust and the Bird: My Mother's Story* by Anchor Books in 2010; Jonathan Wright's translation of Aḥmad Saʿdāwī's *Frānkishtāyn*

fī Baghdād, published as *Frankenstein in Baghdad* by Penguin in 2018; and Elisabeth Jaquette's translation of Dīmah Wannūs's *al-Khā ʾifūn*, published as *The Frightened Ones* by Knopf in 2020.

6. Hassan, "Arabic and the Paradigms of Comparison," 189.

7. A list of such events might include, in addition to the attacks of 9/11, the U.S. war in Iraq from 2003 to 2011; the Arab Spring uprisings in Tunisia, Egypt, Bahrain, and a number of other Arab countries in 2011–2012; ongoing U.S. military operations against the militant group ISIL/ISIS beginning in 2014; the murder of Saudi *Washington Post* columnist Jamal Khashoggi in Istanbul in 2018; ongoing civil unrest in Libya, Syria, and Yemen; and the destruction of the Beirut port in an ammonium nitrate explosion in 2020.

8. Robyn Creswell, "Is Arabic Untranslatable?," *Public Culture* 28, no. 3 (2016): 449.

9. Claudia Roth Pierpont, "Found in Translation," *The New Yorker*, January 18, 2010, 74.

10. See Gilles Deleuze and Félix Guattari, *A Thousand Plateaus: Capitalism and Schizophrenia*, trans. Brian Massumi (Minneapolis: University of Minnesota Press, 1987), 238; see Edward W. Said, "The World, the Text, and the Critic," in *The World, the Text, and the Critic* (Cambridge, MA: Harvard University Press, 1983), 39.

11. Edward W. Said, *Orientalism* (New York: Vintage Books, 1994), 1.

12. Lydia Liu, *Translingual Practice: Literature, National Culture, and Translated Modernity—China, 1900–1937* (Stanford, CA: Stanford University Press, 1995), xv.

13. Ibid., 20.

14. See, for example, Waïl S. Hassan's *Immigrant Narratives: Orientalism and Cultural Translation in Arab American and Arab British Literature* (New York: Oxford University Press, 2011), which examines how the historic legacies of Orientalism manifest in the work of Anglophone Arab writers since the early twentieth century; and David Fieni's *Decadent Orientalisms: The Decay of Colonial Modernity* (New York: Fordham University Press, 2020), which surveys key exemplars of Orientalist thought in Arab and Western intellectual and literary history from the nineteenth century to the present.

15. Hosam Aboul-Ela, "Is There an Arab (Yet) in This Field? Postcolonialism, Comparative Literature, and the Middle Eastern Horizon of Said's Discourse Analysis," *Modern Fiction Studies* 56, no. 4 (2010): 735.

16. Aamir Mufti, *Forget English! Orientalisms and World Literatures* (Cambridge, MA: Harvard University Press, 2016), 57–58.

17. According to the fourteenth-century Arab historian Ibn Khaldūn, *ʿilm al-lughah* refers to the study of language insofar as it is constituted as the set of linguistic elements instituted or emplaced into use ("*al-mawḍū ʿāt al-lughwiyyah*") in a variety of real-world contexts. The practical concerns of *ʿilm al-lughah* are contrasted here with the theoretical study of grammar in *ʿilm al-naḥw* and the study of normative conventions of style in *ʿilm al-bayān*. See A. Hadj-Salah, "Lugha," in *Encyclopaedia of Islam, Second Edition*, ed. P. Bearman et al. (Leiden: Brill, 2012), https://referenceworks.brillonline.com/entries/encyclopaedia-of-islam-2/lugha-SIM_4685.

18. Lara Harb, *Arabic Poetics: Aesthetic Experience in Classical Arabic Literature* (New York: Cambridge University Press, 2020), 23.

19. Mufti, *Forget English!*, 92.

20. Gayatri Chakravorty Spivak, *An Aesthetic Education in the Era of Globalization* (Cambridge, MA: Harvard University Press, 2012), 98.

21. Khaled Furani, *Silencing the Sea: Secular Rhythms in Palestinian Poetry* (Stanford, CA: Stanford University Press, 2012), 2.

22. Adam Zachary Newton, *To Make the Hands Impure: Art, Ethical Adventure, the Difficult and the Holy* (New York: Fordham University Press, 2015), 10, 29; emphasis original.

23. Gayatri Chakravorty Spivak, "The Politics of Translation," in *The Translation Studies Reader*, 3rd ed., ed. Lawrence Venuti (New York: Routledge, 2012), 315.

24. María Puig de la Bellacasa, *Matters of Care: Speculative Ethics in More Than Human Worlds* (Minneapolis: University of Minnesota Press, 2017), 115.

25. Shaden Tageldin, *Disarming Words: Empire and the Seductions of Translation in Egypt* (Berkeley: University of California Press, 2011), 26.

26. See http://www.rochester.edu/College/translation/threepercent/about/. The U.S. publishing industry differs substantially in this respect from the publishing industries of many European countries. In France and Germany, between ten and fifteen percent of all books published between 1990 and 2005 were translations, while in smaller countries like the Czech Republic and Finland, translations comprised 20 to 30 percent of new titles that entered the market during this same period. In the United Kingdom, however, the figures have typically been similar to those of the United States. See Alexandra Büchler and Alice Guthrie, eds., "Literary Translation from Arabic into English in the United Kingdom and Ireland, 1990–2010," Literature Across Frontiers, December 2011, http://www.lit-across-frontiers.org/wp-content/uploads/2013/03/Literary-Translation-from-Arabic-into-English-in-the-United-Kingdom-and-Ireland-1990-2010-final.pdf, 15.

27. See Lawrence Venuti, *The Translator's Invisibility: A History of Translation*, 3rd ed. (New York: Routledge, 2018), 12.

28. Corollary to the vast quantity of literary texts written in English is the enormous number of people globally who can capably read these texts, "once we include second- and third- as well as first-language users [of English] throughout the world," as Rebecca Walkowitz notes. See Rebecca Walkowitz, *Born Translated: The Contemporary Novel in an Age of World Literature* (New York: Columbia University Press, 2015), 11.

29. Among these achievements are the 2018 addition to the U.S. National Book Awards of a category for translated literature, as well as the recent commercial success in the United States of several works of translated fiction, including Japanese author Haruki Murakami's *1Q84* (2011) and Italian author Elena Ferrante's Neapolitan novels (2012–2015), among others.

30. The notion of translation as a "labor of love" is a recurrent trope in translators' accounts of what motivates them to do what they do. See, for example, Gregory Rabassa's use of this formulation to describe a translation undertaken "without a publisher in mind," in his memoir *If This Be Treason: Translation and Its Dyscontents* (New York: New Directions, 2005), 114; and more than a century earlier, in a text that I examine in detail in chapter 2, Richard Francis Burton's characterization of his translation of the Arabic *Alf laylah wa-laylah* stories as having "been to me a labour of love, an unfailing source of solace and satisfaction," in Richard F. Burton, *A Plain and Literal Translation of the Arabian Nights' Entertainments: Now Entituled The Book of the Thousand Nights and a Night*, vol. 1 ([London]: The Burton Club, n.d.), vii.

31. Venuti, *The Translator's Invisibility*, 266.

32. Mufti, *Forget English!*, 16.

33. See, e.g., Spivak's elaboration of this concept in the chapter titled "The Double Bind Starts to Kick In," in Spivak, *An Aesthetic Education*, 97–118.

34. For example, Pascale Casanova in *The World Republic of Letters* describes Moroccan poet Abdellatif Laâbi's decision to compose his poetry first in French before self-translating it into Arabic as characteristic of the kinds of "solutions to literary domination" adopted by "writers on the periphery" for whom allegiance to a native tongue with little international cachet must invariably be weighed against the far greater publishing opportunities available to authors who write in a colonial language. See Pascale Casanova, *The World Republic of Letters*, trans. M. B. DeBevoise (Cambridge, MA: Harvard University Press, 2004), 257–258. Along similar lines, Alexander Beecroft has observed that although Arabic literature "participates in a global circulation of some kind," as a "rival" to other world literary traditions—especially those in English and French—it can make little headway, "given the political and economic power, demographic weight and geographic breadth . . . [these other literatures] possess." See Alexander Beecroft, "World Literature without a Hyphen: Towards a Typology of Literary Systems (2008)," in *World Literature in Theory*, ed. David Damrosch (Chichester, UK: John Wiley and Sons, 2014), 188.

35. See Roger Allen, "The Happy Traitor: Tales of Translation," *Comparative Literature Studies* 47, no. 4 (2010): 472–486, and "Translating Arabic Fiction," *Journal of Arabic Literature* 46, nos. 2–3 (2015): 157–167; Booth, "Translator v. Author" and "'The Muslim Woman' as Celebrity Author and the Politics of Translating Arabic: Girls of Riyadh Go on the Road," *Journal of Middle East Women's Studies* 6 (2010): 149–182; Issa J. Boullata, "The Case for Resistant Translation from Arabic to English," *Translation Review* 65 (2003): 29–33; Michelle Hartman, "Gender, Genre, and the (Missing) Gazelle: Arab Women Writers and the Politics of Translation," *Feminist Studies* 38, no. 1 (2012): 17–49, and "'My Tale Is Too Long to Tell': *The Locust and the Bird* between South Lebanon and New York City," *Journal of Arabic Literature* 46, nos. 2–3 (2015): 168–192; and Nirvana Tanoukhi, "Rewriting Political Commitment for an International Canon: Paul Bowles's *For Bread Alone* as Translation of Mohamed Choukri's *Al-Khubz Al-Hafi*," *Research in African Literatures* 34, no. 2 (2003): 127–144.

36. Hartman, "Missing Gazelle," 22–23.

37. "The Politics of Translation" was published as a chapter in Spivak's monograph *Outside in the Teaching Machine* (1993) and later anthologized as a standalone essay, in a slightly modified version, in Lawrence Venuti's edited volume *The Translation Studies Reader* (2000). Representative of this ethical turn in translation studies were works such as Sandra Bermann and Michael Wood's coedited volume *Nation, Language, and the Ethics of Translation* (Princeton, NJ: Princeton University Press, 2005), which contains contributions from postcolonial critics including Spivak herself as well as from scholars like David Damrosch and Emily Apter; and Mona Baker's *Translation and Conflict: A Narrative Account* (New York: Routledge, 2006). Both of these volumes conceive of translation ethics as rooted in a translator's responsibility to communicate the originary otherness of the source material to a new audience, whether this otherness is ontological or cultural in nature. For Bermann, what ensures that "the translator's task is inevitably an ethical one" is an "'exorbitant' quality of language, that which remains mysteriously 'other' within it;" while for Baker, translators "face a basic ethical choice with every assignment" because the "texts and utterances they produce . . . participate in creating, negotiating and contesting [a] social reality" coded with narrative ideologies to which language gives expres-

sion. See Sandra Bermann, "Introduction," in Bermann and Wood, *Nation, Language, and the Ethics of Translation*, 6; and Baker, *Translation and Conflict*, 105.

38. See Henry Staten, "Tracking the 'Native Informant': Cultural Translation as the Horizon of Literary Translation," in Bermann and Wood, *Nation, Language, and the Ethics of Translation*, 112.

39. Liu, *Translingual Practice*, 25.

40. See Henri Meschonnic, *Ethics and Politics of Translating*, trans. and ed. Pier-Pascale Boulanger (Philadelphia: John Benjamins, 2011), 39: "A code of conduct will not suffice if poetics is missing."

41. Ibid., 69.

42. Douglas Robinson, *The Translator's Turn* (Baltimore, MD: Johns Hopkins University Press, 1991), 18.

43. Pier-Pascale Boulanger laments in the introduction to his edited English translation of Meschonnic's *Éthique et politique du traduire* (2007) that the scholar's work is little known in the Anglophone academy. See Pier-Pascale Boulanger, "Introduction," in Meschonnic, *Ethics and Politics of Translating*, 15–20. In Robinson's case, although he has published more than twenty scholarly monographs and held a tenured faculty position for two decades at the University of Mississippi, I have seldom seen his work cited by mainstream scholars of translation in English.

44. Peter Cole, "Making Sense in Translation: Toward an Ethics of the Art," in *In Translation: Translators on Their Work and What It Means*, ed. Roger Allen and Susan Bernofsky (New York: Columbia University Press, 2013), 8; emphasis original.

45. Elliott Colla, "Translation Theory, Practice, and Transduction," *ElliottColla.com*, April 23, 2018, http://www.elliottcolla.com/blog/2018/4/23/translation-theory-practice-and-transduction.

46. Creswell, "Is Arabic Untranslatable?," 453, 449.

47. Ibid., 453.

48. George Steiner, *After Babel: Aspects of Language and Translation* (New York: Oxford University Press, 1975), 296–297.

49. Jerome, "Letter to Pammachius," trans. Kathleen Davis, in Venuti, *The Translation Studies Reader*, 23.

50. Jerome, "Letter to Pammachius," 24.

51. See Lawrence Venuti, "Genealogies of Translation Theory: Jerome," in Venuti, *The Translation Studies Reader*, 483–502.

52. Maria Tymoczko, "Western Metaphorical Discourses Implicit in Translation Studies," in *Thinking through Translation with Metaphors*, ed. James St. André (New York: Routledge, 2014), 121–123.

53. Jerome, *Sancti Eusebii Hieronymi Epistulae*, ed. Isidorus Hilberg, vol. 1 (Vienna: F. Tempsky and Leipzig: G. Freytag, 1910), Letter LVII: 5, 510, 508.

54. Mohamed-Salah Omri, "Notes on the Traffic between Theory and Arabic Literature," *International Journal of Middle East Studies* 43 (2011): 732.

55. Tarek El-Ariss, "Theory in a Global Context: A Critical Practice in Five Steps," *CARGC Papers* 17 (2022): 9.

56. Dima Ayoub, "Politics of Paratextuality: The Glossary between Translation and the Translational," *Journal of Arabic Literature* 51, nos. 1–2 (2020): 30.

57. Booth, "'The Muslim Woman' as Celebrity Author," 154.

58. See Mona Kareem, "Lily Meyer and Mona Kareem on Their New Series, Close-Up: An Experiment in Reviewing Translation," interview in *Words Without Borders*,

May 14, 2020, https://www.wordswithoutborders.org/dispatches/article/lily-meyer-mona-kareem-close-up-an-experiment-in-reviewing-translation-s?src=landingpage.

59. Michael A. Toler, "The Ethics of Cultural Representation: The Maghribi Novel in English Translation," *The Journal of North African Studies* 6, no. 3 (2001): 50.

60. Jenine Abboushi Dallal, "The Perils of Occidentalism: How Arab Novelists Are Driven to Write for Western Readers," *The Times Literary Supplement*, April 24, 1998, 8.

61. Marilyn Booth quoted in Tarek El-Ariss, *Trials of Arab Modernity: Literary Affects and the New Political* (New York: Fordham University Press, 2013), 10.

62. Magda M. Al-Nowaihi, "Unheard in English," *The MIT Electronic Journal of Middle East Studies: Crossing Boundaries—New Perspectives on the Middle East* 4 (2004): 28.

63. Hosam Aboul-Ela, *Domestications: American Empire, Literary Culture, and the Postcolonial Lens* (Evanston, IL: Northwestern University Press, 2018), 7–8.

64. Heather Love, "Close but not Deep: Literary Ethics and the Descriptive Turn," *New Literary History* 41, no. 2 (2010): 375.

65. Deleuze and Guattari, *A Thousand Plateaus*, 70.

66. Nicholas Dames, *The Physiology of the Novel: Reading, Neural Science, and the Form of Victorian Fiction* (New York: Oxford University Press, 2007), 11.

67. Robyn Warhol, *Having a Good Cry: Effeminate Feelings and Pop-Culture Forms* (Columbus: Ohio State University Press, 2003), ix.

68. Rachel Greenwald Smith, *Affect and American Literature in the Age of Neoliberalism* (New York: Cambridge University Press, 2015), 25–26.

69. Ibid., 18.

70. Benedictus de Spinoza, *Ethics*, trans. and ed. Edwin Curley (London: Penguin Books, 1996), 84, 41.

71. See Pierre Bourdieu, *Distinction: A Social Critique of the Judgement of Taste*, trans. Richard Nice (Cambridge, MA: Harvard University Press, 1984).

72. Sara Ahmed, "Happy Objects," in *The Affect Theory Reader*, ed. Melissa Gregg and Gregory Seigworth (Durham, NC: Duke University Press, 2010), 29, 31.

73. See especially Massumi's discussion of affects that "escape" subjective knowability to figure a body's perception of its own vitality instead in its potential for interactions with other bodies. See Brian Massumi, *Parables for the Virtual: Movement, Affect, Sensation* (Durham, NC: Duke University Press, 2002), 35–36.

74. Mara Naaman, "Disciplinary Divergences: Problematizing the Field of Arabic Literature," *Comparative Literature Studies* 47, no. 4 (2010): 449–450.

75. Jacquemond maintains that "the emergence of . . . [a] 'pan-Arab' literary field does not invalidate a 'national' approach" to understanding the dynamic structures within which Arabic literature has been produced and consumed in recent decades. For example, he writes, while Egyptian authors may be "able to entertain the ambition of 'becoming universal' through translation, and of becoming recognized and published across the Arab region from 'the Gulf to the ocean,' their works and careers are nevertheless in the main determined by their positions in local Egyptian history and society." See Richard Jacquemond, *Conscience of the Nation: Writers, State, and Society in Modern Egypt*, trans. David Tresilian (Cairo: American University in Cairo Press, 2008), 12–13.

76. I return to this point in the conclusion.

77. In an effort to acknowledge this broader definition of Arabic literature, the Modern Language Association in the United States recently expanded Arabic literature into two "forums" within its classificatory schema of scholarly interests with which

members may affiliate themselves: "Global Arab and Arab American" and "Arabic." See https://www.mla.org/Membership/Forums.

78. Michael Allan, *In the Shadow of World Literature: Sites of Reading in Colonial Egypt* (Princeton, NJ: Princeton University Press, 2016), 77; emphasis original.

79. Ibid., 14.

80. Caroline Levine, *Forms: Whole, Rhythm, Hierarchy, Network* (Princeton, NJ: Princeton University Press, 2015), 3, 6–7.

81. Ibid., 6.

82. See Walter Benjamin, "The Task of the Translator," in *Illuminations*, trans. Harry Zohn, ed. Hannah Arendt (New York: Schocken Books, 1969), 77.

83. See Haun Saussy, "Comparative Literature: The Next Ten Years," in *Futures of Comparative Literature: ACLA State of the Discipline Report*, ed. Ursula K. Heise (New York: Routledge, 2017), 25.

84. See his discussion of translation and translatability in David Damrosch, *What Is World Literature?* (Princeton, NJ: Princeton University Press, 2003), 288–297.

85. Franco Moretti, "Conjectures on World Literature," *New Left Review* 1 (2000): 55.

86. Emily Apter, *Against World Literature: On the Politics of Untranslatability* (New York: Verso, 2013), 3.

87. Emily Apter, *The Translation Zone: A New Comparative Literature* (Princeton, NJ: Princeton University Press, 2006), 6.

88. Mark Polizzotti, *Sympathy for the Traitor: A Translation Manifesto* (Cambridge, MA: MIT Press, 2018), 41–42.

89. Lawrence Venuti, "Hijacking Translation: How Comp Lit Continues to Suppress Translated Texts," *boundary 2* 43, no. 2 (2016): 187.

90. The original French volume, titled *Vocabulaire européen des philosophies: Dictionnaire des intraduisibles*, was published in 2004.

91. Barbara Cassin, "Introduction," trans. Michael Wood, in *Dictionary of Untranslatables: A Philosophical Lexicon*, ed. Barbara Cassin et al. (Princeton, NJ: Princeton University Press, 2014), xvii.

92. Walkowitz, *Born Translated*, 33–34.

93. Venuti, "Hijacking Translation," 187–188; emphasis original.

94. Cassin, "Introduction," xviii.

95. Benjamin, "Task of the Translator," 80.

96. The model proposed by Friedrich Schleiermacher in 1813 of a translator who must choose between a practice that "leaves the writer in peace as much as possible and moves the reader toward him," or one that "leaves the reader in peace as much as possible and moves the writer toward him," has remained a centerpiece of such dichotomous views of translation. See Friedrich Schleiermacher, "On the Different Methods of Translating," trans. Susan Bernofsky, in Venuti, *The Translation Studies Reader*, 49.

97. Bellos draws a distinction between the self-evident "truth" of translation "that everything is effable" and the "anguished engagement with the problem of ineffable essences . . . [that] has preoccupied secular [translation] scholars of the twentieth century." See David Bellos, *Is That a Fish in Your Ear? Translation and the Meaning of Everything* (New York: Faber and Faber, 2011), 151–153.

98. Elspeth Probyn, "Shame in the Habitus," *The Sociological Review* 52, no. 2, supplement (2004): 228.

99. Gregory J. Seigworth and Melissa Gregg, "An Inventory of Shimmers," in Gregg and Seigworth, *The Affect Theory Reader*, 2.

100. Eve Kosofsky Sedgwick, *Touching Feeling: Affect, Pedagogy, Performativity* (Durham, NC: Duke University Press, 2003), 145.

101. Ibid., 8.

102. Jeffrey Sacks, *Iterations of Loss: Mutilation and Aesthetic Form, Al-Shidyaq to Darwish* (New York: Fordham University Press, 2015), 1–3.

103. Kathleen Stewart, "Worlding Refrains," in *The Affect Theory Reader*, ed. Melissa Gregg and Gregory J. Seigworth (Durham, NC: Duke University Press, 2010), 339.

104. I employ the notion of "worlding" throughout this book in a manner approximate to what I understand Stewart's sense of the term to be: as designating an act or process of bringing-into-mattering, to a capacious and generous extent, a thing that is in crucial respects other to the one who performs the worlding act. In this regard, "worlding" signifies here somewhat (although not wholly) differently than it does for Martin Heidegger, for whom worlding is the hallmark activity of a work of art that brings things in themselves into meaningful presence, in a way analogous to how the world-as-such sets forth the things within *it* so as to reveal *their* unconcealed natures. See Martin Heidegger, "The Origin of the Work of Art," in *Poetry, Language, Thought*, trans. Albert Hofstadter (New York: Harper Perennial, 2001).

105. Philip E. Lewis, "The Measure of Translation Effects," in Venuti, *The Translation Studies Reader*, 227.

1. Sonics of *Lafẓ*: Translating Arabic Acoustics for Anglophone Ears

1. The original 1855 edition of the book was printed in Paris by Benjamin Duprat under al-Shidyāq's supervision and bore the bilingual title *Kitāb al-sāq ʿalā al-sāq fī mā huwa al-Fāriyāq: aw ayyām wa-shuhūr wa-aʿwām fī ʿajam al-ʿArab wa-al-aʿjām / La vie et les aventures de Fariac: Relation de ses voyages avec ses observations critiques sur les arabes et sur les autres peuples*. See Geoffrey Roper, "Fāris al-Shidyāq and the Transition from Scribal to Print Culture," in *The Book in the Islamic World: The Written Word and Communication in the Middle East*, ed. George Atiyeh (Albany: State University of New York Press, 1995), 213.

2. Patricia Storace, "After Rabelais," review of *Leg over Leg* by Ahmad Faris al-Shidyaq, trans. Humphrey Davies, *TLS*, November 18, 2015, https://www.the-tls.co.uk/articles/private/after-rabelais/.

3. John Yargo, "More Steps Than the Stairway of a Minaret," review of *Leg over Leg* by Ahmad Faris al-Shidyaq, trans. Humphrey Davies, *Los Angeles Review of Books*, May 10, 2014, https://lareviewofbooks.org/article/steps-stairway-minaret-humphrey-davies-translation-faris-al-shidyaqs-leg-leg/.

4. Martin Riker, "A Ramshackle Modernity," review of *The Time Regulation Institute* by Ahmet Hamdi Tanpinar, trans. Maureen Freely and Alexander Dawe, *New York Times*, January 3, 2014, https://www.nytimes.com/2014/01/05/books/review/the-time-regulation-institute-by-ahmet-hamdi-tanpinar.html?searchResultPosition=3.

5. "Best Books of 2015—Part Two," *The Guardian*, November 29, 2015, https://www.theguardian.com/books/ng-interactive/2015/nov/29/best-books-of-2015-part-two.

6. See Edward W. Said, "Embargoed Literature," *The Nation*, September 17, 1990, 278–280.

7. According to Venuti, domesticating translations are those that strive to blend in seamlessly with mainstream English-language fiction by evincing an "absence of any linguistic or stylistic peculiarities" and "adhering to current usage, maintaining con-

tinuous syntax, [and] fixing a precise meaning." See Lawrence Venuti, *The Translator's Invisibility: A History of Translation*, 3rd ed. (New York: Routledge, 2018), 1.

8. See ibid., 20.

9. The Library of Arabic Literature's website includes a complete up-to-date list of titles published so far, at https://www.libraryofarabicliterature.org/books/.

10. Shawkat Toorawa, "A Corpus, Not a Canon (Nor an Anthology): Creating a 'Library of Arabic Literature,'" *Journal of World Literature* 2 (2017): 370.

11. Montgomery gave this assessment of the Library's founding mission during a panel discussion at the Conceptions and Configurations of the Arabic Literary Canon Workshop in Paris on June 19, 2019. He was joined on the panel by Toorawa, the Library of Arabic Literature's general editor Philip Kennedy, and LAL's editorial director Chip Rossetti.

12. See Toorawa, "A Corpus, Not a Canon," 370, 366.

13. Chip Rossetti, email, November 4, 2019.

14. Ahmad Faris al-Shidyaq, *Leg over Leg or, The Turtle in the Tree, concerning The Fāriyāq; What Manner of Creature Might He Be; otherwise entitled Days, Months, and Years spent in Critical Examination of the Arabs and Their Non-Arab Peers*, trans. and ed. Humphrey Davies (New York: New York University Press, 2013–2014), 1:36. I take the Arabic text of *al-Sāq ʿalā al-sāq* that appears alongside Davies's translation in the bilingual Library of Arabic Literature edition published in 2013–2014—and which is intended to hew as closely as possible to the text of *al-Sāq ʿalā al-sāq*'s first 1855 printing (see "A Note on the Text," xxxi–xxxiii)—to be authoritative for the purposes of the Arabic quotations given in this chapter. Because the Arabic text is printed on alternating pages of each volume of the bilingual LAL edition, page ranges when they refer to Arabic passages spanning more than one page are thus discontinuous to allow for the interruption of the corresponding page(s) in English. I have amended the orthography very slightly in some of my transcriptions (marking the *hamza* over initial *alif*, placing two dots under all word-final instances of *yāʾ*, and so on) to reflect current scholarly conventions for transcribing Arabic.

15. Rana Issa, "The Insomniac Feast: Al-Shidyaq's Reading Digest," paper presented at the Conceptions and Configurations of the Arabic Literary Canon Workshop, Paris, June 19, 2019, 12.

16. Angela Leighton, *Hearing Things: The Work of Sound in Literature* (Cambridge, MA: The Belknap Press of Harvard University Press, 2018), 2.

17. Al-Shidyaq, *Leg over Leg*, 1:36.

18. See Muḥammad ibn Mukarram ibn Manẓūr, *Lisān al-ʿArab* (Beirut: Dār Ṣādir, 2005), 13:216.

19. See M. G. Carter and J. van Ess, "Lafẓ," in *Encyclopaedia of Islam, Second Edition*, ed. P. Bearman et al. (Leiden: Brill, 2012), https://referenceworks.brillonline.com/entries/encyclopaedia-of-islam-2/lafz-COM_1420.

20. See C. H. M. Versteegh, O. N. H. Leaman, and J. E. Bencheikh, "Maʿnā," in ibid., https://referenceworks.brillonline.com/entries/encyclopaedia-of-islam-2/mana-COM_0659.

21. See D. E. Kouloughli, "A propos de lafẓ et maʿnā," *Bulletin d'Études Orientales* 35 (1983): 48.

22. Ramzi Baalbaki, "Arabic Linguistic Tradition I: Naḥw and ṣarf," in *The Oxford Handbook of Arabic Linguistics*, ed. Jonathan Owens (New York: Oxford University Press, 2013), 99.

23. See Lara Harb, "Form, Content, and the Inimitability of the Qur'an in 'Abd al-Qahir al-Jurjani's Works," *Middle Eastern Literatures* 18, no. 3 (2015): 313. It is worth noting that al-Jurjānī's understanding of the inimitability of the Qur'an, as Harb describes it, rests on a somewhat less narrowly circumscribed notion of form than that traditionally associated with *lafẓ*, wherein he endeavors to account also for form's interdependence with content in creating the specific constructions or orderings of language (*naẓm*) found in the sacred text.

24. Humphrey Davies, "Translator's Afterword," in al-Shidyaq, *Leg over Leg*, 4:486.

25. Ibid., 1:37.

26. Ibid.

27. Deborah Kapchan, "Body," in *Keywords in Sound*, ed. David Novak and Matt Sakakeeny (Durham, NC: Duke University Press, 2015), 38, 41.

28. Victor Shklovsky, "Art as Technique," in *Russian Formalist Criticism: Four Essays*, trans. Lee T. Lemon and Marion J. Reis (Lincoln: University of Nebraska Press, 1965), 12.

29. See René Wellek and Austin Warren, *Theory of Literature* (New York: Harcourt, Brace and Company, 1942), 141.

30. Rebecca C. Johnson, "Archive of Errors: Aḥmad Fāris al-Shidyāq, Literature, and the World," *Middle Eastern Literatures* 20, no. 1 (2017): 40.

31. See al-Shidyaq, *Leg over Leg*, 1:52. When al-Shidyāq asserts in the same passage that "I hope that in the description of beauty alone there is enough polish and luster and decoration [in this book] to take the place of these embellishments [*tilka al-muḥassināt*]," I view this statement as a tacit acknowledgement of the inadequacy of mere representations of beauty ("*waṣf al-jamāl*") to accomplish what linguistic ornamentation can in terms of producing aesthetic effects in the text, especially as this statement follows a conditional clause that begins "If someone were to insist to me that my expression [in writing] lacked rhetorical flourish" ("*Idhā taʿannata ʿalayya aḥad bi-kawn ʿibāratī ghayr balīghah*")—an accusation that no one reading *al-Sāq ʿalā al-sāq* could possibly make. My interpretation of these lines is contra that of Fawwaz Traboulsi, who understands them literally and therefore claims that al-Shidyāq "rejected stylistic ornamentation" and "sought simplicity and naturalness" in his writing. See Fawwaz Traboulsi, "Ahmad Faris Al-Shidyaq (1804–87): The Quest for Another Modernity," in *Arabic Thought Beyond the Liberal Age: Towards an Intellectual History of the Nahda*, ed. Jens Hanssen and Max Weiss (New York: Cambridge University Press, 2016), 185–186.

32. Sabry Hafez, *The Genesis of Arabic Narrative Discourse: A Study in the Sociology of Modern Arabic Literature* (London: Saqi Books, 1993), 118.

33. See Fruma Zachs, *The Making of a Syrian Identity: Intellectuals and Merchants in Nineteenth Century Beirut* (Leiden: Brill, 2005), 187–188.

34. See Geoffrey Roper, "Aḥmad Fāris al-Shidyāq and the Libraries of Europe and the Ottoman Empire," *Libraries & Culture* 33, no. 3 (1990): 233–234.

35. Sherif Ismail provides a partial list of these words and suggests that al-Shidyāq's neologisms were widely accepted because in their "morphology, and hence also phonology," each "derives organically from extant Arabic roots, hence they emanate from and merge seamlessly into Arabic, and they thus sound natural and 'native' in both sound and form." See Sherif Ismail, "Multiple Encounters: Philology, Exile, and Hospitality, from Fāris al-Shidyāq to Auerbach and Edward Said," *Philological Encounters* 3, nos. 1–2 (2018): 81.

36. See Kamran Rastegar, *Literary Modernity between the Middle East and Europe: Textual Transactions in Nineteenth-Century Arabic, English, and Persian Literatures* (New York: Routledge, 2007), 108.

37. See Roper, "Libraries of Europe," 234.

38. See Rastegar, *Literary Modernity*, 108.

39. See "A Note on the Text," in al-Shidyaq, *Leg over Leg*, 1:xxxi.

40. See Roper, "Transition from Scribal to Print Culture," 213.

41. Dima Ayoub, "Politics of Paratextuality: The Glossary between Translation and the Translational," *Journal of Arabic Literature* 51, nos. 1–2 (2020): 27.

42. Kwame Anthony Appiah, "Thick Translation," in *The Translation Studies Reader*, 3rd ed., ed. Lawrence Venuti (New York: Routledge, 2012), 341.

43. "lexical synonymy . . . without doubt a universal phenomenon"; see Kouloughli, "A propos de lafẓ et maʿnā," 47.

44. Abī ʿUthmān ʿAmru ibn Baḥr al-Jāḥiẓ, *Kitāb al-ḥayawān*, ed. ʿAbd al-Salām Muḥammad Hārūn (Cairo: Muṣṭafā al-Bābī al-Ḥalabī, 1965), 3:131–132.

45. James E. Montgomery, *Al-Jāḥiẓ: In Praise of Books* (Edinburgh: Edinburgh University Press, 2013), 9, 6.

46. See also Jeannie Miller, *The Quibbler: Al-Jahiz's Equivocations in Kitab al-Hayawan and Beyond* (Edinburgh: Edinburgh University Press, forthcoming).

47. Al-Jāḥiẓ, *Kitāb al-ḥayawān*, 1:74–75.

48. See ʿAbd al-Fattāḥ Kīlīṭū, *Lan tatakallama lughatī* (Beirut: Dār al-Talīʿah, 2002), 30–31.

49. Montgomery, *Al-Jāḥiẓ*, 12.

50. Gayatri Chakravorty Spivak, "The Politics of Translation," in Venuti, *The Translation Studies Reader*, 313.

51. Emily Apter, *Against World Literature: On the Politics of Untranslatability* (New York: Verso, 2013), 8, 11, 14–15, 3.

52. Jacques Derrida, *Monolingualism of the Other; or, The Prosthesis of Origin*, trans. Patrick Mensah (Stanford, CA: Stanford University Press, 1998), 56.

53. See Harb, "Form, Content, and the Inimitability of the Qur'an," 304.

54. See Anna Ziajka Stanton, "Feeling the Grammar: Literary Translations of the Dual Inflection in Arabic," *Philological Encounters* 4, nos. 1–2 (2019): 26–54.

55. Mohamed-Salah Omri, "Notes on the Traffic between Theory and Arabic Literature," *International Journal of Middle East Studies* 43 (2011): 732.

56. Hosam Aboul-Ela, "Is There an Arab (Yet) in This Field? Postcolonialism, Comparative Literature, and the Middle Eastern Horizon of Said's Discourse Analysis," *Modern Fiction Studies* 56, no. 4 (2010): 744.

57. Tarek El-Ariss, "Theory in a Global Context: A Critical Practice in Five Steps," *CARGC Papers* 17 (2022): 10.

58. Emily Apter, "Philosophical Translation and Untranslatability: Translation as Critical Pedagogy," *Profession* (2010), 55, 57–58; see also note 6.

59. See Waïl Hassan, "Translator's Introduction," in Abdelfattah Kilito, *Thou Shalt Not Speak My Language*, trans. Waïl S. Hassan (Syracuse, NY: Syracuse University Press, 2008), x.

60. See ibn Manẓūr, *Lisān al-ʿArab*, 2:219; and 6:116–117. There is also evidence tying the etymology of *turjumān* to the quadriliteral Hebrew root *trgm*, "which has cognates in other Semitic languages but is likely to have had an Indo-European origin." See

Steven D. Fraade, "Targum, Targumim," in *The Eerdmans Dictionary of Early Judaism*, ed. John J. Collins and Daniel C. Harlow (Grand Rapids, MI: Eerdmans, 2010), 1278.

61. Sandra Bermann, "Introduction," in *Nation, Language, and the Ethics of Translation*, ed. Sandra Bermann and Michael Wood (Princeton, NJ: Princeton University Press, 2005), 5.

62. See Apter, *Against World Literature*, 3.

63. Deborah Kapchan, "The Splash of Icarus: Theorizing Sound Writing/Writing Sound Theory," in *Theorizing Sound Writing*, ed. Deborah Kapchan (Middletown, CT: Wesleyan University Press, 2017), 1–2.

64. Ibid., 2.

65. Al-Shidyaq, *Leg over Leg*, 1:89, 91.

66. See W. Wright, *Arabic Grammar*, 3rd ed. (Mineola, NY: Dover Publications, 2005), 47.

67. Al-Shidyaq, *Leg over Leg*, 1:88.

68. These are the definitions given in the *Hans Wehr Dictionary of Modern Written Arabic*, 4th ed., ed. J. Milton Cowan (Ithaca, NY: Spoken Language Services, 1994), 667, 339, 304.

69. Mattityahu Peled, "The Enumerative Style in Al-sâq ʿalâ al-sâq," *Journal of Arabic Literature* 22, no. 2 (1991), 134.

70. Ibid., 140.

71. Rebecca C. Johnson, "Foreword," in al-Shidyaq, *Leg over Leg*, 1:xxvi–xxvii.

72. Christian Junge, "Doing Things with Lists—Enumeration in Arabic Prose," *Journal of Arabic Literature* 50 (2019): 293.

73. Al-Shidyaq, *Leg over Leg*, 1:46, 48.

74. Johnson, "Foreword," 1:xxvii.

75. Al-Shidyaq, *Leg over Leg*, 1:89.

76. Jean-Luc Nancy, *Listening*, trans. Charlotte Mandell (New York: Fordham University Press, 2007), 14.

77. See al-Shidyaq, *Leg over Leg*, 1:178.

78. See ibid., 2:63.

79. Johnson, "Archive of Errors," 43–44.

80. Al-Shidyaq, *Leg over Leg*, 2:62, 64.

81. Wright, *Arabic Grammar*, 5.

82. Al-Shidyaq, *Leg over Leg*, 2:63, 65.

83. See J. L. Austin, *How to Do Things with Words* (London: Oxford University Press, 1962), 99–100.

84. Storace, "After Rabelais," 28.

85. Jeffrey Sacks, *Iterations of Loss: Mutilation and Aesthetic Form, Al-Shidyaq to Darwish* (New York: Fordham University Press, 2015), 91.

86. Ibid., 97.

87. Stefan Helmreich, "Transduction," in *Keywords in Sound*, ed. David Novak and Matt Sakakeeny (Durham, NC: Duke University Press, 2015), 222.

88. Humphrey Davies, "Translator's Afterword," 491–492.

89. Al-Shidyaq, *Leg over Leg*, 4:112–113; emphasis original.

90. In Arabic:

"ما هذه اللغة التي تتكلمون بها لعمر الله ما فهمت شيا مما قلتم."

See al-Shidyaq, *Leg over Leg*, 4:114.

91. According to the *Oxford English Dictionary*, the etymology of "risible" (s.v.) is as follows: "Middle French *risible* that provokes laughter, laughable (c1370), capable of laughing (1550) and its etymon post-classical Latin *risibilis* capable of laughing (4th cent.), laughable (5th cent.) < classical Latin *rīs-*, past participial stem of *rīdēre* to laugh."

92. *Aslaqa* = "to hunt wolves;" see J. G. Hava, *Arabic-English Dictionary for the Use of Students* (Beirut: Catholic Press, 1899), 324.

93. Robyn Creswell, "The First Great Arabic Novel," review of *Leg over Leg* by Ahmad Faris al-Shidyaq, trans. Humphrey Davies, *The New York Review of Books*, October 8, 2015, https://www.nybooks.com/articles/2015/10/08/first-great-arabic-novel/.

94. Hilary Kilpatrick, review of *Leg over Leg* by Ahmad Faris al-Shidyaq, trans. Humphrey Davies, *Journal of the American Oriental Society* 138, no. 3 (2018): 660–661.

95. Elspeth Carruthers, review of *Leg over Leg* by Ahmad Faris al-Shidyaq, trans. Humphrey Davies, *Banipal* 49 (2014), https://www.banipal.co.uk/book_reviews/106/leg-over-leg/.

96. Tarek El-Ariss, review of *Leg over Leg* by Ahmad Faris al-Shidyaq, trans. Humphrey Davies, *Arab Studies Journal* 24, no. 1 (2016): 286–287.

97. See Spivak, "The Politics of Translation," 313; Venuti, *The Translator's Invisibility*, 15.

98. Al-Shidyaq, *Leg over Leg*, 1:8.

99. Rana Issa, "Scripture as Literature: The Bible, the Qurʾān, and Aḥmad Fāris al-Shidyāq," *Journal of Arabic Literature* 50 (2019): 36.

100. See Samah Selim, "The Narrative Craft: Realism and Fiction in the Arabic Canon," *Edebiyat: Journal of M.E. Literatures* 14, nos. 1–2 (2003): 114–115.

101. Johnson, "Archive of Errors," 32.

102. Tarek El-Ariss, *Trials of Arab Modernity: Literary Affects and the New Political* (New York: Fordham University Press, 2013), 58.

103. See Nadia Al-Bagdadi, "The Cultural Function of Fiction: From the Bible to Libertine Literature—Historical Criticism and Social Critique in Aḥmad Fāris al-Šidyāq," *Arabica* 46 (1999): 378.

104. See Raḍwā ʿĀshūr, *al-Ḥadāthah al-mumkinah: Al-Shidyāq wa-al-Sāq ʿalā al-sāq* (Cairo: Dār al-Shurūq, 2009), 10.

105. Rastegar, *Literary Modernity*, 103.

106. Peled, "The Enumerative Style," 127.

107. Talal Asad, "The Concept of Cultural Translation in British Anthropology," in *Writing Culture: The Poetics and Politics of Ethnography*, ed. James Clifford and George E. Marcus (Berkeley: University of California Press, 1986), 157–158.

108. See "About the Typefaces," in al-Shidyaq, *Leg over Leg*, 1:367. The Arabic portion of the text was later removed for a two-volume English-only paperback edition of *Leg over Leg* published in 2015.

109. See Stephen Greenblatt, "Resonance and Wonder," *Bulletin of the American Academy of Arts and Sciences* 43, no. 4 (1990): 20.

110. Laura U. Marks, "Haptic Visuality: Touching with the Eyes," *Framework: The Finnish Art Review* 2 (2004): 79.

111. Michelle Hartman, *Native Tongue, Stranger Talk: The Arabic and French Literary Landscapes of Lebanon* (Syracuse, NY: Syracuse University Press, 2014), 54.

112. Storace, "After Rabelais," 28.

113. Wai Chee Dimock, "A Theory of Resonance," *PMLA* 112, no. 5 (1997): 1064.
114. Nancy, *Listening*, 43.

2. Vulgarity of *Saj*ʿ: The Scandalous Pleasures of Burton's *The Book of the Thousand Nights and a Night*

1. The biographies include Byron Farwell's *Burton: A Biography of Sir Richard Francis Burton* (London: Longmans,1963), Fawn Brodie's *The Devil Drives: A Life of Sir Richard Burton* (New York: Norton, 1967), Edward Rice's *Captain Sir Richard Francis Burton: The Secret Agent Who Made the Pilgrimage to Mecca, Discovered the Kama Sutra, and Brought the Arabian Nights to the West* (New York: Charles Scribner's Sons, 1990), Mary Lovell's *A Rage to Live: A Biography of Richard and Isabel Burton* (New York: Norton, 1998), and Dane Kennedy's *The Highly Civilized Man: Richard Burton and the Victorian World* (Cambridge, MA: Harvard University Press, 2005). The first book in Mark Hodder's six-volume "Burton & Swinburne" series, *The Strange Affair of Spring-Heeled Jack* (2010), reimagines Burton as a renegade detective called upon to use his esoteric knowledge and personal panache to stop a murderous time-traveling cyborg who is terrorizing a dystopically mechanized version of Victorian London. Bulgarian author Iliya Troyanov's novel *Der Weltensammler* (2006), translated into English as *The Collector of Worlds* (2008), offers a romantic portrait of Burton as an aesthete, cosmopolite, and modernist avant la lettre. And the film *Mountains of the Moon* (dir. Bob Rafelson, 1990) chronicles Burton's 1857–1858 expedition to locate the source of the Nile River; it stars Irish actor Patrick Bergin as Burton, opposite Iain Glen (later known for his roles in the PBS series *Downton Abbey* and HBO's *Game of Thrones*) as Burton's co-adventurer and rival John Hanning Speke.

2. Edwards H. Metcalf letter to William Davis, 3 November 1989, RFB Box 57, Folder 4, Sir Richard Francis Burton Papers, Huntington Library, San Marino, CA.

3. The initial set of ten volumes was released in 1885–1886, followed by six additional volumes, titled *Supplemental Nights to the Book of the Thousand Nights and a Night with Note Anthropological and Explanatory*, in 1886–1888.

4. See David Damrosch, *What Is World Literature?* (Princeton, NJ: Princeton University Press, 2003), 5–6.

5. Jorge Luis Borges, "The Aleph," in *The Aleph and Other Stories: 1933–1969*, trans. Norman Thomas di Giovanni (New York: Dutton, 1970), 30.

6. Salman Rushdie, *Shame* (London: Jonathan Cape, 1983), 33.

7. See Robert Irwin, *The Arabian Nights: A Companion* (New York: Tauris Parke Paperbacks, 2004), 19.

8. See Suzanne Jill Levine, "Jorge Luis Borges and the Translators of the *Nights*," *Translation Review* 77–78 (2009): 17, 19. Her analysis is based on a close reading of Borges's 1935 essay "The Translators of *The 1001 Nights*" (originally, "Los traductores de las 1001 Noches"). In his own short stories, Borges frequently invoked themes, characters, and stylistic elements associated with the *Alf laylah wa-laylah* tales.

9. Martin Puchner, *The Written World: The Power of Stories to Shape People, History, Civilization* (New York: Random House, 2017), 121.

10. Since the text of Puchner's book contains neither in-text note callouts nor parenthetical citations, in the convention of mass-market titles, one must already know something about the origins of the *Nights* stories to realize that the lengthy passage that he quotes must inevitably come from a translation and must then go through the fur-

ther effort of referring to the notes section in the back of the book to ascertain which translation Puchner used.

11. An additional volume of *Nights* stories translated by Payne, titled *Alaeddin and the Enchanted Lamp; Zein ul Asnam and the King of the Jinn*, was published in 1885.

12. Thomas Wright, *The Life of Sir Richard Burton* (London: Everett and Co., 1906), 1:xii.

13. "Burton's Life Told Anew; Thomas Wright's Perfectly Impartial Biography of the Great Orientalist—His Relations with Payne," review of *The Life of Sir Richard Burton* by Thomas Wright, *New York Times*, June 23, 1906.

14. Wright, *The Life of Sir Richard Burton*, 2:106.

15. See Paulo Lemos Horta, *Marvellous Thieves: Secret Authors of the Arabian Nights* (Cambridge, MA: Harvard University Press, 2017), 240. Lengthy excerpts from Payne's translation were published in *The New Quarterly Magazine* in January 1879 (150–174) and April 1879 (377–401), embedded within a pair of unsigned essays—presumably also written by Payne—on the history of the *Alf laylah wa-laylah* stories and their European translations.

16. Given the enormous variation, since earliest times, among printed volumes purporting to include *Alf laylah wa-laylah* stories in both Arabic and European languages, few if any of the nineteenth-century European translations of these tales could be considered faithful to any Arabic source text(s). See Dwight F. Reynolds, "A Thousand and One Nights: A History of the Text and Its Reception," in *Arabic Literature in the Post-Classical Period*, ed. Roger Allen and D. S. Richards (New York: Cambridge University Press, 2006), 270–291.

17. See Horta, *Marvellous Thieves*, 219, and more generally the chapter of his book entitled "Stealing with Style."

18. The quotation is from Thomas J. Assad, *Three Victorian Travelers: Burton, Blunt, Doughty* (London: Routledge and Kegan Paul, 1964), 50. On Victorian views of bodies and sex, see Michel Foucault, *The History of Sexuality: Volume I—An Introduction*, trans. Robert Hurley (New York: Vintage, 1990), as well as Laura Ann Stoler's analysis of the pivotal role of non-European bodies in informing these views, in *Race and the Education of Desire: Foucault's* History of Sexuality *and the Colonial Order of Things* (Durham, NC: Duke University Press, 1995).

19. See Antoinette Burton, "Introduction: Archive Fever, Archive Stories," in *Archive Stories: Facts, Fictions, and the Writing of History*, ed. Antoinette Burton (Durham, NC: Duke University Press, 2005), 8. As far as I know, Antoinette Burton bears no familial relation to Sir Richard.

20. Carolyn Steedman, *Dust* (Manchester: Manchester University Press, 2001), 19.

21. Edward Rice, *Captain Sir Richard Francis Burton: The Secret Agent Who Made the Pilgrimage to Mecca, Discovered the Kama Sutra, and Brought the Arabian Nights to the West* (New York: Charles Scribner's Sons, 1990), 104.

22. Mary Lovell, for instance, is convinced that Burton was circumcised even though the "operation is not mentioned in any of . . . [his] published works" and "we do not know where the operation was performed." See Mary Lovell, *A Rage to Live*, 85. Fawn Brodie asserts simply that "all his friends with some knowledge of the area knew that Burton would also have to be circumcised." See Brodie, *The Devil Drives*, 88.

23. In this regard, Burton as he has often been portrayed by his biographers and in fictional characterizations resembles an earlier T. E. Lawrence, the British diplomat personified by Peter O'Toole in the 1962 film *Lawrence of Arabia*, whose "ability,

and . . . desire, to become the Other," in Steven Caton's words, led him to adopt Arab dress and ultimately to sympathize with the cause of Arab independence over British colonial claims in the Middle East in the aftermath of World War I. See Steven C. Caton, *Lawrence of Arabia: A Film's Anthropology* (Berkeley: University of California Press, 1999), 161.

24. Edward W. Said, *Orientalism* (New York: Vintage Books, 1994), 195–196.

25. Assad, *Three Victorian Travelers*, 50; Kwame Anthony Appiah, *Cosmopolitanism: Ethics in a World of Strangers* (New York: Norton, 2006), 4–5.

26. For example, in *Personal Narrative of a Pilgrimage to El Medinah and Meccah* (1855–1856)—Burton's account of traveling to the holy cities of Islam in the guise of a Muslim pilgrim—he recounts passing himself off as "an Indo-British subject named Abdullah," a doctor whose trademarks include "much unclean dressing and an unlimited expenditure of broken English" (19), and whom Burton plays as an abject personage who, while en route by boat from Alexandria to Cairo, "squatted apart, smoking perpetually, with occasional interruptions to say his prayers and to tell his beads upon the mighty rosary, [and who] . . . drank the muddy water of the canal out of a leathern bucket, and . . . munched his bread and garlic with a desperate sanctimoniousness" (32). See Richard F. Burton, *Personal Narrative of a Pilgrimage to El Medinah and Meccah*, 2nd ed., vol. 1 (London: Longman, Brown, Green, Longmans, and Roberts, 1857).

27. Wright, *Life of Sir Richard Burton*, 1:225.

28. Ibid., 1:104.

29. Said, *Orientalism*, 195.

30. Horta, *Marvellous Thieves*, 263.

31. I reviewed Burton's personal copies of the Bulaq, Calcutta I, and Breslau editions of *Alf laylah wa-laylah*, listed in the Huntington Library's catalog under the reference numbers RB 634492, RB 634514, and RB 634491, respectively.

32. See Horta, *Marvellous Thieves*, 244.

33. See Burton's annotations in the volumes listed in the Huntington Library's catalog as RB 634495 (Scott's *Nights*, especially vol. 6), RB 634496 (Lane's *Nights*), and RB 634503 (Payne's *Alaeddin*); RB 634381, an Arabic grammar textbook penned by none other than Aḥmad Fāris al-Shidyāq; and RB 634076 and RB 634080 (Burton's personal copies of his own *Nights* and its supplemental volumes).

34. See Burton's notes on the title-page verso in F. Steingass, *The Student's Arabic-English Dictionary: Companion Volume to the Author's English-Arabic Dictionary*, RB 634401, Huntington Library, San Marino, CA. The definitions of these Arabic terms are given on pages 125, 137, 228, 235, and 464 of the dictionary, respectively.

35. Rana Kabbani, *Imperial Fictions: Europe's Myths of Orient* (London: Saqi, 2008), 100.

36. Wright takes pains in his biography of Burton to insist that the famed linguist would have been "quite capable of translating the *Nights* without drawing upon the work of another," framing Burton's decision to plagiarize from Payne as an error in judgment rather than as an admission of his inability to do the work himself. See Wright, *Life of Sir Richard Burton*, 2:116.

37. Saree Makdisi and Felicity Nussbaum, "Introduction," in *The Arabian Nights in Historical Context: Between East and West*, ed. Saree Makdisi and Felicity Nussbaum (New York: Oxford University Press, 2008), 1. Muhsin Mahdi locates the probable origins of the text known as *Alf laylah wa-laylah* "at a midpoint between the ninth century when Arab authors first report on the *Nights* and the nineteenth century when

all the four first editions of the Arabic *Nights* were produced." In Mahdi's estimation, the surviving Arabic manuscript that comes closest to reproducing "the original core of the work" dates to the fourteenth century. See Muhsin Mahdi, "Introduction," in *The Thousand and One Nights (Alf Layla wa-Layla): From the Earliest Known Sources*, ed. Muhsin Mahdi (Leiden: Brill, 1994), 3:8.

38. Wright, *Life of Sir Richard Burton*, 2:52–53.

39. Richard F. Burton, "The Arabian Nights," *The Atheneaum*, November 26, 1881, 703. Although Burton claimed here to have begun his translation in collaboration with the Arabist John Frederick Steinhaeuser before the latter's untimely death in 1866—a story that he would repeat in his foreword to volume 1 of the *Nights*—scholars concur that this story is almost undoubtedly false. See, e.g., Horta, *Marvellous Thieves*, 240; Irwin, *Arabian Nights*, 29; Wright, *Life of Sir Richard Burton*, vol. 2, 30–31.

40. Burton's biographers offer slightly different versions of this story: see Lovell, *A Rage to Live*, 662; Rice, *Captain Sir Richard Francis Burton*, 453; Wright, *Life of Sir Richard Burton*, 2:31, 33–35.

41. Excepting the first volume of Payne's *Nights*, which was already about to go to press at the time of the two men's first correspondence. See Richard Francis Burton letter to John Payne (#2), n.d. 1882, Sir Richard Francis Burton Papers, Huntington Library, San Marino, CA, RFB 313, Box 26.

42. Richard Francis Burton letter to John Payne (#12), 21 October 1882, Sir Richard Francis Burton Papers, Huntington Library, San Marino, CA, RFB 313, Box 26.

43. Richard Francis Burton letter to John Payne (#26), 12 May 1884, Sir Richard Francis Burton Papers, Huntington Library, San Marino, CA, RFB 313, Box 26.

44. Richard Francis Burton letter to John Payne (#28), 20 June 1884, Sir Richard Francis Burton Papers, Huntington Library, San Marino, CA, RFB 313, Box 26.

45. Richard Francis Burton letter to John Payne (#21), 1 October 1883, Sir Richard Francis Burton Papers, Huntington Library, San Marino, CA, RFB 313, Box 26.

46. Richard F. Burton, *A Plain and Literal Translation of the Arabian Nights' Entertainments: Now Entituled The Book of the Thousand Nights and a Night* (London: The Burton Club, n.d.), 1:xxi.

47. Brandon LaBelle, *Lexicon of the Mouth: Poetics and Politics of Voice and the Oral Imaginary* (New York: Bloomsbury, 2014), 4.

48. Ibid., 104.

49. Mladen Dolar, *A Voice and Nothing More* (Cambridge, MA: MIT Press, 2006), 15.

50. See Ferial Ghazoul, *Nocturnal Poetics:* The Arabian Nights *in Comparative Context* (Cairo: American University in Cairo Press, 1996), 153. On the oral transmission of the stories in Arabic, see also Husain Haddawy, "Introduction," in *The Arabian Nights*, trans. Husain Haddawy (New York: Norton, 1990), xii, xiv.

51. Muhsin J. al-Musawi, *The Islamic Context of* The Thousand and One Nights (New York: Columbia University Press, 2009), 197.

52. Jorge Luis Borges, "The Translators of *The Thousand and One Nights*," trans. Esther Allen, in *The Translation Studies Reader*, 3rd ed., ed. Lawrence Venuti (New York: Routledge, 2012), 99.

53. Lawrence Venuti, *The Translator's Invisibility: A History of Translation*, 3rd ed. (New York: Routledge, 2018), 269.

54. Tarek Shamma, "The Exotic Dimension of Foreignizing Strategies: Burton's Translation of the Arabian Nights," *The Translator* 11, no. 1 (2005): 61.

55. Haun Saussy, *The Ethnography of Rhythm: Orality and Its Technologies* (New York: Fordham University Press), 2016), 107.

56. See Sir Richard Francis Burton Papers, Huntington Library, San Marino, CA, RFB 105, Box 20.

57. See Richard Francis Burton, *Supplemental Nights to the Book of the Thousand Nights and a Night with Notes Anthropological and Explanatory* (London: The Burton Club, n.d.), 2:269–277; and John Payne, *Tales from the Arabic: Of the Breslau and Calcutta (1814–18) Editions of the Book of the Thousand Nights and One Night Not Occurring in the Other Printed Texts of the Work, Now First Done into English by John Payne* (London: n.p., 1901), 3:159–170.

58. See Quentin Keynes letter to Fawn Brodie, 9 June 1966, Sir Richard Francis Burton Papers, Huntington Library, San Marino, CA, Box 52 (10).

59. In this regard, I disagree with Horta's conclusion that "the discordant elements of his [Burton's] translation . . . particularly the use of assonance, alliteration, and rhyming prose" reflect "a generic attempt to 'Arabize' rather than a real engagement with the language of the original." See Horta, *Marvellous Thieves*, 246–247.

60. John Payne, *The Book of the Thousand Nights and One Night: Now First Completely Done into English Prose and Verse, from the Original Arabic* (London: n.p., 1901), 1:1–2.

61. Burton, *The Book of the Thousand Nights*, 1:2.

62. See Jaakko Hämeen-Anttila, "Adab a) Arabic, early developments," in *Encyclopaedia of Islam, THREE*, ed. Kate Fleet et al. (Leiden: Brill, 2014), https://referenceworks.brillonline.com/entries/encyclopaedia-of-islam-3/adab-a-arabic-early-developments-COM_24178.

63. *Alf laylah wa-laylah*, 2nd ed., ed. Muḥammad Qiṭṭah al-ʿAdawī (Bulaq: Maṭbaʿat ʿAbd al-Raḥmān Rushdī, 1279 [1862]), 1:2.

64. 'Abdallah Ibrahim, "The Role of the Pre-Modern: The Generic Characteristics of the *Band*," in *Arabic Literature in the Post-Classical Period*, ed. Roger Allen and D. S. Richards (New York: Cambridge University Press, 2006), 92.

65. Adonis, *An Introduction to Arab Poetics*, trans. Catherine Cobham (London: Saqi Books, 1990), 17.

66. Mia Gerhardt, *The Art of Story-Telling: A Literary Study of the Thousand and One Nights* (Leiden: E. J. Brill, 1963), 46.

67. See Theodore Preston, "Introduction," in *Makamat; or, Rhetorical Anecdotes of Al Hariri of Basra*, trans. Theodore Preston (London: J. Deighton, 1850), 2.

68. Payne, *The Book of the Thousand Nights*, 9:383.

69. Burton, *The Book of the Thousand Nights*, 1:xiv.

70. Ibid., 10:255.

71. Michael Cooperson, "Note on the Translation," in Al-Ḥarīrī, *Impostures*, trans. Michael Cooperson (New York: New York University Press, 2020), xxxix– xli; emphasis original.

72. *Al-Qur'ān: A Contemporary Translation*, trans. Ahmed Ali (Princeton, NJ: Princeton University Press, 1993), Q 1.1–3, 11.

73. "Perhaps the most notable way in which the Qur'an functions in Muslim religious life is in the five required daily ritual prayers. Since each of the five daily prayers consists of a different number of cycles or units of prostration (two at dawn, four at noon, four in the afternoon, three at sunset, and four in the evening), there are in all

seventeen daily cycles of prayer, and in each of them one must recite the first sura of the Qur'an (al-Fatiha, 'The Opening')." See Carl W. Ernst, *How to Read the Qur'an: A New Guide, with Select Translations* (Chapel Hill, NC: University of North Carolina Press, 2011), 59.

74. Saussy, *Ethnography of Rhythm*, 32.

75. Tarek Shamma, *Translation and the Manipulation of Difference: Arabic Literature in Nineteenth-Century England* (Manchester: St. Jerome Publishing, 2009), 65–66. The passage quoted here appears in Burton, *The Book of the Thousand Nights*, 1:10–11. Cf. Payne's "a damsel slender of form and dazzlingly beautiful, as she were a shining sun," in Payne, *The Book of the Thousand Nights*, 1:5.

76. Payne, *The Book of the Thousand Nights*, 1:viii.

77. In other Arabic editions of *Alf laylah wa-laylah*, this story is titled variously "Ḥikāyat al-ḥammāl wa-al-thalāth banāt," "Ḥikāyat al-ḥammāl wa-al-ṣabāyā al-thalāth," or "Qiṣṣat al-ḥammāl wa-al-ṣabāyā al-thalāth."

78. Payne, *The Book of the Thousand Nights*, 1:76–77.

79. Burton, *The Book of the Thousand Nights*, 1:90.

80. Ghazoul, *Nocturnal Poetics*, 90.

81. *Alf laylah wa-laylah*, 1:37.

82. Referring more generally to a gap or opening, *farj* is deployed numerous times as a designation for female genitalia in, for example, Aḥmad al-Tīfāshī's early thirteenth-century erotic treatise *Nuzhat al-albāb fī-mā lā yūjad fī kitāb*, ed. Jamāl Jumʿah (London: Riyāḍ al-Rayyis, 1992). In 2021, a Google search returned primarily pornographic results for *kuss*, with a lesser quantity of the same for *farj* and for *zunbūr* when it was paired with the standard Arabic word for woman (*marʾah*). *Raḥim* turned up mostly anatomical diagrams and medical information.

83. Gordon Williams, *Shakespeare's Sexual Language: A Glossary* (London: Continuum, 1997), 77, 143.

84. Jonathon Green, *Cassell's Dictionary of Slang*, 2nd ed. (London: Weidenfeld and Nicolson, 2005), 248; Geoffrey Hughes, *An Encyclopedia of Swearing: The Social History of Oaths, Profanity, Foul Language, and Ethnic Slurs in the English-Speaking World* (Armonk, NY: M. E. Sharpe, 2006), 112, 405.

85. Elliott Colla, "The Porter and Portability: Figure and Narrative in the *Nights*," in *Scheherazade's Children: Global Encounters with the Arabian Nights*, ed. Philip F. Kennedy and Marina Warner (New York: NYU Press, 2013), 97.

86. In this regard, Kabbani speculates that because the Arabic stories "were originally recounted to an all-male audience desiring bawdy entertainment . . . [they] were purposefully crude." See Kabbani, *Imperial Fictions*, 86.

87. Sahar Amer, *Crossing Borders: Love between Women in Medieval French and Arabic Literatures* (Philadelphia: University of Pennsylvania Press, 2008), 25.

88. On the financial windfall that the publication of the *Nights* brought to Burton in the final decade of his life, see Wright, *Life of Sir Richard Burton*, 2:85.

89. Burton, *The Book of the Thousand Nights*, 1:viii.

90. Shamma, *Translation and the Manipulation of Difference*, 62.

91. Robyn Creswell, *City of Beginnings: Poetic Modernism in Beirut* (Princeton, NJ: Princeton University Press, 2019), 124.

92. A. J. Racy, *Making Music in the Arab World: The Culture and Artistry of Ṭarab* (New York: Cambridge University Press, 2004), 78–80.

93. Adonis, *Introduction to Arab Poetics*, 27.

94. George Sawa, *Music Performance Practice in the Early ʿAbbāsid Era: 132–320 AH / 750–932 AD*, 2nd ed. (Ottawa: The Institute of Mediaeval Music, 2004), 192–193.

95. Jonathan H. Shannon, "Emotion, Performance, and Temporality in Arab Music: Reflections on Tarab," *Cultural Anthropology* 18, no. 1 (2003): 72, 74.

96. "The Arabian Nights," *The Edinburgh Review* 335, July 1886, 178–179.

97. "Pantagruelism or Pornography?," *Pall Mall Gazette*, September 14, 1885, 2–3.

98. Dane Kennedy, *The Highly Civilized Man: Richard Burton and the Victorian World* (Cambridge, MA: Harvard University Press, 2005), 225.

99. See Lovell, *A Rage to Live*, 621–622.

100. Judith Walkowitz, *City of Dreadful Delight: Narratives of Sexual Danger in Late-Victorian London* (Chicago: University of Chicago Press, 1992), 123.

101. Ellen Bayuk Rosenman, *Unauthorized Pleasures: Accounts of Victorian Erotic Experience* (Ithaca, NY: Cornell University Press, 2003), 22.

102. Rosenman, *Unauthorized Pleasures*, 175.

103. Karen Moukheiber, "Gendering Emotions: *Ṭarab*, Women and Musical Performance in Three Biographical Narratives from 'The Book of Songs,'" *Cultural History* 8, no. 2 (2019): 167.

104. Brian Massumi, *Parables for the Virtual: Movement, Affect, Sensation* (Durham, NC: Duke University Press, 2002), 5.

105. See Wright, *Life of Sir Richard Burton*, 2:118.

106. "The Arabian Nights," *The Edinburgh Review*, 181.

107. Nicholas Dames, *The Physiology of the Novel: Reading, Neural Science, and the Form of Victorian Fiction* (New York: Oxford University Press, 2007), 8.

108. Benjamin Morgan, "Critical Empathy: Vernon Lee's Aesthetics and the Origins of Close Reading," *Victorian Studies* 55, no. 1 (2012): 31, 34.

109. "Multiple News Items," *The Standard*, September 12, 1885, 5.

110. Roland Barthes, *Le plaisir du texte* (Paris: Éditions du Seuil, 1973), 51, 25.

111. "The Arabian Nights," *The Liverpool Mercury*, March 26, 1887, 7.

112. Farwell, *Burton*, 366.

113. Kabbani, *Imperial Fictions*, 94.

114. See Norman Penzer, *An Annotated Bibliography of Sir Richard Francis Burton* (London: A. M. Philpot, 1923), 316–317.

115. See Brodie, *The Devil Drives*, 342.

116. Tarek El-Ariss, "Fiction of Scandal," *Journal of Arabic Literature* 43 (2012): 520.

117. Wright, *Life of Sir Richard Burton*, 1:xii.

118. Gregory Seigworth and Melissa Gregg, "An Inventory of Shimmers," in *The Affect Theory Reader*, ed. Melissa Gregg and Gregory J. Seigworth (Durham, NC: Duke University Press, 2010), 2.

119. Harold Bloom, *The Anxiety of Influence: A Theory of Poetry*, 2nd ed. (New York: Oxford University Press, 1997), xxvii.

120. Jacques Derrida, *The Post Card: From Socrates to Freud and Beyond*, trans. Alan Bass (Chicago: University of Chicago Press, 1987), 266.

121. Ibid., 289, 293.

122. *Alf laylah wa-laylah*, 1:39.

123. Ibid.

3. Ethics of the *Muthannā*: Caring for the Other in a Mother Tongue

1. Lawrence Venuti, *The Translator's Invisibility: A History of Translation* (New York: Routledge, 1995), 311.

2. Susan Bassnett, "When Is a Translation Not a Translation?," in *Constructing Cultures: Essays on Literary Translation*, ed. Susan Bassnett and André Lefevere (Clevedon, UK: Multilingual Matters, 1998), 25–26.

3. See Brian Massumi, *Parables for the Virtual: Movement, Affect, Sensation* (Durham, NC: Duke University Press, 2002), 59.

4. Richard Shusterman, *Thinking through the Body: Essays in Somaesthetics* (New York: Cambridge University Press, 2012), 47.

5. Massumi, *Parables for the Virtual*, 14.

6. Venuti, *The Translator's Invisibility*, 311.

7. See Gregory Rabassa, *If This Be Treason: Translation and Its Dyscontents* (New York: New Directions, 2005), 10.

8. "In this sense, the function of an author is to characterize the existence, circulation, and operation of certain discourses within a society." See Michel Foucault, "What Is an Author?," in *Language, Counter-memory, Practice: Selected Essays and Interviews*, ed. Donald F. Bouchard, trans. Donald F. Bouchard and Sherry Simon (Ithaca, NY: Cornell University Press, 1977), 124. Venuti at times verges on endorsing this definition of a translator in *The Translator's Invisibility*.

9. See Douglas Robinson, *Who Translates? Translator Subjectivities Beyond Reason* (Albany: State University of New York Press, 2001), 2–3.

10. Mark Polizzotti, *Sympathy for the Traitor: A Translation Manifesto* (Cambridge, MA: MIT Press, 2018), 12.

11. Douglas Robinson, *The Translator's Turn* (Baltimore, MD: Johns Hopkins University Press, 1991), 21–22.

12. Ibid., 22.

13. See Shusterman, *Thinking through the Body*, 27.

14. Ibid., 31.

15. Robinson, *The Translator's Turn*, 200–201.

16. Abī ʿUthmān ʿAmr ibn Baḥr al-Jāḥiẓ, *al-Bayān wa-al-tabyīn*, ed. ʿAbd al-Salām Muḥammad Hārūn (Cairo: Maktabat al-Khānjī, 1960), 1:368.

17. Emmanuel Levinas, *Ethics and Infinity: Conversations with Philippe Nemo*, trans. Richard A. Cohen (Pittsburgh, PA: Duquesne University Press, 1985), 85–86. I offer this understanding of the Levinasian other contra those critics who view it as a theoretical rather than corporeal figure, an abstract manifestation of pure and unbridled alterity, such as Alain Badiou, who ascribes to Levinas's other a quasi-religious quality of difference that "transcends mere finite experience." See Alain Badiou, *Ethics: An Essay on the Understanding of Evil*, trans. Peter Hallward (London: Verso, 2001), 22.

18. Cathryn Vasseleu, *Textures of Light: Vision and Touch in Irigaray, Levinas and Merleau Ponty* (New York: Routledge, 1998), 98.

19. The novel has received modest acclaim in both languages: *Līmbū Bayrūt*'s initial print run was supported by a grant from the Arab Fund for Arts and Culture (AFAC), while my English translation was longlisted for the 2017 PEN Translation Prize in the United States and shortlisted for the 2017 Saif Ghobash Banipal Prize for Arabic Literary Translation in the United Kingdom.

20. See Shusterman, *Thinking through the Body*, 5.

21. Polizzotti, *Sympathy for the Traitor*, 98.

22. See, for example, Spivak's explanation that she chose to draw upon "Indian material" to support her arguments in this book because "I was born in India and received my primary, secondary, and tertiary education there, including two years of graduate work." Gayatri Chakravorty Spivak, *A Critique of Postcolonial Reason: Toward a History of the Vanishing Present* (Cambridge, MA: Harvard University Press, 1999), 209.

23. See Henry Staten, "Tracking the 'Native Informant': Cultural Translation as the Horizon of Literary Translation," in *Nation, Language, and the Ethics of Translation*, ed. Sandra Bermann and Michael Wood (Princeton, NJ: Princeton University Press, 2005), 111.

24. Venuti, *The Translator's Invisibility*, ix.

25. See psychoanalyst Christopher Bollas's account of treating patients whose affects he experienced as though they were his own, as quoted in Teresa Brennan, *The Transmission of Affect* (Ithaca, NY: Cornell University Press, 2004), 28.

26. Sara Ahmed, "Happy Objects," in *The Affect Theory Reader*, ed. Melissa Gregg and Gregory Seigworth (Durham, NC: Duke University Press, 2010), 32.

27. Judith Butler, *The Force of Nonviolence: An Ethico-Political Bind* (New York: Verso, 2020), 16.

28. Barbara Johnson, *Mother Tongues: Sexuality, Trials, Motherhood, Translation* (Cambridge, MA: Harvard University Press, 2003), 34.

29. Ibid., 66.

30. The Future Movement is a powerful political faction led by Saʿd al-Ḥarīrī (b. 1970), the son of Lebanon's assassinated prime minister Rafīq al-Ḥarīrī (1944–2005). The younger al-Ḥarīrī served as Lebanon's prime minister himself from 2009 to 2011 and 2016 to 2020.

31. Hilāl Shūmān, *Līmbū Bayrūt* (Beirut: Dār al-Tanwīr, 2013), 11.

32. Ibid., 11.

33. Lauren Berlant, *Cruel Optimism* (Durham, NC: Duke University Press, 2011), 116.

34. For a cogent explanation of the dual in Arabic, see Karin Ryding, *A Reference Grammar of Modern Standard Arabic* (Cambridge: Cambridge University Press, 2005), 129–131.

35. Kristen Brustad, *The Syntax of Spoken Arabic: A Comparative Study of Moroccan, Egyptian, Syrian, and Kuwaiti Dialects* (Washington, DC: Georgetown University Press, 2000), 87. Whether the dual has been "lost" in the modern dialects or was never fully attested among Arabic speakers at any point in history, and whether its somewhat vestigial formations in today's dialects derive from an older Arabic "koine" that developed alongside classical Arabic in the early era of Islam as a lingua franca enabling communication among the geographically dispersed populations of the Muslim world (as Charles Ferguson argues in "The Arabic Koine," *Language* 35, no. 4 [1959], 620–621), remains a matter of debate among scholars of the language.

36. See Brustad, *Syntax of Spoken Arabic*, 45; Haim Blanc, "Dual and Pseudo-Dual in the Arabic Dialects," *Language* 46, no. 1 (1970): 43. I have altered Blanc's transcription slightly to conform to modern conventions for transliterating Arabic.

37. Blanc, "Dual and Pseudo-Dual," 43.

38. These modern English words are all thought to be derived from the Proto-Indo-European word designating the number two, reconstructed as **dwoh*, which as the language evolved "was progressively extended by suffixes to indicate 'duality,' i.e. a dual

ending, and markers to indicate gender distinctions as it was declined," thus supplying the language with at least a partially comprehensive dual system. See J. P. Mallory and D. Q. Adams, *The Oxford Introduction to Proto-Indo-European and the Proto-Indo-European World* (New York: Oxford University Press, 2006), 310.

39. Roman Jakobson, "On Linguistic Aspects of Translation," in *The Translation Studies Reader*, 3rd ed., ed. Lawrence Venuti (New York: Routledge, 2012), 128–129; emphasis added. For Jakobson, the reverse situation of translating "into a language provided with a certain grammatical category from a language devoid of such a category" presents the greater problem for the translator, as when translating the English "She has brothers" into a language that differentiates dual from plural, in which case, he writes, "we are compelled [as translators] either to make our own choice between two statements 'She has two brothers'—'She has more than two' or to leave the decision to the listener and say: 'She has either two or more than two brothers'" (129).

40. Jareer Abu-Haidar, "'Qifā nabki': The Dual Form of Address in Arabic Poetry in a New Light," *Journal of Arabic Literature* 19, no. 1 (1988): 42.

41. Ibid., 43, 47.

42. *Al-Qur'ān: A Contemporary Translation*, trans. Ahmed Ali (Princeton, NJ: Princeton University Press, 1993), Q 55.13, 461. In Arabic:

فَبِأَيِّ ءَالَآءِ رَبِّكُمَا تُكَذِّبَانِ {13}

43. Michael Sells, *Approaching the Qur'an: The Early Revelations* (Ashland, OR: White Cloud Press, 1999), 146.

44.

وَيَا آدَمُ اسْكُنْ أَنْتَ وَزَوْجُكَ الْجَنَّةَ فَكُلَا مِنْ حَيْثُ شِئْتُمَا وَلَا تَقْرَبَا هَٰذِهِ الشَّجَرَةَ فَتَكُونَا مِنَ الظَّالِمِينَ {19}
فَوَسْوَسَ لَهُمَا الشَّيْطَانُ لِيُبْدِيَ لَهُمَا مَا وُورِيَ عَنْهُمَا مِنْ سَوْآتِهِمَا وَقَالَ مَا نَهَاكُمَا رَبُّكُمَا عَنْ هَٰذِهِ الشَّجَرَةِ إِلَّا أَنْ
تَكُونَا مَلَكَيْنِ أَوْ تَكُونَا مِنَ الْخَالِدِينَ {20}

45. *Al-Qur'ān*, Q 7.19–20, 134; translation slightly modified to approximate the syntax of the Arabic lines more closely. There are thirteen dual-inflected words in these two verses and an additional fifteen in verses 21–22.

46. Amina Wadud, *Qur'an and Woman: Rereading the Sacred Text from a Woman's Perspective* (New York: Oxford University Press, 1999), 25.

47. Hoda El Shakry, *The Literary Qur'an: Narrative Ethics in the Maghreb* (New York: Fordham University Press, 2020), 3.

48. Kees Versteegh, "The Development of Argumentation in Arabic Grammar: The Declension of the Dual and the Plural," *Zeitschrift für Arabische Linguistik* 15 (1985): 154.

49. Mel Y. Chen, *Animacies: Biopolitics, Racial Mattering, and Queer Affect* (Durham, NC: Duke University Press, 2012), 24.

50. Hilal Chouman, *Limbo Beirut*, trans. Anna Ziajka Stanton (Austin: Center for Middle Eastern Studies, University of Texas at Austin, 2016), 3.

51. Shūmān, *Līmbū Bayrūt*, 11.

52. Ibid.

53. Ibid.

54. Philip Lewis, "The Measure of Translation Effects," in Venuti, *The Translation Studies Reader*, 227.

55. Shūmān, *Līmbū Bayrūt*, 90; Chouman, *Limbo Beirut*, 82.

56. Aurelia Plath quoted in Johnson, *Mother Tongues*, 89.

57. Shūmān, *Līmbū Bayrūt*, 92.

58. Ibid., 97.

59. See *Hans Wehr Dictionary of Modern Written Arabic*, 4th ed., ed. J. Milton Cowan (Ithaca, NY: Spoken Language Services, 1994), 1299; F. Steingass, *The Student's Arabic-English Dictionary: Companion Volume to the Author's English-Arabic Dictionary* (London: Crosby Lockwood and Son, 1884), 1241.

60. Susan Bassnett, *Translation Studies*, 4th ed. (New York: Routledge, 2014), 25–26.

61. M. M. Bakhtin, "Discourse in the Novel," in *The Dialogic Imagination: Four Essays by M. M. Bakhtin*, ed. Michael Holquist, trans. Caryl Emerson and Michael Holquist (Austin: University of Texas Press, 1981), 276.

62. Shūmān, *Līmbū Bayrūt*, 109–110.

63. Ibid., 121.

64. See G. R. Driver, *Semitic Writing: From Pictogram to Alphabet*, rev. ed. (London: Oxford University Press, 1976), 156–171; and John F. Healey, "The Early Alphabet," in *Reading the Past: Ancient Writing from Cuneiform to the Alphabet* (Berkeley: University of California Press, 1990), 210–213.

65. Driver, *Semitic Writing*, 157–158.

66. W. J. T. Mitchell, *Picture Theory: Essays on Verbal and Visual Representation* (Chicago: University of Chicago Press, 1994), 113.

67. Sybille Krämer, "Writing, Notational Iconicity, Calculus: On Writing as a Cultural Technique," trans. Anita McChesney, *MLN* 118 (2003): 518–519.

68. The dot underneath the *bā'* was introduced at a somewhat later stage in the history of the Arabic alphabet to distinguish it from other letters with the same basic shape. See Healey, "The Early Alphabet," 251–253. For a summary overview of the development of the modern Arabic letters from these earlier alphabets, see John F. Healey and G. Rex Smith, *A Brief Introduction to the Arabic Alphabet: Its Origins and Various Forms* (London: Saqi, 2009), 51–72.

69. See Healey and Smith, *A Brief Introduction*, 29, 33–36, 49.

70. Muḥammad ibn Mukarram ibn Manẓūr, *Lisān al-ʿArab* (Beirut: Dār Ṣādir, 2005), 15:323.

71. *Al-Qur'ān*, Q 28.7, 329; translation slightly modified.

72. Tablets discovered among the ruins of the prehistoric Syrian port city of Ugarit describe a seasonal conflict between Baal, the god of rain and wind, and the sea deity Yamm (sometimes spelled "Yam"). As a result of their fight, Yamm dies and Baal ascends to his throne, thus bringing an end to the fierce coastal storms of winter and restoring fertility to the land with the rains of spring. See J. C. L. Gibson, *Canaanite Myths and Legends*, 2nd ed. (London: T & T Clark International, 2004), 2–8.

73. Chouman, *Limbo Beirut*, 83, 91.

74. Ibid., 100.

75. Ibid., 111.

76. Johnson, *Mother Tongues*, 160–161. See Sylvia Plath, *The Bell Jar* (New York: Harper & Row, 1971), 102.

77. See Michel de Certeau, *The Practice of Everyday Life*, trans. Steven Rendall (Berkeley: University of California Press, 1984), 97–98.

78. For a critique of sectarianism as a conceptual framework for understanding the politics of the contemporary Middle East, see Ussama Makdisi, *The Culture of Sectarianism: Community, History, and Violence in Nineteenth-Century Ottoman Lebanon* (Berkeley: University of California Press, 2000).

79. Shūmān, *Līmbū Bayrūt*, 231; Chouman, *Limbo Beirut*, 214–215.

80. Berlant, *Cruel Optimism*, 262–263.

81. Ibid.

82. Shūmān, *Līmbū Bayrūt*, 232.

83. Chouman, *Limbo Beirut*, 216.

84. Butler, *The Force of Nonviolence*, 49–50.

85. Rachel Cusk, *A Life's Work: On Becoming a Mother* (New York: Picador, 2001), 70–71.

86. Julia Kristeva, "Stabat Mater," trans. Léon Roudiez, in *The Kristeva Reader*, ed. Toril Moi (New York: Columbia University Press, 1986), 178.

87. Sarah Ruhl, *100 Essays I Don't Have Time to Write: On Umbrellas and Sword Fights, Parades and Dogs, Fire Alarms, Children, and Theater* (New York: Farrar, Straus and Giroux, 2014), 3–4.

88. See Friedmann's discussion of writing the essays contained in *Things That Helped: On Postpartum Depression* (2017) in the *Literary Hub* roundtable "What It Means to Write about Motherhood, Part Two," October 25, 2018, https://lithub.com/what-it-means-to-write-about-motherhood-part-two/.

89. Butler, *The Force of Nonviolence*, 49.

90. Al-Jāḥiẓ, *al-Bayān wa-al-tabyīn*, 368.

91. Massumi, *Parables for the Virtual*, 57–58.

4. ʿ*Ajamī* Politics and Aesthetic Experience: Translating the Body in Pain

1. See "Theater of Operations: The Gulf Wars 1991–2011," https://www.moma.org/calendar/exhibitions/5084.

2. The artworks referred to here are Jamal Penjweny's *Saddam Is Here* (2010); Susan Meiselas's *Concrete blocks mark the mass grave in Koreme. Northern Iraq, Kurdistan* (1992), *Clothes found around exhumed bones mark unknown grave in Erbil cemetery. Northern Iraq, Kurdistan* (1992), and *Koreme, Northern Iraq, Kurdistan* (1992); Thomas Hirschhorn's *Touching Reality* (2012); and Hanaa Malallah's *She/He Has No Picture* (2019).

3. See Allen Feldman, "Violence and Vision: The Prosthetics and Aesthetics of Terror," *Public Culture* 10, no. 1 (1997): 56. The United States deployed its military to Iraq first in 1990 (under President George H. W. Bush) in response to Iraq's invasion of Kuwait, and again in 2003 (under President George W. Bush) under the pretense that Saddam Hussein's regime had played a role in the terrorist attacks of September 11, 2001. The second war officially concluded in 2011, but American troops have remained in Iraq ever since, initially to support the new postwar Iraqi government and more recently to conduct ongoing operations against the militant group known variously as ISIL, ISIS, the Islamic State, or, in Arabic, Daesh (al-Dawlah al-Islāmiyyah fī al-ʿIrāq wa-al-Shām).

4. These figures come respectively from the Associated Press (see Allegra Stratton, "2007 Is America's Deadliest Year in Iraq," *The Guardian*, December 31, 2007, https://www.theguardian.com/world/2007/dec/31/usa.iraq?CMP=share_btn_link) and the Iraq Body Count project, which maintains a public online database of violent civilian deaths in Iraq since the start of the 2003 U.S. invasion; the database is searchable by month, year, region of Iraq, and cause of death, and includes figures to the year 2022 (see https://www.iraqbodycount.org/database/).

5. Jean Baudrillard, "The Gulf War Did Not Take Place," in *The Gulf War Did Not Take Place*, trans. Paul Patton (Bloomington: Indiana University Press, 1995), 73–74.

Baudrillard first advanced this view of the war in a series of three essays published in the French newspaper *Libération* between January and March 1991, titled "La guerre du Golfe n'aura pas lieu" ("The Gulf War will not take place"), "La guerre du Golfe a-t-elle vraiment lieu?" ("The Gulf War: is it really taking place?"), and "La guerre du Golfe n'a pas eu lieu" ("The Gulf War did not take place").

6. Elizabeth Dauphinée, "The Politics of the Body in Pain: Reading the Ethics of Imagery," *Security Dialogue* 38, no. 2 (2007): 145. For an account of the abuses at Abu Ghraib, see Seymour M. Hersh, "Torture at Abu Ghraib," *The New Yorker*, May 10, 2004, 42–47.

7. See Jason Farago and Tim Arango, "These Artists Refuse to Forget the Wars in Iraq," review of *Theater of Operations: The Gulf Wars 1991–2011* at MoMA PS1, New York (November 3, 2019–March 1, 2020), *New York Times*, November 14, 2019, https://www.nytimes.com/2019/11/14/arts/design/iraq-wars-art-momaps1-review.html.

8. See Peter Schjeldahl, "Casualties,'" review of *Theater of Operations: The Gulf Wars 1991–2011* at MoMA PS1, New York (November 3, 2019–March 1, 2020), *The New Yorker*, December 2, 2019, 71.

9. Dauphinée, "Politics of the Body in Pain," 147.

10. Susan Sontag, "In Plato's Cave," in *On Photography* (New York: Penguin, 1977), 20.

11. See Jacques Rancière, *Dissensus: On Politics and Aesthetics*, trans. Steven Corcoran (New York: Bloomsbury Academic, 2015), 146.

12. Pierre Bourdieu, *Pascalian Meditations*, trans. Richard Nice (Stanford, CA: Stanford University Press, 2000), 134–135; emphasis original.

13. Brian Massumi, *Parables for the Virtual: Movement, Affect, Sensation* (Durham, NC: Duke University Press, 2002), 60.

14. Bourdieu, *Pascalian Meditations*, 142.

15. Talal Asad, *Formations of the Secular: Christianity, Islam, Modernity* (Stanford, CA: Stanford University Press, 2003), 84–85.

16. As visual culture theorist Mieke Bal has cautioned, it can be perilously "bad scholarship" to analyze works from multiple aesthetic media within a single theoretical framework; and yet, I am encouraged to do so here by her corollary allowance that there "are also many instances of good scholarship where the difference [between media] must be suspended, precisely in order to 'get at' the questions of representation the scholar wishes to address." See Mieke Bal, "The Commitment to Look," *Journal of Visual Culture* 4, no. 2 (2005): 148.

17. See Jenelle Troxell, "Torture, Terror, Digitality: A Conversation with Tony Cokes," *Afterimage* 43, no. 3 (2015): 22.

18. See Moustafa Bayoumi, "Disco Inferno," *The Nation*, December 8, 2005, https://www.thenation.com/article/archive/disco-inferno/.

19. Tarek El-Ariss, "Return of the Beast: From Pre-Islamic Ode to Contemporary Novel," *Journal of Arabic Literature* 47, nos. 1–2 (2016): 80.

20. As defined in Lawrence Venuti, *The Translator's Invisibility: A History of Translation*, 3rd ed. (New York: Routledge, 2018), 15–16.

21. Annette Damayanti Lienau, "Reframing Vernacular Culture on Arabic Fault Lines: Bamba, Senghor, and Sembene's Translingual Legacies in French West Africa," *PMLA* 130, no. 2 (2015): 420.

22. On the history of the Arabic script's adoption of diacritic dots to differentiate among letters, see John F. Healey, "The Early Alphabet," in *Reading the Past: Ancient*

Writing from Cuneiform to the Alphabet (Berkeley: University of California Press, 1990), 250; and John F. Healey and G. Rex Smith, *A Brief Introduction to the Arabic Alphabet: Its Origins and Various Forms* (London: Saqi, 2009), 78.

23. See ʿAbd al-ʿAzīz Maṭar, *Laḥn al-ʿāmmah fī ḍawʾ al-dirāsāt al-lughawiyyah al-ḥadīthah* (Cairo: al-Dār al-Qawmiyyah lil-Tibāʿah wa-al-Nashr, 1966), 19.

24. Wall placard for Hanaa Malallah, "She/He Has No Picture" (2019), *Theater of Operations: The Gulf Wars 1991–2011* at MoMA PS1, New York (November 3, 2019–March 1, 2020).

25. Al-Furāt is the Arabic name for the river known in English as the Euphrates, the waterway that, together with the Tigris, has enabled humans to flourish in the geographic vicinity of present-day Iraq since prehistoric times.

26. Ikram Masmoudi, *War and Occupation in Iraqi Fiction* (Edinburgh: Edinburgh University Press, 2015), 3–4.

27. Ibid., 20.

28. Sinān Anṭūn, *Iʿjām* (Beirut: Dār al-Ādāb, 2004), 14, 37, 91, 109.

29. A. F. L. Beeston, *The Arabic Language Today* (Washington, DC: Georgetown University Press, 2006), 15.

30. Ofra Bengio, *Saddam's Word: Political Discourse in Iraq* (New York: Oxford University Press, 1998), 9. For examples of Arabic terminology coopted by the Ba'athist state for its own purposes, see 12–16.

31. See Jacques Derrida, "Structure, Sign and Play in the Discourse of the Human Sciences," in *Writing and Difference*, trans. Alan Bass (Chicago: University of Chicago Press, 1978), 292.

32. Friederike Pannewick, "Dancing Letters: The Art of Subversion in Sinān Anṭūn's Novel *Iʿjām*," in *Conflicting Narratives: War, Trauma and Memory in Iraqi Culture*, ed. Stephan Milich, Friederike Pannewick, and Leslie Tramontini (Wiesbaden: Reichert Verlag, 2012), 71.

33. Ibid., 66.

34. Saad A. Albazei, review of *I'jaam: An Iraqi Rhapsody* by Sinan Antoon, trans. Rebecca C. Johnson and Sinan Antoon, *World Literature Today* 82, no. 6 (2008): 58.

35. Derrida, "Structure, Sign and Play," 292–293.

36. Elaine Scarry, *The Body in Pain: The Making and Unmaking of the World* (New York: Oxford University Press, 1985), 5.

37. See Gilles Deleuze and Félix Guattari, *A Thousand Plateaus: Capitalism and Schizophrenia*, trans. Brian Massumi (Minneapolis: University of Minnesota Press, 1987), 203.

38. Anṭūn, *Iʿjām*, 115–116.

39. Ibid., 38.

40. Ibid., 106.

41. See Emile Benveniste, "Subjectivity in Language," trans. Mary E. Meek, in *Critical Theory since 1965*, ed. Hazard Adams and Leroy Searle (Tallahassee: Florida State University Press, 1986), 729.

42. Achille Mbembe, "The Banality of Power and the Aesthetics of Vulgarity in the Postcolony," trans. Janet Roitman, *Public Culture* 4, no. 2 (1992): 11–12.

43. See Jacques Derrida, *Of Grammatology*, trans. Gayatri Chakravorty Spivak, rev. ed. (Baltimore, MD: Johns Hopkins University Press, 1997), 7.

44. Immanuel Kant, *Groundwork for the Metaphysics of Morals*, trans. and ed. Allen W. Wood (New Haven, CT: Yale University Press, 2002), 46.

45. Sinan Antoon, "Sinan Antoon: 'I think of myself as a global citizen,'" interview by Dina Omar, *The Electronic Intifada*, April 7, 2010, https://electronicintifada.net/content/sinan-antoon-i-think-myself-global-citizen/8760.

46. See the Iraq Body Count database at https://www.iraqbodycount.org/database/.

47. John M. Broder, "A Nation at War: The Casualties; U.S. Military Has No Count of Iraqi Dead in Fighting," *New York Times*, April 2, 2003, http://www.nytimes.com/2003/04/02/world/nation-war-casualties-us-military-has-no-count-iraqi-dead-fighting.html.

48. Sinan Antoon, *I'jaam: An Iraqi Rhapsody*, trans. Rebecca C. Johnson and Sinan Antoon (San Francisco: City Lights, 2007), 21–22.

49. Suzanne Keen, *Empathy and the Novel* (New York: Oxford University Press, 2007), 4.

50. Tarek El-Ariss, *Trials of Arab Modernity: Literary Affects and the New Political* (New York: Fordham University Press, 2013), 5.

51. Keen, *Empathy and the Novel*, 4.

52. Raymond Williams, *Marxism and Literature* (New York: Oxford University Press, 1977), 132.

53. State of the Union Address delivered by President George W. Bush to a nationally televised joint session of Congress on January 20, 2004, https://georgewbush-whitehouse.archives.gov/news/releases/2004/01/20040120-7.html.

54. See, for example, Rumsfeld's remarks to the Council on Foreign Relations on May 27, 2003, as quoted in Tom McCarthy, "Donald Rumsfeld Denies He Thought Democracy in Iraq Was 'Realistic' Goal," *The Guardian*, June 9, 2015, https://www.theguardian.com/us-news/2015/jun/09/donald-rumsfeld-iraq-war-democracy-contradiction: "'This much is clear: we have a stake in their success,' Rumsfeld said then, referring to the people of Iraq. 'For if Iraq—with its size, capabilities, resources and its history—is able to move to the path of representative democracy, however bumpy the road, then the impact in the region and the world could be dramatic.'" A video of the speech is archived at https://www.cfr.org/event/meeting-donald-h-rumsfeld.

55. Alain Badiou, *Ethics: An Essay on the Understanding of Evil*, trans. Peter Hallward (London: Verso, 2001), 10.

56. Ibid., 13.

57. Ibid., 32, 34.

58. See Elspeth Probyn, "Shame in the Habitus," *The Sociological Review* 52, no. 2 supplement (2004): 224.

59. Williams, *Marxism and Literature*, 133–134.

60. See Antoon, *I'jaam*, 3, 20, 28, 54.

61. See Wolfgang Iser, "The Repertoire," in Adams and Searle, *Critical Theory since 1965*, 367.

62. Sinan Antoon, "A Note about *I'jaam*," in *I'jaam: An Iraqi Rhapsody* by Sinan Antoon, trans. Rebecca C. Johnson and Sinan Antoon (San Francisco: City Lights, 2007).

63. See Antoon, *I'jaam*, 75.

64. Rancière, *Dissensus*, 165.

65. Drawing on Bourdieu's definition of habitus as well as that of the sociologist Marcel Mauss, Probyn proposes the notion of an affective habitus to underscore the

degree to which affect is experienced "as simultaneously social and physical." See Probyn, "Shame in the Habitus," 225, 235.

66. Teresa Brennan, *The Transmission of Affect* (Ithaca, NY: Cornell University Press, 2004), 13.

67. See Asad, *Formations of the Secular*, 68.

68. Rancière, *Dissensus*, 148.

69. Ibid., 156.

70. Fredric Jameson, "Third-World Literature in the Era of Multinational Capitalism," *Social Text* 15 (1986): 69. An early critique of the essentializing terms of Jameson's argument came from Aijaz Ahmad, who accused Jameson of having overlooked the heterogeneity of the Western canon as well as that of non-Western literary traditions. See Aijaz Ahmad, "Jameson's Rhetoric of Otherness and the 'National Allegory,'" *Social Text* 17 (1987): 3–25.

71. Mai Al-Nakib, "Arab Literature: Politics and Nothing But?," *World Literature Today* 90, no. 1 (2016): 30–31; emphasis original.

72. See Susan Salter Reynolds, review of *I'jaam: An Iraqi Rhapsody* by Sinan Antoon, trans. Rebecca C. Johnson and Sinan Antoon, *Los Angeles Times*, June 17, 2007, https://www.latimes.com/archives/la-xpm-2007-jun-17-bk-discoveries17-story.html; Emily Weinstein, "Letter Imperfect: Dreams from Prison in an Orwellian Iraqi Novel," review of *I'jaam: An Iraqi Rhapsody* by Sinan Antoon, trans. Rebecca C. Johnson and Sinan Antoon, *Village Voice*, June 13–19, 2007, 55; Sarah Chenoweth, review of *I'jaam: An Iraqi Rhapsody* by Sinan Antoon, trans. Rebecca C. Johnson and Sinan Antoon, *Counterpoise* 13, nos. 1/2 (2009): 61.

73. Al-Nakib, "Arab Literature," 31.

74. Masmoudi, *War and Occupation in Iraqi Fiction*, 1.

75. See Ann Marlowe, review of *I'jaam: An Iraqi Rhapsody* by Sinan Antoon, trans. Rebecca C. Johnson and Sinan Antoon, *San Francisco Chronicle*, August 30, 2007, https://www.sfgate.com/books/article/Outcast-I-jaam-offer-outsiders-looks-at-2506373.php.

76. Marilyn Booth, "'The Muslim Woman' as Celebrity Author and the Politics of Translating Arabic: Girls of Riyadh Go on the Road," *Journal of Middle East Women's Studies* 6 (2010): 154.

77. Claudia Roth Pierpont, "Found in Translation," *The New Yorker*, January 18, 2010, 76–77.

78. Ibid., 75–76.

79. See Jameson, "Third-World Literature," 69.

80. Booth, "The Muslim Woman," 151.

81. As an academic, Anṭūn's reputation rests largely on his association with the ezine *Jadaliyya*, a multilingual open-access online platform that publishes original scholarship and news features about the Middle East, which he helped to found in 2010 and where he remains today a principal editor.

82. Anṭūn has stridently disavowed the notion that his religious background should inform in any way his work as a scholar and public intellectual. See Sinan Antoon, "A Barbarian in Rome: Excerpts from a Diary," in *We Are Iraqis: Aesthetics and Politics in a Time of War*, ed. Nadje Al-Ali and Deborah Al-Najjar (Syracuse, NY: Syracuse University Press, 2013), 27; and Sinān Anṭūn, "Barbarī fī Rūmā," *Jadaliyya*, April 9, 2013, http://www.jadaliyya.com/pages/index/11129.

83. This description comes from the summary provided on *About Baghdad*'s now-defunct official website, at http://www.aboutbaghdad.com/. The film was codirected by Anṭūn along with Bassam Haddad, Maya Mikdashi, Suzy Salamy, and Adam Shapiro and distributed by InCounter Productions.

84. Antoon, "I think of myself as a global citizen"; Sinan Antoon, "Dead Poets Society," *The Nation*, May 26, 2003, 25; Sinan Antoon, "Iraq: 5 Years Later," *The Charlie Rose Show*, PBS, March 19, 2008, https://charlierose.com/videos/28940, 6:00.

85. Waïl S. Hassan, *Immigrant Narratives: Orientalism and Cultural Translation in Arab American and Arab British Literature* (New York: Oxford University Press, 2011), 29.

86. Rebecca Johnson collaborated with Anṭūn on the translation of *I'jām* while she was a graduate student at NYU. As of 2022, she was an associate professor of English at Northwestern University.

87. Susan Bassnett, "Rejoinder," *Orbis Litterarum* 68, no. 3 (2013): 288.

88. See, for example, Marilyn Booth's assessment of Rajā' al-Ṣāni''s role in co-translating her novel *Banāt al-Riyāḍ* (2005), published as *Girls of Riyadh* in 2007, with Booth herself, in Marilyn Booth, "Translator v. Author (2007): *Girls of Riyadh* Go to New York," *Translation Studies* 1, no. 2 (2008): 197–211; Michelle Hartman's examination of the part played by Ḥanān al-Shaykh in the translation of her memoir *Ḥikāyatī sharḥun yaṭūl* (2005) into English as *The Locust and the Bird* (2009), in Michelle Hartman, "'My Tale Is Too Long to Tell': *The Locust and the Bird* between South Lebanon and New York City," *Journal of Arabic Literature* 46, nos. 2–3 (2015): 168–192; and Diya Abdo's remarks on Laylā Abū Zayd's self-translation of her autobiography *Rujū' ilā al-ṭufūlah* (1993) as *Return to Childhood: The Memoir of a Modern Moroccan Woman* (1998), in Diya M. Abdo, "Textual Migration: Self-Translation and Translation of the Self in Leila Abouzeid's *Return to Childhood: The Memoir of a Modern Moroccan Woman* and *Ruju' 'Ila Al-Tufulah*," *Frontiers: A Journal of Women Studies* 30, no. 2 (2009): 1–42.

89. See Michael Boyden and Liesbeth De Bleeker, "Introduction," *Orbis Litterarum* 68, no. 3 (2013): 179–180.

90. In Hans Robert Jauss's definition, the "coherence of literature as an event is primarily mediated in the horizon of expectations of the literary experience of contemporary and later readers, critics, and authors." See Hans Robert Jauss, "Literary History as a Challenge to Literary Theory," in *Toward an Aesthetic of Reception*, trans. Timothy Bahti (Minneapolis: University of Minnesota Press, 1982), 22.

91. Haytham Bahoora, "Writing the Dismembered Nation: The Aesthetics of Horror in Iraqi Narratives of War," *The Arab Studies Journal* 23, no. 1 (2015): 186.

92. Ibid., 188, 194, 199.

93. Yasmeen Hanoosh, "Unnatural Narratives and Transgressing the Normative Discourses of Iraqi History: Translating Murtaḍā Gzār's *Al-Sayyid Aṣghar Akbar*," *Journal of Arabic Literature* 44 (2013): 146–148.

94. See Sinān Anṭūn, "al-Riwā'ī al-'Irāqī Sinān Anṭūn li-*Al-Ḥiwār Al-Mutamaddin*: Al-bunyah fī riwāyat *I'jām* dā'iriyyah tadākhuliyyah wa-lā ajwibah fī nihāyat al-maṭāf," interview by 'Adnān Ḥusayn Aḥmad, *Al-Ḥiwār Al-Mutamaddin*, August 6, 2005, http://www.ahewar.org/debat/show.art.asp?aid=42533&r=0.

95. Sinan Antoon, *The Corpse Washer*, trans. Sinan Antoon (New Haven, CT: Yale University Press, 2013), 144–145.

96. Ibid., 156.

97. These are *Yā Maryam* (2012), translated into English as *The Baghdad Eucharist* (2017) by Maia Tabet; and *Fihris* (2016), translated into English as *The Book of Collateral Damage* (2019) by Jonathan Wright.

98. Sinan Antoon, "Translation as Mourning," lecture, American University in Cairo, March 4, 2014, https://www.youtube.com/watch?v=f9ehd8nbFFY, 58:50–59:06. See also his discussion of taking "the easy way out" by relying on others to translate his later novels into English, in Sinan Antoon, "In 'The Book of Collateral Damage,' An Accounting of What Baghdad Lost," interview by Steve Inskeep, *Morning Edition*, NPR, July 9, 2019, https://www.npr.org/2019/07/09/739613519/in-the-book-of-collateral-damage-an-accounting-of-what-baghdad-lost.

99. See Anṭūn, "al-Riwāʾī al-ʿIrāqī."

100. See El-Ariss, "Return of the Beast," 65.

101. Sianne Ngai, *Ugly Feelings* (Cambridge, MA: Harvard University Press, 2005), 10–11.

102. Ibid., 26.

103. Badiou, *Ethics*, 42.

104. See Pierpont, "Found in Translation," 74.

Conclusion: Beyond Untranslatability

1. Roger Allen, review of *Modern Arabic Short Stories* and *Egyptian Short Stories*, trans. and ed. Denys Johnson-Davies, *Al-ʿArabiyya* 12 (1979): 89. On Johnson-Davies's critical role in promoting Ṣāliḥ's work to Anglophone audiences, see Elizabeth Holt, "Al-Ṭayyib Ṣāliḥ's *Season of Migration to the North*, the CIA, and the Cultural Cold War after Bandung," *Research in African Literatures* 50, no. 3 (2019): 78–79.

2. Denys Johnson-Davies and Ferial Ghazoul, "On Translating Arabic Literature: An Interview with Denys Johnson-Davies," *Alif: Journal of Comparative Poetics* 3 (1983): 85–86.

3. David Damrosch, *What Is World Literature?* (Princeton, NJ: Princeton University Press, 2003), 6; emphasis original.

4. Haun Saussy, "Exquisite Cadavers Stitched from Fresh Nightmares: Of Memes, Hives, and Selfish Genes," in *Comparative Literature in an Age of Globalization*, ed. Haun Saussy (Baltimore, MD: Johns Hopkins University Press, 2006), 17–18; emphasis original.

5. Kathleen Stewart, "Worlding Refrains," in *The Affect Theory Reader*, ed. Melissa Gregg and Gregory J. Seigworth (Durham, NC: Duke University Press, 2010), 340.

6. Pheng Cheah, *What Is a World?* (Durham, NC: Duke University Press, 2016), 5, 2.

7. Roger Allen, "Translating Arabic Literature," *Translation Review* 65, no. 1 (2003): 1. Allen taught Arabic language and literature at the University of Pennsylvania from 1968 to 2011. He has translated many works of Arabic fiction into English, in addition to publishing numerous scholarly books and articles about Arabic literature.

8. See Benedict Anderson, *Imagined Communities: Reflections on the Origin and Spread of Nationalism*, rev. ed. (New York: Verso, 1991), 35.

9. Sarah Brouillette, "World Literature and Market Dynamics," in *Institutions of World Literature: Writing, Translation, Markets*, ed. Stefan Helgesson and Pieter Vermeulen (New York: Routledge, 2016), 93–94.

10. See "World Lite," *n+1* 17 (2013), https://nplusonemag.com/issue-17/the-intellectual-situation/world-lite/.

11. Emily Apter, *Against World Literature: On the Politics of Untranslatability* (New York: Verso, 2013), 83.

12. See Timothy Brennan, *At Home in the World: Cosmopolitanism Now* (Cambridge, MA: Harvard University Press, 1997), 203.

13. Jenine Abboushi Dallal, "The Perils of Occidentalism: How Arab Novelists Are Driven to Write for Western Readers," *The Times Literary Supplement*, April 24, 1998, 8.

14. See Brennan, *At Home in the World*, 204. According to Appadurai—contra the prevailing view of many literary critics then and now—globalization does "not necessarily or even frequently imply homogenization" to a single international or Western cultural standard, for "different societies appropriate the materials of modernity differently." See Arjun Appadurai, *Modernity at Large: Cultural Dimensions of Globalization* (Minneapolis: University of Minnesota Press, 1996), 17.

15. In Arabic, *al-Būkar al-ʿArabiyyah*. Like the Booker, the IPAF also recognizes a longlist and shortlist of nominees in addition to a single ultimate winner. Moreover, the IPAF's inaugural board of trustees was chaired by Jonathan Taylor, who was at the time also the chair of the Booker Prize Foundation (a post he held from 2001 to 2015). Despite these connections, the IPAF's administrators have insisted repeatedly that their prize "is not in any way connected with the Booker Prize" (see https://www.arabicfiction.org/).

16. The high monetary value of most of these new awards far outstrips that of the longest-running Arabic literary prize, the American University in Cairo Press's Naguib Mahfouz Medal for Literature, which was first awarded in 1996 and is worth only a comparatively paltry $5,000.

17. Mohamed-Salah Omri, "Notes on the Traffic between Theory and Arabic Literature," *International Journal of Middle East Studies* 43 (2011): 732. My article examining the 2013 IPAF-winning novel *Sāq al-bāmbū* by Kuwaiti writer Saʿūd al-Sanʿūsī as an exemplary case study for investigating the globalizing effects of the International Prize for Arabic Fiction aims to go some way toward addressing this lacuna. See Anna Ziajka Stanton, "Eyes on the Prize: The Global Readability of an IPAF-Winning Modern Arabic Novel," *Middle Eastern Literatures* 24, no. 1 (2021): 20–39.

18. Muḥsin al-Mūsawī, "Simāt riwāyat al-jawāʾiz," *Al-Ḥayāt*, July 24, 2014, https://aljasrah.net/aljasra3489/سمات-رواية-الجوائز.

19. Rebecca Walkowitz, *Born Translated: The Contemporary Novel in an Age of World Literature* (New York: Columbia University Press, 2015), 2.

20. At the time of writing, a published English translation existed for every novel that had won the IPAF from 2008 to 2019, excepting two (the 2012 and 2018 winners).

21. See, for example, the account of the origins of the Arabic novel given by Roger Allen in *The Arabic Novel: An Historical and Critical Introduction*, 2nd ed. (Syracuse, NY: Syracuse University Press, 1995), 11–12. For a more critical take on this master narrative, see Samah Selim, "The Narrative Craft: Realism and Fiction in the Arabic Canon," *Edebiyat: Journal of M.E. Literatures* 14, nos. 1–2 (2003): 114–115.

22. Rebecca C. Johnson, *Stranger Fictions: A History of the Novel in Arabic Translation* (Ithaca, NY: Cornell University Press, 2020), 4.

23. Ibid., 3.

24. Ibid., 8.

25. See, e.g., Mohamed-Salah Omri, "Local Narrative Form and Constructions of the Arabic Novel," *Novel: A Forum on Fiction* 41 (2008): 244–263.

26. See "Plus de kutub, please," *The Economist*, June 18, 2016, 54; Ursula Lindsey, "Why Don't Arabs Read?," *Al-Fanar Media*, July 7, 2016, https://www.al-fanarmedia.org/2016/07/why-dont-arabs-read/.

27. See, for example, a recent Arabic-language blog post on the Al Jazeera website titled "*Lā yaqra'ūn*" ("They Don't Read"), in which this statistic is cited to confirm the author's diagnosis of a widespread intellectual malaise afflicting the Arabophone population of the contemporary Middle East. See Lubnā Maz'āsh, "Lā yaqra'ūn," *Aljazeera.net*, September 8, 2017, https://www.aljazeera.net/blogs/2017/9/8/لا-يقرأون.

28. On the enigmatic origins of this statistic, see Leah Caldwell, "The Arab Reader and the Myth of Six Minutes," *Al-Akhbar English*, January 10, 2012, http://www.pcp.ps/article/156/The-Arab-Reader-and-the-Myth-of-Six-Minutes; Khadija Hamouchi, "'Arabs Don't Read': A Myth Made Real by the Internet?," *The Arab Weekly*, January 21, 2018, https://thearabweekly.com/arabs-dont-read-myth-made-real-internet; and N. P. Krishna Kumar, "Reading Index Results Reveal Arabs Read 35 Hours a Year," *Al Arabiya English*, December 5, 2015, https://english.alarabiya.net/en/business/economy/2016/12/05/Reading-Index-results-reveal-Arabs-read-35-hours-a-year.

29. See Next Page Foundation, *What Arabs Read: A Pan-Arab Survey on Readership*, "Phase One: Egypt, Lebanon, Saudi Arabia, Tunisia, Morocco," January 2007, https://menadoc.bibliothek.uni-halle.de/menalib/content/titleinfo/1303340; and Next Page Foundation, *What Arabs Read: A Pan-Arab Survey on Readership*, "Phase Two: Algeria, Jordan, Palestine and Syria," September 2007, https://menadoc.bibliothek.uni-halle.de/menalib/content/titleinfo/1303343.

30. See Saḥar al-Malījī and Maḥmūd Jāwīsh, "'Khitām ma'riḍ al-kitāb' bi-3.5 milyūn zā'ir," *Al-Maṣrī Al-Yawm*, February 5, 2020, https://www.almasryalyoum.com/news/details/1481920. The 2019 Sharjah International Book Fair reportedly hosted more than 2.5 million visitors over eleven days, while the 2018 Algiers International Book Fair recorded 2.3 million visitors over thirteen days. See Porter Anderson, "Sharjah International Book Fair Draws a Record-Breaking 2.52 Million Visitors," *Publishing Perspectives*, November 11, 2019, https://publishingperspectives.com/2019/11/sharjah-international-book-2019-fair-draws-record-breaking-2-52-million-visitors/; and Mark Williams, "In Algeria the Biggest Cultural Event Is a Book Fair," *The New Publishing Standard*, October 20, 2019, https://thenewpublishingstandard.com/2019/10/20/in-algeria-the-biggest-cultural-event-is-a-book-fair-will-the-algiers-ibf-break-its-2-3-million-visitor-record-this-year-with-its-focus-on-young-authors/.

31. See Aḥmad Nāgī, "2.5 milyūn dūlār sanawiyyan yunfiquhā al-'Arab 'alā al-jawā'iz al-adabiyyah," *Akhbār Al-Adab*, July 5, 2015, 6.

32. See al-Mūsawī, "Simāt riwāyat al-jawā'iz"; Muḥsin al-Mūsawī, "Riwāyat al-jawā'iz," *Al-Ḥayāt*, July 23, 2014, https://aljasrah.net/aljasra3440/رواية-الجوائز; Khalīl Ṣuwayliḥ, "Riwā'īyūn bi-lā jawā'iz . . . riwā'īyūn mansīyun," *Al-Akhbār*, January 18, 2016, http://ar.theasian.asia/archives/29887. See also Sharīf Ṣāliḥ, "'Ashr naṣā'iḥ lil-fawz bi-jā'izat 'al-Būkar,'" *Al-Nahār*, May 12, 2015, 32. The titles of the last two articles translate respectively to "Novelists without Prizes . . . Forgotten Novelists" and "Ten Pieces of Advice for Winning the 'Booker' Prize."

33. Roger Allen, "Fiction and Publics: The Emergence of the 'Arabic Best-Seller,'" in *Viewpoints: The State of the Arts in the Middle East* (Washington, DC: The Middle East Institute, 2009), 10.

34. James F. English, *The Economy of Prestige: Prizes, Awards, and the Circulation of Cultural Value* (Cambridge, MA: Harvard University Press, 2005), 329.

35. Ibid., 263.

36. Anne-Marie McManus, "Scale in the Balance: Reading with the International Prize for Arabic Fiction ('The Arabic Booker')," *International Journal of Middle East Studies* 48 (2016): 219.

37. Brennan intends to designate by this phrase, invoked in the title of his book *At Home in the World: Cosmopolitanism Now*, a quality of cosmopolitan orientation characteristic of literature in the age of globalization.

38. Rechristened as simply the International Booker Prize after the partnership between the Booker Foundation and the Man Group ended in mid-2019, this award is the younger, more globally minded cousin of the Booker Prize (formerly the Man Booker Prize). It is "awarded annually for a single book, translated into English and published in the UK or Ireland." See https://thebookerprizes.com/fiction/about.

39. See Beejay Silcox, "The First Arabic Novel to Win the International Booker Prize," review of *Celestial Bodies* by Jokha Alharthi, trans. Marilyn Booth, *New York Times*, October 21, 2019, https://www.nytimes.com/2019/10/21/books/review/celestial-bodies-jokha-alharthi.html; James Wood, "Lifelines," review of *Celestial Bodies* by Jokha Alharthi, trans. Marilyn Booth, *The New Yorker*, October 14, 2019, 78–79; Ruth Franklin, "Ladies of the Moon," review of *Celestial Bodies* by Jokha Alharthi, trans. Marilyn Booth, *New York Review of Books*, December 5, 2019, https://www.nybooks.com/articles/2019/12/05/jokha-alharthi-celestial-bodies/.

40. See, for example, John Updike's infamous 1988 review of Peter Theroux's translation of *Mudun al-milḥ* (1984) by Saudi writer ʿAbd al-Raḥmān Munīf, published in English as *Cities of Salt* in 1987. In this thoroughly racist assessment of Munīf's novel, Updike refers to the Arab Gulf nations as "stark and backward" and deems Munīf "insufficiently Westernized to produce a narrative that feels much like what we call a novel." See John Updike, "Satan's Work and Silted Cisterns," review of *Cities of Salt* by Abdelrahman Munif, trans. Peter Theroux, *The New Yorker*, October 17, 1988, 117.

41. Marcia Lynx Qualey, "Women in Translation Month: 10 Recommended Books from 2020," *ArabLit.org*, August 1, 2020, https://arablit.org/2020/08/01/women-in-translation-month-8-recommended-books-from-2020/; emphasis original.

42. See Joan Gaylord, "'Celestial Bodies' Reveals Cracks in the Patriarchy," review of *Celestial Bodies* by Jokha Alharthi, trans. Marilyn Booth, *The Christian Science Monitor*, December 31, 2019, https://www.csmonitor.com/Books/Book-Reviews/2019/1231/Celestial-Bodies-reveals-cracks-in-the-patriarchy; Franklin, "Ladies of the Moon."

43. See Bilāl Ramaḍān, "Intiqādāt ḥāddah li-'*Sayyidāt al-qamar*' awwal riwāyah tafūz bi-jāʾizat Mān Būkar al-ʿAlamiyyah," *al-Yawm al-Sābiʿ*, May 27, 2019, https://www.youm7.com/story/2019/5/27/4260408/انتقادات-حادة-لـ-سيدات-القمر-أول-رواية-تفوز-بجائزة-مان-.

44. Harish Trivedi, "Translation and World Literature: The Indian Context," in *Translation and World Literature*, ed. Susan Bassnett (New York: Routledge, 2019), 16.

45. Omani prose literature appeared as a distinct entity in the Arabic literary field only in the late twentieth century, "coinciding with the impressive economic, political, social, and cultural development" ushered in by the country's oil boom. See Barbara Michalak-Pikulska and Waïl S. Hassan, "Oman," in *The Oxford Handbook of Arab Novelistic Traditions*, ed. Waïl S. Hassan (New York: Oxford University Press, 2017), 359.

46. Marilyn Booth, "Arab Writers–Going Global: Hoda Barakat, Jokha Alharthi & Marilyn Booth" (panel discussion at the Emirates Airline Festival of Literature, Dubai, February 5, 2020), https://www.youtube.com/watch?v=4rDudm1usE4&fbclid

=IwAR3Pdw462h3tYXeLgDuKffqoxohg3f9_9b6lh4IlPLnFCDkQqmQGOzBTVrI, 23:30–24:24.

47. Marilyn Booth, "'The Muslim Woman' as Celebrity Author and the Politics of Translating Arabic: Girls of Riyadh Go on the Road," *Journal of Middle East Women's Studies* 6 (2010): 168.

48. Marilyn Booth, "On Translation and Madness," *Translation Review* 65, no. 1 (2003): 50–51.

49. This novel was *Awrāq al-narjis* by Egyptian writer Sumayyah Ramaḍān, which Booth translated as *Leaves of Narcissus*. See Booth, "On Translation and Madness," 52.

50. Booth, "Arab Writers," 43:17–43:25.

51. Personal communication, July 2015.

52. In an interview with the online literary magazine *Words Without Borders*, Abu-Zeid admitted that "when I was on a more academic path in life . . . I had a lot of metaphors, and a lot of theories [about translation]. But now I have less of them." See Kareem James Abu-Zeid, "The Translator Relay: Kareem James Abu-Zeid," interview by Jessie Chaffee, *Words Without Borders*, September 22, 2016, https://www.wordswithoutborders.org/dispatches/article/the-translator-relay-kareem-james-abu-zeid-jessie-chaffee. Abu-Zeid has also described his disillusionment with the metrics by which translations tend to be evaluated in the Anglophone academy, noting, "it's called literary *criticism* for a reason." See Kareem James Abu-Zeid, "A Very Long Road to Publication. Or: Why You Shouldn't Give Up on Your 'Failed' Translation Projects," *Asymptote*, October 2019, https://www.asymptotejournal.com/criticism/adonis-songs-of-mihyar-the-damascene; emphasis original.

53. Elisabeth Jaquette, "Taking Something Unconventional and Making It Beautiful," interview by Graham Oliver, *Ploughshares*, June 24, 2016, http://blog.pshares.org/index.php/taking-something-unconventional-and-making-it-beautiful-an-interview-with-elisabeth-jaquette.

54. Ibid.; Elisabeth Jaquette, "A Talk with TA First Translation Prize Shortlistee Elisabeth Jaquette: 'Outside of a Narrow Norm,'" interview by Marcia Lynx Qualey, *ArabLit.org*, February 28, 2018, https://arablit.org/2018/02/28/a-talk-with-ta-first-translation-prize-shortlistee-elisabeth-jaquette-outside-of-a-narrow-norm; Olivia Snaije, "The Politics of Translation: 'Arabic Literatures in Europe,'" *Publishing Perspectives*, October 26, 2019, https://publishingperspectives.com/2019/10/politics-of-translation-arabic-literatures-in-europe-frankfurt-2019-show-daily.

55. Kareem James Abu-Zeid, interview by *Epicenter*, March 3, 2016, https://www.youtube.com/watch?v=yo9U6doBHjw&feature=youtu.be, 6:36–6:45; Abu-Zeid, "A Very Long Road," emphasis original.

56. See Abu-Zeid, "The Translator Relay."

57. Elliott Colla, "Dragomen and Checkpoints," *The Translator* 21, no. 2 (2015): 134.

58. See the MLA's searchable online Language Enrollment Database, which gives enrollment figures for classes in languages other than English at U.S. colleges and universities between 1958 and 2016, at https://apps.mla.org/flsurvey_search.

59. Booth, "Arab Writers," 42:33–42:40.

60. Sara Ahmed, "Happy Objects," in Gregg and Seigworth, *The Affect Theory Reader*, 32.

61. Ibid., emphasis original.

Bibliography

Abdo, Diya M. "Textual Migration: Self-Translation and Translation of the Self in Leila Abouzeid's *Return to Childhood: The Memoir of a Modern Moroccan Woman* and *Ruju' 'Ila Al-Tufulah*." *Frontiers: A Journal of Women Studies* 30, no. 2 (2009): 1–42.

Abou Rached, Ruth. "Pathways of Solidarity in Transit: Iraqi Women Writers' Story-Making in English Translation." In *The Routledge Handbook of Translation, Feminism and Gender*, edited by Luise von Flotow and Hala Kamal, 48–63. New York: Routledge, 2020.

Aboul-Ela, Hosam. "Challenging the Embargo: Arabic Literature in the US Market." *Middle East Report* 219 (2001): 42–44.

———. *Domestications: American Empire, Literary Culture, and the Postcolonial Lens*. Evanston, IL: Northwestern University Press, 2018.

———. "Is There an Arab (Yet) in This Field? Postcolonialism, Comparative Literature, and the Middle Eastern Horizon of Said's Discourse Analysis." *Modern Fiction Studies* 56, no. 4 (2010): 729–750.

Abu-Haidar, Jareer. "'Qifā nabki': The Dual Form of Address in Arabic Poetry in a New Light." *Journal of Arabic Literature* 19, no. 1 (1988): 40–48.

Abu-Zeid, Kareem James. Interview by *Epicenter*, March 3, 2016. https://www.youtube.com/watch?v=yo9U6doBHjw&feature=youtu.be.

———. "The Translator Relay: Kareem James Abu-Zeid." Interview by Jessie Chaffee. *Words Without Borders*, September 22, 2016. https://www.wordswithoutborders.org/dispatches/article/the-translator-relay-kareem-james-abu-zeid-jessie-chaffee.

———. "A Very Long Road to Publication. Or: Why You Shouldn't Give Up on Your 'Failed' Translation Projects." *Asymptote*, October 2019. https://www.asymptotejournal.com/criticism/adonis-songs-of-mihyar-the-damascene.

Adams, Hazard, and Leroy Searle, eds. *Critical Theory since 1965*. Tallahassee: Florida State University Press, 1986.

Adonis. *An Introduction to Arab Poetics*. Translated by Catherine Cobham. London: Saqi Books, 1990.

Ahmad, Aijaz. "Jameson's Rhetoric of Otherness and the 'National Allegory.'" *Social Text* 17 (1987): 3–25.

Ahmed, Sara. "Happy Objects." In Gregg and Seigworth, *The Affect Theory Reader*, 29–51.

Al-Bagdadi, Nadia. "The Cultural Function of Fiction: From the Bible to Libertine Literature. Historical Criticism and Social Critique in Aḥmad Fāris al-Šidyāq." *Arabica* 46 (1999): 375–401.

Albazei, Saad A. Review of *I'jaam: An Iraqi Rhapsody* by Sinan Antoon, translated by Rebecca C. Johnson and Sinan Antoon. *World Literature Today* 82, no. 6 (2008), 58.

Alf laylah wa-laylah. Edited by Muḥammad Qiṭṭah al-ʿAdawī. 2nd ed. 4 vols. Bulaq: Maṭbaʿat ʿAbd al-Raḥmān Rushdī, 1862.

Allan, Michael. *In the Shadow of World Literature: Sites of Reading in Colonial Egypt*. Princeton, NJ: Princeton University Press, 2016.

Allen, Roger. *The Arabic Novel: An Historical and Critical Introduction*. 2nd ed. Syracuse, NY: Syracuse University Press, 1995.

———. "Fiction and Publics: The Emergence of the 'Arabic Best-Seller.'" In *Viewpoints: The State of the Arts in the Middle East*, 9–12. Washington, DC: The Middle East Institute, 2009.

———. "The Happy Traitor: Tales of Translation." *Comparative Literature Studies* 47, no. 4 (2010): 472–486.

———. Review of *Modern Arabic Short Stories* and *Egyptian Short Stories*, translated and edited by Denys Johnson-Davies. *Al-'Arabiyya* 12 (1979): 89–91.

———. "Translating Arabic Fiction." *Journal of Arabic Literature* 46, nos. 2–3 (2015): 157–167.

———. "Translating Arabic Literature." *Translation Review* 65, no. 1 (2003): 1–5.

Al-Nakib, Mai. "Arab Literature: Politics and Nothing But?" *World Literature Today* 90, no. 1 (2016): 30–32.

Al-Nowaihi, Magda M. "Unheard in English." *The MIT Electronic Journal of Middle East Studies: Crossing Boundaries—New Perspectives on the Middle East* 4 (2004): 23–29.

Al-Qur'ān: A Contemporary Translation. Translated by Ahmed Ali. Princeton, NJ: Princeton University Press, 1993.

Al-Shidyaq, Ahmad Faris. *Leg over Leg or, The Turtle in the Tree, concerning The Fāriyāq; What Manner of Creature Might He Be; otherwise entitled Days, Months, and Years spent in Critical Examination of the Arabs and Their Non-Arab Peers*, translated and edited by Humphrey Davies. New York: New York University Press, 2013–2014.

Amer, Sahar. *Crossing Borders: Love between Women in Medieval French and Arabic Literatures*. Philadelphia: University of Pennsylvania Press, 2008.

Anderson, Benedict. *Imagined Communities: Reflections on the Origin and Spread of Nationalism*. Rev. ed. New York: Verso, 1991.

Anderson, Porter. "Sharjah International Book Fair Draws a Record-Breaking 2.52 Million Visitors." *Publishing Perspectives*, November 11, 2019. https://publishingperspectives.com/2019/11/sharjah-international-book-2019-fair-draws-record-breaking-2-52-million-visitors/.

Antoon, Sinan (Anṭūn, Sinān). "A Barbarian in Rome: Excerpts from a Diary." In *We Are Iraqis: Aesthetics and Politics in a Time of War*, edited by Nadje Al-Ali and Deborah Al-Najjar, 24–34. Syracuse, NY: Syracuse University Press, 2013.

———. *The Corpse Washer*. Translated by Sinan Antoon. New Haven, CT: Yale University Press, 2013.

———. "Dead Poets Society." *The Nation*, May 26, 2003, 25–29.

———. *I'jaam: An Iraqi Rhapsody*. Translated by Rebecca C. Johnson and Sinan Antoon. San Francisco: City Lights, 2007.

———. "In 'The Book Of Collateral Damage,' An Accounting Of What Baghdad Lost." Interview by Steve Inskeep. *Morning Edition*, NPR, July 9, 2019. https://www.npr.org/2019/07/09/739613519/in-the-book-of-collateral-damage-an-accounting-of-what-baghdad-lost.

———. "Iraq: 5 Years Later." *The Charlie Rose Show*, PBS, March 19, 2008. https://charlierose.com/videos/28940.

———. "Sinan Antoon: 'I think of myself as a global citizen.'" Interview by Dina Omar. *The Electronic Intifada*, April 7, 2010. https://electronicintifada.net/content/sinan-antoon-i-think-myself-global-citizen/8760.

———. "Translation as Mourning." Lecture at The American University in Cairo, March 4, 2014. https://www.youtube.com/watch?v=f9ehd8nbFFY.

Anṭūn, Sinān (Antoon, Sinan). "Al-Riwā'ī al-ʿIrāqī Sinān Anṭūn li-*Al-Ḥiwār Al-Mutamaddin*: Al-bunyah fī riwāyat *Iʿjām* dā'iriyyah tadākhuliyyah wa-lā ajwibah fī nihāyat al-maṭāf." Interview by ʿAdnān Ḥusayn Aḥmad. *Al-Ḥiwār Al-Mutamaddin*, August 6, 2005. http://www.ahewar.org/debat/show.art.asp?aid=42533&r=0.

———. "Barbarī fī Rūmā." *Jadaliyya*, April 9, 2013. http://www.jadaliyya.com/pages/index/11129.

———. *Iʿjām*. Beirut: Dār al-Ādāb, 2004.

Appadurai, Arjun. *Modernity at Large: Cultural Dimensions of Globalization*. Minneapolis: University of Minnesota Press, 1996.

Appiah, Kwame Anthony. *Cosmopolitanism: Ethics in a World of Strangers*. New York: Norton, 2006.

———. "Thick Translation." In Venuti, *The Translation Studies Reader*, 331–343.

Apter, Emily. *Against World Literature: On the Politics of Untranslatability*. New York: Verso, 2013.

———. "Philosophical Translation and Untranslatability: Translation as Critical Pedagogy." *Profession* (2010): 50–63.
———. *The Translation Zone: A New Comparative Literature*. Princeton, NJ: Princeton University Press, 2006.
"The Arabian Nights." *The Edinburgh Review*, July 1886, 166–199.
"The Arabian Nights." *The Liverpool Mercury*, March 26, 1887, 7.
Asad, Talal. "The Concept of Cultural Translation in British Anthropology." In *Writing Culture: The Poetics and Politics of Ethnography*, edited by James Clifford and George E. Marcus, 141–164. Berkeley: University of California Press, 1986.
———. *Formations of the Secular: Christianity, Islam, Modernity*. Stanford, CA: Stanford University Press, 2003.
ʿĀshūr, Raḍwā. *Al-Ḥadāthah al-mumkinah: Al-Shidyāq wa-al-Sāq ʿalā al-sāq*. Cairo: Dār al-Shurūq, 2009.
Assad, Thomas J. *Three Victorian Travelers: Burton, Blunt, Doughty*. London: Routledge and Kegan Paul, 1964.
Austin, J. L. *How to Do Things with Words*. London: Oxford University Press, 1962.
Ayoub, Dima. "Politics of Paratextuality: The Glossary between Translation and the Translational." *Journal of Arabic Literature* 51, nos. 1–2 (2020): 27–52.
Baalbaki, Ramzi. "Arabic Linguistic Tradition I: Naḥw and ṣarf." In *The Oxford Handbook of Arabic Linguistics*, edited by Jonathan Owens, 92–114. New York: Oxford University Press, 2013.
Badiou, Alain. *Ethics: An Essay on the Understanding of Evil*. Translated by Peter Hallward. London: Verso, 2001.
Bahoora, Haytham. "Writing the Dismembered Nation: The Aesthetics of Horror in Iraqi Narratives of War." *The Arab Studies Journal* 23, no. 1 (2015): 184–208.
Baker, Mona. *Translation and Conflict: A Narrative Account*. New York: Routledge, 2006.
Bakhtin, M. M. "Discourse in the Novel." In *The Dialogic Imagination: Four Essays by M. M. Bakhtin*, edited by Michael Holquist, translated by Caryl Emerson and Michael Holquist, 259–422. Austin: University of Texas Press, 1981.
Bal, Mieke. "The Commitment to Look." *Journal of Visual Culture* 4, no. 2 (2005): 145–162.
Barthes, Roland. *Le plaisir du texte*. Paris: Éditions du Seuil, 1973.
Bassnett, Susan. *Translation Studies*. 4th ed. New York: Routledge, 2014.
———. "Rejoinder." *Orbis Litterarum* 68, no. 3 (2013): 282–289.
———. "When Is a Translation Not a Translation?" In *Constructing Cultures: Essays on Literary Translation*, edited by Susan Bassnett and André Lefevere, 25–40. Clevedon, UK: Multilingual Matters, 1998.
Baudrillard, Jean. *The Gulf War Did Not Take Place*. Translated by Paul Patton. Bloomington: Indiana University Press, 1995.

Bayoumi, Moustafa. "Disco Inferno." *The Nation*, December 8, 2005. https://www.thenation.com/article/archive/disco-inferno/.

Beecroft, Alexander. "World Literature Without a Hyphen: Towards a Typology of Literary Systems (2008)." In *World Literature in Theory*, edited by David Damrosch, 180–191. Chichester, UK: John Wiley and Sons, 2014.

Beeston, A. F. L. *The Arabic Language Today*. Washington, DC: Georgetown University Press, 2006.

Bellos, David. *Is That a Fish in Your Ear? Translation and the Meaning of Everything*. New York: Faber and Faber, 2011.

Bengio, Ofra. *Saddam's Word: Political Discourse in Iraq*. New York: Oxford University Press, 1998.

Benjamin, Walter. "The Task of the Translator." In *Illuminations*, translated by Harry Zohn, edited by Hannah Arendt, 69–82. New York: Schocken Books, 1969.

Benveniste, Emile. "Subjectivity in Language." Translated by Mary E. Meek. In Adams and Searle, *Critical Theory since 1965*, 728–732.

Berlant, Lauren. *Cruel Optimism*. Durham, NC: Duke University Press, 2011.

Bermann, Sandra. "Introduction." In *Nation, Language, and the Ethics of Translation*, edited by Sandra Bermann and Michael Wood, 1–10. Princeton, NJ: Princeton University Press, 2005.

"Best Books of 2015—Part Two." *The Guardian*, November 29, 2015. https://www.theguardian.com/books/ng-interactive/2015/nov/29/best-books-of-2015-part-two.

Blanc, Haim. "Dual and Pseudo-Dual in the Arabic Dialects." *Language* 46, no. 1 (1970): 42–57.

Bloom, Harold. *The Anxiety of Influence: A Theory of Poetry*. 2nd ed. New York: Oxford University Press, 1997.

Booth, Marilyn. "Arab Writers–Going Global: Hoda Barakat, Jokha Alharthi & Marilyn Booth." Panel discussion at the Emirates Airline Festival of Literature, Dubai, February 5, 2020. https://www.youtube.com/watch?v=4rDudm1usE4&fbclid=IwAR3Pdw462h3tYXeLgDuKffqoxohg3f9_9b61h4IlPLnFCDkQqmQGOzBTVrI.

———. "'The Muslim Woman' as Celebrity Author and the Politics of Translating Arabic: Girls of Riyadh Go on the Road." *Journal of Middle East Women's Studies* 6 (2010): 149–182.

———. "On Translation and Madness." *Translation Review* 65, no. 1 (2003): 47–53.

———. "Translator v. Author (2007): *Girls of Riyadh* Go to New York." *Translation Studies* 1, no. 2 (2008): 197–211.

Borges, Jorge Luis. "The Aleph." In *The Aleph and Other Stories: 1933–1969*, translated by Norman Thomas di Giovanni, 15–30. New York: Dutton, 1970.

———. "The Translators of *The Thousand and One Nights*." Translated by Esther Allen. In Venuti, *The Translation Studies Reader*, 92–106.

Boulanger, Pier-Pascale. "Introduction." In Henri Meschonnic, *Ethics and Politics of Translating*, translated and edited by Pier-Pascale Boulanger, 11–33. Philadelphia: John Benjamins, 2011.

Boullata, Issa J. "The Case for Resistant Translation from Arabic to English." *Translation Review* 65 (2003): 29–33.

Bourdieu, Pierre. *Distinction: A Social Critique of the Judgement of Taste*. Translated by Richard Nice. Cambridge, MA: Harvard University Press, 1984.

———. *Pascalian Meditations*. Translated by Richard Nice. Stanford, CA: Stanford University Press, 2000.

Boyden, Michael, and Liesbeth De Bleeker. "Introduction." *Orbis Litterarum* 68, no. 3 (2013): 177–187.

Brennan, Teresa. *The Transmission of Affect*. Ithaca, NY: Cornell University Press, 2004.

Brennan, Timothy. *At Home in the World: Cosmopolitanism Now*. Cambridge, MA: Harvard University Press, 1997.

Briggs, Kate. *This Little Art*. London: Fitzcarraldo Editions, 2017.

Broder, John M. "A Nation at War: The Casualties; U.S. Military Has No Count of Iraqi Dead in Fighting." *New York Times*, April 2, 2003. http://www.nytimes.com/2003/04/02/world/nation-war-casualties-us-military-has-no-count-iraqi-dead-fighting.html.

Brodie, Fawn. *The Devil Drives: A Life of Sir Richard Burton*. New York: Norton, 1967.

Brouillette, Sarah. "World Literature and Market Dynamics." In *Institutions of World Literature: Writing, Translation, Markets*, edited by Stefan Helgesson and Pieter Vermeulen, 93–106. New York: Routledge, 2016.

Brustad, Kristen. *The Syntax of Spoken Arabic: A Comparative Study of Moroccan, Egyptian, Syrian, and Kuwaiti Dialects*. Washington, DC: Georgetown University Press, 2000.

Büchler, Alexandra, and Alice Guthrie, eds. "Literary Translation from Arabic into English in the United Kingdom and Ireland, 1990–2010." Literature Across Frontiers, December 2011. http://www.lit-across-frontiers.org/wp-content/uploads/2013/03/Literary-Translation-from-Arabic-into-English-in-the-United-Kingdom-and-Ireland-1990–2010-final.pdf.

Burton, Antoinette. "Introduction: Archive Fever, Archive Stories." In *Archive Stories: Facts, Fictions, and the Writing of History*, edited by Antoinette Burton, 1–24. Durham, NC: Duke University Press, 2005.

Burton, Richard F. "The Arabian Nights." *The Atheneaum*, November 26, 1881, 703.

———. *Personal Narrative of a Pilgrimage to El Medinah and Meccah*. 2nd ed. 2 Vols. London: Longman, Brown, Green, Longmans, and Roberts, 1857.

———. *A Plain and Literal Translation of the Arabian Nights' Entertainments: Now Entituled The Book of the Thousand Nights and a Night*. 10 Vols. [London]: The Burton Club, n.d.

———. *Supplemental Nights to the Book of the Thousand Nights and a Night with Notes Anthropological and Explanatory*. 6 Vols. [London]: The Burton Club, n.d.

"Burton's Life Told Anew; Thomas Wright's Perfectly Impartial Biography of the Great Orientalist—His Relations with Payne." Review of *The Life of Sir Richard Burton* by Thomas Wright. *New York Times*, June 23, 1906.

Bush, George W. State of the Union Address, January 20, 2004. https://georgewbush-whitehouse.archives.gov/news/releases/2004/01/20040120-7.html.

Butler, Judith. *The Force of Nonviolence: An Ethico-Political Bind*. New York: Verso, 2020.

Caldwell, Leah. "The Arab Reader and the Myth of Six Minutes." *Al-Akhbar English*, January 10, 2012. http://www.pcp.ps/article/156/The-Arab-Reader-and-the-Myth-of-Six-Minutes.

Carruthers, Elspeth. Review of *Leg over Leg* by Ahmad Faris al-Shidyaq, translated by Humphrey Davies. *Banipal* 49 (2014). https://www.banipal.co.uk/book_reviews/106/leg-over-leg/.

Carter, M. G., and J. van Ess. "Lafẓ." In *Encyclopaedia of Islam, Second Edition*, edited by P. Bearman et al. Leiden: Brill, 2012. https://referenceworks.brillonline.com/entries/encyclopaedia-of-islam-2/lafz-COM_1420.

Casanova, Pascale. *The World Republic of Letters*. Translated by M. B. DeBevoise. Cambridge, MA: Harvard University Press, 2004.

Cassin, Barbara. "Introduction." Translated by Michael Wood. In *Dictionary of Untranslatables: A Philosophical Lexicon*, edited by Barbara Cassin, Emily Apter, Jacques Lezra, and Michael Wood, xvii–xx. Princeton, NJ: Princeton University Press, 2014.

Caton, Steven C. *Lawrence of Arabia: A Film's Anthropology*. Berkeley: University of California Press, 1999.

de Certeau, Michel. *The Practice of Everyday Life*. Translated by Steven Rendall. Berkeley: University of California Press, 1984.

Cheah, Pheng. *What Is a World*? Durham, NC: Duke University Press, 2016.

Chen, Mel Y. *Animacies: Biopolitics, Racial Mattering, and Queer Affect*. Durham, NC: Duke University Press, 2012.

Chenoweth, Sarah. Review of *I'jaam: An Iraqi Rhapsody* by Sinan Antoon, translated by Rebecca C. Johnson and Sinan Antoon. *Counterpoise* 13, nos. 1–2 (2009): 61–62.

Chouman, Hilal. *Limbo Beirut*. Translated by Anna Ziajka Stanton. Austin: Center for Middle Eastern Studies, University of Texas at Austin, 2016.

Cole, Peter. "Making Sense in Translation: Toward an Ethics of the Art." In *In Translation: Translators on Their Work and What It Means*, edited by Roger Allen and Susan Bernofsky, 3–16. New York: Columbia University Press, 2013.

Colla, Elliott. "Dragomen and Checkpoints." *The Translator* 21, no. 2 (2015): 132–153.

———. "The Porter and Portability: Figure and Narrative in the *Nights*." In *Scheherazade's Children: Global Encounters with the Arabian Nights*, edited by Philip F. Kennedy and Marina Warner, 89–107. New York: NYU Press, 2013.

———. "Translation Theory, Practice, and Transduction." *ElliottColla.com*, April 23, 2018. http://www.elliottcolla.com/blog/2018/4/23/translation-theory-practice-and-transduction.

Cooperson, Michael. "Note on the Translation." In Al-Ḥarīrī, *Impostures*, translated by Michael Cooperson, xxix–xlv. New York: New York University Press, 2020.

Creswell, Robyn. *City of Beginnings: Poetic Modernism in Beirut*. Princeton, NJ: Princeton University Press, 2019.

———. "The First Great Arabic Novel." Review of *Leg over Leg* by Ahmad Faris al-Shidyaq, translated by Humphrey Davies. *New York Review of Books*, October 8, 2015. https://www.nybooks.com/articles/2015/10/08/first-great-arabic-novel/.

———. "Is Arabic Untranslatable?" *Public Culture* 28, no. 3 (2016): 447–456.

Croft, Jennifer. *Homesick: A Memoir*. Los Angeles: Unnamed Press, 2019.

Cusk, Rachel. *A Life's Work: On Becoming a Mother*. New York: Picador, 2001.

Dallal, Jenine Abboushi. "The Perils of Occidentalism: How Arab Novelists Are Driven to Write for Western Readers." *The Times Literary Supplement*, April 24, 1998, 8–9.

Dames, Nicholas. *The Physiology of the Novel: Reading, Neural Science, and the Form of Victorian Fiction*. New York: Oxford University Press, 2007.

Damrosch, David. *What Is World Literature*? Princeton, NJ: Princeton University Press, 2003.

Dauphinée, Elizabeth. "The Politics of the Body in Pain: Reading the Ethics of Imagery." *Security Dialogue* 38, no. 2 (2007): 139–155.

Davies, Humphrey. "Translator's Afterword." In Ahmad Faris al-Shidyaq, *Leg over Leg or, The Turtle in the Tree*, translated and edited by Humphrey Davies, 4:485–494. New York: New York University Press, 2014.

Deleuze, Gilles, and Félix Guattari. *A Thousand Plateaus: Capitalism and Schizophrenia*. Translated by Brian Massumi. Minneapolis: University of Minnesota Press, 1987.

Derrida, Jacques. *Monolingualism of the Other; or, The Prosthesis of Origin*. Translated by Patrick Mensah. Stanford, CA: Stanford University Press, 1998.

———. *Of Grammatology*. Translated by Gayatri Chakravorty Spivak. Rev. ed. Baltimore, MD: Johns Hopkins University Press, 1997.

———. *The Post Card: From Socrates to Freud and Beyond*. Translated by Alan Bass. Chicago: University of Chicago Press, 1987.

———. "Structure, Sign and Play in the Discourse of the Human Sciences." In *Writing and Difference*, translated by Alan Bass, 278–293. Chicago: University of Chicago Press, 1978.

Dimock, Wai Chee. "A Theory of Resonance." *PMLA* 112, no. 5 (1997): 1060–1071.

Dolar, Mladen. *A Voice and Nothing More*. Cambridge, MA: MIT Press, 2006.

Driver, G. R. *Semitic Writing: From Pictogram to Alphabet*. Rev. ed. London: Oxford University Press, 1976.

El-Ariss, Tarek. "Fiction of Scandal." *Journal of Arabic Literature* 43 (2012): 510–531.

———. *Leaks, Hacks, and Scandals: Arab Culture in the Digital Age*. Princeton, NJ: Princeton University Press, 2019.

———. "Return of the Beast: From Pre-Islamic Ode to Contemporary Novel." *Journal of Arabic Literature* 47, nos. 1–2 (2016): 62–90.

———. Review of *Leg over Leg* by Ahmad Faris al-Shidyaq, translated by Humphrey Davies. *Arab Studies Journal* 24, no. 1 (2016): 286–290.

———. "Theory in a Global Context: A Critical Practice in Five Steps." *CARGC Papers* 17 (2022): 1–18.

———. *Trials of Arab Modernity: Literary Affects and the New Political*. New York: Fordham University Press, 2013.

El Shakry, Hoda. *The Literary Qur'an: Narrative Ethics in the Maghreb*. New York: Fordham University Press, 2020.

English, James F. *The Economy of Prestige: Prizes, Awards, and the Circulation of Cultural Value*. Cambridge, MA: Harvard University Press, 2005.

Ernst, Carl W. *How to Read the Qur'an: A New Guide, with Select Translations*. Chapel Hill: University of North Carolina Press, 2011.

Farago, Jason, and Tim Arango. "These Artists Refuse to Forget the Wars in Iraq." Review of *Theater of Operations: The Gulf Wars 1991–2011* at MoMA PS1, New York (November 3, 2019–March 1, 2020). *New York Times*, November 14, 2019. https://www.nytimes.com/2019/11/14/arts/design/iraq-wars-art-momaps1-review.html.

Farwell, Byron. *Burton: A Biography of Sir Richard Francis Burton*. London: Longmans, 1963.

Feldman, Allen. "Violence and Vision: The Prosthetics and Aesthetics of Terror." *Public Culture* 10, no. 1 (1997): 24–60.

Ferguson, Charles. "The Arabic Koine." *Language* 35. no. 4 (1959): 616–630.

Foucault, Michel. *The History of Sexuality: Volume I–An Introduction*. Translated by Robert Hurley. New York: Vintage, 1990.

———. "What Is an Author?" In *Language, Counter-memory, Practice: Selected Essays and Interviews*, edited by Donald F. Bouchard, translated by Donald F. Bouchard and Sherry Simon, 113–138. Ithaca, NY: Cornell University Press, 1977.

Fraade, Steven D. "Targum, Targumim." In *The Eerdmans Dictionary of Early Judaism*, edited by John J. Collins and Daniel C. Harlow, 1278–1281. Grand Rapids, MI: William B. Eerdmans, 2010.

Franklin, Ruth. "Ladies of the Moon." Review of *Celestial Bodies* by Jokha Alharthi, translated by Marilyn Booth. *New York Review of Books*, December 5, 2019. https://www.nybooks.com/articles/2019/12/05/jokha-alharthi-celestial-bodies/.

Friedmann, Jessica. *Things That Helped: On Postpartum Depression*. New York: Farrar, Straus and Giroux, 2018.

———. "What It Means to Write About Motherhood, Part Two." Roundtable in *Literary Hub*, October 25, 2018. https://lithub.com/what-it-means-to-write-about-motherhood-part-two/.

Furani, Khaled. *Silencing the Sea: Secular Rhythms in Palestinian Poetry*. Stanford, CA: Stanford University Press, 2012.

Gaylord, Joan. "'Celestial Bodies' Reveals Cracks in the Patriarchy." Review of *Celestial Bodies* by Jokha Alharthi, translated by Marilyn Booth. *The Christian Science Monitor*, December 31, 2019. https://www.csmonitor.com/Books/Book-Reviews/2019/1231/Celestial-Bodies-reveals-cracks-in-the-patriarchy.

Gerhardt, Mia. *The Art of Story-Telling: A Literary Study of the Thousand and One Nights*. Leiden: E. J. Brill, 1963.

Ghazoul, Ferial. *Nocturnal Poetics:* The Arabian Nights *in Comparative Context*. Cairo: American University in Cairo Press, 1996.

Gibson, J. C. L. *Canaanite Myths and Legends*. 2nd ed. London: T & T Clark International, 2004.

Green, Jonathon. *Cassell's Dictionary of Slang*. 2nd ed. London: Weidenfeld and Nicolson, 2005.

Greenblatt, Stephen. "Resonance and Wonder." *Bulletin of the American Academy of Arts and Sciences* 43, no. 4 (1990): 11–34.

Gregg, Melissa, and Gregory Seigworth, eds. *The Affect Theory Reader*. Durham, NC: Duke University Press, 2010.

Haddawy, Husain. "Introduction." In *The Arabian Nights*, translated by Husain Haddawy, xi–xxxvi. New York: Norton, 1990.

Hadj-Salah, A. "Lugha." In *Encyclopaedia of Islam, Second Edition*, edited by P. Bearman et al. Leiden: Brill, 2012. https://referenceworks.brillonline.com/entries/encyclopaedia-of-islam-2/lugha-SIM_4685.

Hafez, Sabry. *The Genesis of Arabic Narrative Discourse: A Study in the Sociology of Modern Arabic Literature*. London: Saqi Books, 1993.

Hämeen-Anttila, Jaakko. "Adab a) Arabic, Early Developments." In *Encyclopaedia of Islam, THREE*, edited by Kate Fleet et al. Leiden: Brill, 2014. https://referenceworks.brillonline.com/entries/encyclopaedia-of-islam-3/adab-a-arabic-early-developments-COM_24178.

Hamouchi, Khadija. "'Arabs Don't Read': A Myth Made Real by the Internet?" *The Arab Weekly*, January 21, 2018. https://thearabweekly.com/arabs-dont-read-myth-made-real-internet.

Hanoosh, Yasmeen. "Unnatural Narratives and Transgressing the Normative Discourses of Iraqi History: Translating Murtaḍā Gzār's *Al-Sayyid Aṣghar Akbar*." *Journal of Arabic Literature* 44 (2013): 145–180.

Hans Wehr Dictionary of Modern Written Arabic. Edited by J. Milton Cowan. 4th ed. Ithaca, NY: Spoken Language Services, 1994.

Harb, Lara. *Arabic Poetics: Aesthetic Experience in Classical Arabic Literature*. New York: Cambridge University Press, 2020.

———. "Form, Content, and the Inimitability of the Qur'an in 'Abd al-Qahir al-Jurjani's Works." *Middle Eastern Literatures* 18, no. 3 (2015): 301–321.

Hartman, Michelle. "Gender, Genre, and the (Missing) Gazelle: Arab Women Writers and the Politics of Translation." *Feminist Studies* 38, no. 1 (2012): 17–49.

———. "'My Tale Is Too Long to Tell': *The Locust and the Bird* between South Lebanon and New York City." *Journal of Arabic Literature* 46, nos. 2–3 (2015): 168–192.

———. *Native Tongue, Stranger Talk: The Arabic and French Literary Landscapes of Lebanon*. Syracuse, NY: Syracuse University Press, 2014.

Hassan, Waïl S. "Agency and Translational Literature: Ahdaf Soueif's *The Map of Love*." *PMLA* 121, no. 3 (2006): 753–768.

———. "Arabic and the Paradigms of Comparison." In *Futures of Comparative Literature: ACLA State of the Discipline Report*, edited by Ursula K. Heise, 187–194. New York: Routledge, 2017.

———. *Immigrant Narratives: Orientalism and Cultural Translation in Arab American and Arab British Literature*. New York: Oxford University Press, 2011.

———. "Translator's Introduction." In Abdelfattah Kilito, *Thou Shalt Not Speak My Language*, translated by Waïl S. Hassan, vii–xxvi. Syracuse, NY: Syracuse University Press, 2008.

Hava, J. G. *Arabic-English Dictionary for the Use of Students*. Beirut: Catholic Press, 1899.

Healey, John F. "The Early Alphabet." In *Reading the Past: Ancient Writing from Cuneiform to the Alphabet*, 197–257. Berkeley: University of California Press, 1990.

Healey, John F., and G. Rex Smith. *A Brief Introduction to the Arabic Alphabet: Its Origins and Various Forms*. London: Saqi, 2009.

Heidegger, Martin. "The Origin of the Work of Art." In *Poetry, Language, Thought*, translated by Albert Hofstadter, 17–86. New York: Harper Perennial, 2001.

Helmreich, Stefan. "Transduction." In *Keywords in Sound*, edited by David Novak and Matt Sakakeeny, 222–231. Durham, NC: Duke University Press, 2015.

Holt, Elizabeth. "Al-Ṭayyib Ṣāliḥ's *Season of Migration to the North*, the CIA, and the Cultural Cold War after Bandung." *Research in African Literatures* 50, no. 3 (2019): 70–90.

Horta, Paulo Lemos. *Marvellous Thieves: Secret Authors of the Arabian Nights*. Cambridge, MA: Harvard University Press, 2017.

Hughes, Geoffrey. *An Encyclopedia of Swearing: The Social History of Oaths, Profanity, Foul Language, and Ethnic Slurs in the English-Speaking World*. Armonk, NY: M. E. Sharpe, 2006.

Ibn Manẓūr, Muḥammad ibn Mukarram. *Lisān al-ʿArab*. 18 Vols. Beirut: Dār Ṣādir, 2005.

Ibrahim, 'Abdallah. "The Role of the Pre-Modern: The Generic Characteristics of the *Band*." In *Arabic Literature in the Post-Classical Period*, edited by Roger

Allen and D. S. Richards, 87–98. New York: Cambridge University Press, 2006.

Irwin, Robert. *The Arabian Nights: A Companion*. New York: Tauris Parke Paperbacks, 2004.

Iser, Wolfgang. "The Repertoire." In Adams and Searle, *Critical Theory since 1965*, 360–380.

Ismail, Sherif. "Multiple Encounters: Philology, Exile, and Hospitality, from Fāris al-Shidyāq to Auerbach and Edward Said." *Philological Encounters* 3, nos. 1–2 (2018): 67–104.

Issa, Rana. "The Insomniac Feast: Al-Shidyaq's Reading Digest." Paper presented at the Conceptions and Configurations of the Arabic Literary Canon Workshop, Paris, June 19, 2019.

———. "Scripture as Literature: The Bible, the Qurʾān, and Aḥmad Fāris al-Shidyāq." *Journal of Arabic Literature* 50 (2019): 29–55.

Jacquemond, Richard. *Conscience of the Nation: Writers, State, and Society in Modern Egypt*. Translated by David Tresilian. Cairo: American University in Cairo Press, 2008.

Jāḥiẓ, Abī ʿUthmān ʿAmru ibn Baḥr al-. *Al-Bayān wa-al-tabyīn*. Edited by ʿAbd al-Salām Muḥammad Hārūn. 4 Vols. Cairo: Maktabat al-Khānjī, 1960.

———. *Kitāb al-ḥayawān*. Edited by ʿAbd al-Salām Muḥammad Hārūn. 8 Vols. Cairo: Muṣṭafā al-Bābī al-Ḥalabī, 1965.

Jakobson, Roman. "On Linguistic Aspects of Translation." In Venuti *The Translation Studies Reader*, 126–131.

Jameson, Fredric. "Third-World Literature in the Era of Multinational Capitalism." *Social Text* 15 (1986): 65–88.

Jaquette, Elisabeth. "A Talk with TA First Translation Prize Shortlistee Elisabeth Jaquette: 'Outside of a Narrow Norm.'" Interview by Marcia Lynx Qualey. *ArabLit.org*, February 28, 2018. https://arablit.org/2018/02/28/a-talk-with-ta-first-translation-prize-shortlistee-elisabeth-jaquette-outside-of-a-narrow-norm.

———. "Taking Something Unconventional and Making It Beautiful." Interview by Graham Oliver. *Ploughshares*, June 24, 2016. http://blog.pshares.org/index.php/taking-something-unconventional-and-making-it-beautiful-an-interview-with-elisabeth-jaquette.

Jauss, Hans Robert. "Literary History as a Challenge to Literary Theory." In *Toward an Aesthetic of Reception*, translated by Timothy Bahti, 3–45. Minneapolis: University of Minnesota Press, 1982.

Jerome. "Letter to Pammachius." Translated by Kathleen Davis. In Venuti, *The Translation Studies Reader*, 21–30.

———. *Sancti Eusebii Hieronymi Epistulae*. Edited by Isidorus Hilberg. 3 vols. Vienna: F. Tempsky, 1910.

Johnson, Barbara. *Mother Tongues: Sexuality, Trials, Motherhood, Translation*. Cambridge, MA: Harvard University Press, 2003.

Johnson, Rebecca C. "Archive of Errors: Aḥmad Fāris al-Shidyāq, Literature, and the World." *Middle Eastern Literatures* 20, no. 1 (2017): 31–50.

———. "Foreword." In Ahmad Faris al-Shidyaq, *Leg over Leg or, The Turtle in the Tree*, translated and edited by Humphrey Davies, 1:ix–xxx. New York: New York University Press, 2013.

———. *Stranger Fictions: A History of the Novel in Arabic Translation*. Ithaca, NY: Cornell University Press, 2020.

Johnson-Davies, Denys, and Ferial Ghazoul. "On Translating Arabic Literature: An Interview with Denys Johnson-Davies." *Alif: Journal of Comparative Poetics* 3 (1983): 80–93.

Junge, Christian. "Doing Things with Lists—Enumeration in Arabic Prose." *Journal of Arabic Literature* 50 (2019): 278–297.

Kabbani, Rana. *Imperial Fictions: Europe's Myths of Orient*. London: Saqi, 2008.

Kant, Immanuel. *Groundwork for the Metaphysics of Morals*. Translated and edited by Allen W. Wood. New Haven, CT: Yale University Press, 2002.

Kapchan, Deborah. "Body." In *Keywords in Sound*, edited by David Novak and Matt Sakakeeny, 33–44. Durham, NC: Duke University Press, 2015.

———. "The Splash of Icarus: Theorizing Sound Writing/Writing Sound Theory." In *Theorizing Sound Writing*, edited by Deborah Kapchan, 1–22. Middletown, CT: Wesleyan University Press, 2017.

Kareem, Mona. "Lily Meyer and Mona Kareem on Their New Series, Close-Up: An Experiment in Reviewing Translation." Interview in *Words Without Borders*, May 14, 2020. https://www.wordswithoutborders.org/dispatches/article/lily-meyer-mona-kareem-close-up-an-experiment-in-reviewing-translation-s?src=landingpage.

Keen, Suzanne. *Empathy and the Novel*. New York: Oxford University Press, 2007.

Kennedy, Dane. *The Highly Civilized Man: Richard Burton and the Victorian World*. Cambridge, MA: Harvard University Press, 2005.

Kīlīṭū, ʿAbd al-Fattāḥ. *Lan tatakallama lughatī*. Beirut: Dār al-Talīʿah, 2002.

Kilpatrick, Hilary. Review of *Leg over Leg* by Ahmad Faris al-Shidyaq, translated by Humphrey Davies. *Journal of the American Oriental Society* 138, no. 3 (2018): 659–662.

Kouloughli, D. E. "A propos de lafẓ et maʿnā." *Bulletin d'Études Orientales* 35 (1983): 43–63.

Krämer, Sybille. "Writing, Notational Iconicity, Calculus: On Writing as a Cultural Technique." Translated by Anita McChesney. *MLN* 118 (2003): 518–537.

Kristeva, Julia. "Stabat Mater." Translated by Léon Roudiez. In *The Kristeva Reader*, edited by Toril Moi, 160–186. New York: Columbia University Press, 1986.

Kumar, N. P. Krishna. "Reading Index Results Reveal Arabs Read 35 Hours a Year." *Al Arabiya English*, December 5, 2015. https://english.alarabiya.net/en/business/economy/2016/12/05/Reading-Index-results-reveal-Arabs-read-35-hours-a-year.

LaBelle, Brandon. *Lexicon of the Mouth: Poetics and Politics of Voice and the Oral Imaginary*. New York: Bloomsbury, 2014.

Leighton, Angela. *Hearing Things: The Work of Sound in Literature*. Cambridge, MA: The Belknap Press of Harvard University Press, 2018.

Levinas, Emmanuel. *Ethics and Infinity: Conversations with Philippe Nemo*. Translated by Richard A. Cohen. Pittsburgh, PA: Duquesne University Press, 1985.

Levine, Caroline. *Forms: Whole, Rhythm, Hierarchy, Network*. Princeton, NJ: Princeton University Press, 2015.

Levine, Suzanne Jill. "Jorge Luis Borges and the Translators of the Nights." *Translation Review* 77–78 (2009): 15–21.

Lewis, Philip E. "The Measure of Translation Effects." In Venuti, *The Translation Studies Reader*, 220–239.

Lienau, Annette Damayanti. "Reframing Vernacular Culture on Arabic Fault Lines: Bamba, Senghor, and Sembene's Translingual Legacies in French West Africa." *PMLA* 130, no. 2 (2015): 419–429.

Lindsey, Ursula. "Why Don't Arabs Read?" *Al-Fanar Media*, July 7, 2016. https://www.al-fanarmedia.org/2016/07/why-dont-arabs-read/.

Liu, Lydia. *Translingual Practice: Literature, National Culture, and Translated Modernity—China, 1900–1937*. Stanford, CA: Stanford University Press, 1995.

Love, Heather. "Close but not Deep: Literary Ethics and the Descriptive Turn." *New Literary History* 41, no. 2 (2010): 371–391.

Lovell, Mary. *A Rage to Live: A Biography of Richard and Isabel Burton*. New York: Norton, 1998.

Mahdi, Muhsin. "Introduction." In *The Thousand and One Nights (Alf Layla wa-Layla): From the Earliest Known Sources*, edited by Muhsin Mahdi, 3:1–10. Leiden: Brill, 1994.

Makdisi, Saree, and Felicity Nussbaum. "Introduction." In *The Arabian Nights in Historical Context: Between East and West*, edited by Saree Makdisi and Felicity Nussbaum, 1–23. New York: Oxford University Press, 2008.

Makdisi, Ussama. *The Culture of Sectarianism: Community, History, and Violence in Nineteenth-Century Ottoman Lebanon*. Berkeley: University of California Press, 2000.

Malījī, Saḥar al-, and Maḥmūd Jāwīsh. "'Khitām maʿriḍ al-kitāb' bi-3.5 milyūn zāʾir." *Al-Maṣrī Al-Yawm*, February 5, 2020. https://www.almasryalyoum.com/news/details/1481920.

Mallory, J. P., and D. Q. Adams. *The Oxford Introduction to Proto-Indo-European and the Proto-Indo-European World*. New York: Oxford University Press, 2006.

Marks, Laura U. "Haptic Visuality: Touching with the Eyes." *Framework: The Finnish Art Review* 2 (2004): 79–82.

Marlowe, Ann. Review of *I'jaam: An Iraqi Rhapsody* by Sinan Antoon, translated by Rebecca C. Johnson and Sinan Antoon. *San Francisco Chronicle*,

August 30, 2007. https://www.sfgate.com/books/article/Outcast-I-jaam-offer-outsiders-looks-at-2506373.php.

Masmoudi, Ikram. *War and Occupation in Iraqi Fiction*. Edinburgh: Edinburgh University Press, 2015.

Massumi, Brian. *Parables for the Virtual: Movement, Affect, Sensation*. Durham, NC: Duke University Press, 2002.

Maṭar, ʿAbd al-ʿAzīz. *Laḥn al-ʿāmmah fī ḍawʾ al-dirāsāt al-lughawiyyah al-ḥadīthah*. Cairo: al-Dār al-Qawmiyyah lil-Tibāʿah wa-al-Nashr, 1966.

Mazʿāsh, Lubnā. "Lā yaqraʾūn." *Aljazeera.net*, September 8, 2017. https://www.aljazeera.net/blogs/2017/9/8/لا-يقرأون.

Mbembe, Achille. "The Banality of Power and the Aesthetics of Vulgarity in the Postcolony." Translated by Janet Roitman. *Public Culture* 4, no. 2 (1992): 1–30.

McCarthy, Tom. "Donald Rumsfeld Denies He Thought Democracy in Iraq Was 'Realistic' Goal." *The Guardian*, June 9, 2015. https://www.theguardian.com/us-news/2015/jun/09/donald-rumsfeld-iraq-war-democracy-contradiction.

McManus, Anne-Marie. "Scale in the Balance: Reading with the International Prize for Arabic Fiction ('The Arabic Booker')." *International Journal of Middle East Studies* 48 (2016): 217–241.

Meschonnic, Henri. *Ethics and Politics of Translating*. Translated and edited by Pier-Pascale Boulanger. Philadelphia: John Benjamins, 2011.

Michalak-Pikulska, Barbara, and Waïl S. Hassan. "Oman." In *The Oxford Handbook of Arab Novelistic Traditions*, edited by Waïl S. Hassan, 359–370. New York: Oxford University Press, 2017.

Mitchell, W. J. T. *Picture Theory: Essays on Verbal and Visual Representation*. Chicago: University of Chicago Press, 1994.

Montgomery, James E. *Al-Jāḥiẓ: In Praise of Books*. Edinburgh: Edinburgh University Press, 2013.

Moretti, Franco. "Conjectures on World Literature." *New Left Review* 1 (2000): 54–68.

Morgan, Benjamin. "Critical Empathy: Vernon Lee's Aesthetics and the Origins of Close Reading." *Victorian Studies* 55, no. 1 (2012): 31–56.

Moukheiber, Karen. "Gendering Emotions: Ṭarab, Women and Musical Performance in Three Biographical Narratives from 'The Book of Songs.'" *Cultural History* 8, no. 2 (2019): 164–183.

Mufti, Aamir R. *Forget English! Orientalisms and World Literatures*. Cambridge, MA: Harvard University Press, 2016.

Muharram, Mohammed Abdullah Hussein. "The Marginalization of Arabic Fiction in the Postcolonial and World English Curriculum: Slips? Or Orientalism and Racism?," *the minnesota review* 78 (2012): 130–145.

"Multiple News Items." *The Standard*, September 12, 1885, 4–5.

al-Musawi, Muhsin J. (al-Mūsawī, Muḥsin). *The Islamic Context of The Thousand and One Nights*. New York: Columbia University Press, 2009.

Mūsawī, Muḥsin al- (al-Musawi, Muhsin J.). "Riwāyat al-jawāʾiz," *Al-Ḥayāt*, July 23, 2014. https://aljasrah.net/aljasra3440/رواية-الجوائز.

———. "Simāt riwāyat al-jawā'iz." *Al-Ḥayāt*, July 24, 2014. https://aljasrah.net/aljasra3489/سمات-رواية-الجوائز.

Naaman, Mara. "Disciplinary Divergences: Problematizing the Field of Arabic Literature." *Comparative Literature Studies* 47, no. 4 (2010): 446–471.

Nāgī, Aḥmad. "2.5 milyūn dūlār sanawiyyan yunfiquhā al-ʿArab ʿalā al-jawā'iz al-adabiyyah." *Akhbār Al-Adab*, July 5, 2015, 5–7.

Nancy, Jean-Luc. *Listening*. Translated by Charlotte Mandell. New York: Fordham University Press, 2007.

Newton, Adam Zachary. *To Make the Hands Impure: Art, Ethical Adventure, the Difficult and the Holy*. New York: Fordham University Press, 2015.

Next Page Foundation. *What Arabs Read: A Pan-Arab Survey on Readership*, "Phase One: Egypt, Lebanon, Saudi Arabia, Tunisia, Morocco." January 2007. https://menadoc.bibliothek.uni-halle.de/menalib/content/titleinfo/1303340.

———. *What Arabs Read: A Pan-Arab Survey on Readership*, "Phase Two: Algeria, Jordan, Palestine and Syria." September 2007. https://menadoc.bibliothek.uni-halle.de/menalib/content/titleinfo/1303343.

Ngai, Sianne. *Ugly Feelings*. Cambridge, MA: Harvard University Press, 2005.

Omri, Mohamed-Salah. "Local Narrative Form and Constructions of the Arabic Novel." *Novel: A Forum on Fiction* 41 (2008): 244–263.

———. "Notes on the Traffic between Theory and Arabic Literature." *International Journal of Middle East Studies* 43 (2011): 731–733.

Pannewick, Friederike. "Dancing Letters: The Art of Subversion in Sinān Anṭūn's Novel *Iʿjām*." In *Conflicting Narratives: War, Trauma and Memory in Iraqi Culture*, edited by Stephan Milich, Friederike Pannewick, and Leslie Tramontini, 65–74. Wiesbaden: Reichert Verlag, 2012.

"Pantagruelism or Pornography?" *Pall Mall Gazette*, September 14, 1885, 2–3.

Payne, John. *The Book of the Thousand Nights and One Night: Now First Completely Done into English Prose and Verse, from the Original Arabic*. 9 vols. London: n.p., 1901.

———. *Tales from the Arabic: of the Breslau and Calcutta (1814–18) Editions of the Book of the Thousand Nights and One Night Not Occurring in the Other Printed Texts of the Work, Now First Done into English by John Payne*. 3 vols. London: n.p., 1901.

Peled, Mattityahu. "The Enumerative Style in Al-sâq ʿalâ al-sâq." *Journal of Arabic Literature* 22, no. 2 (1991): 127–145.

Penzer, Norman. *An Annotated Bibliography of Sir Richard Francis Burton*. London: A. M. Philpot, 1923.

Pierpont, Claudia Roth. "Found in Translation." *The New Yorker*, January 18, 2010, 74–80.

Plath, Sylvia. *The Bell Jar*. New York: Harper & Row, 1971.

"Plus de kutub, please." *The Economist*, June 18, 2016, 54.

Polizzotti, Mark. *Sympathy for the Traitor: A Translation Manifesto*. Cambridge, MA: MIT Press, 2018.

Preston, Theodore. “Introduction.” In *Makamat; or, Rhetorical Anecdotes of Al Hariri of Basra*, translated by Theodore Preston, 1–19. London: J. Deighton, 1850.

Probyn, Elspeth. “Shame in the Habitus.” *The Sociological Review* 52, no. 2, supplement (2004): 224–248.

Puchner, Martin. *The Written World: The Power of Stories to Shape People, History, Civilization*. New York: Random House, 2017.

Puig de la Bellacasa, María. *Matters of Care: Speculative Ethics in More Than Human Worlds*. Minneapolis: University of Minnesota Press, 2017.

Qualey, Marcia Lynx. “Women in Translation Month: 10 Recommended Books from 2020.” *ArabLit.org*, August 1, 2020. https://arablit.org/2020/08/01/women-in-translation-month-8-recommended-books-from-2020/.

Rabassa, Gregory. *If This Be Treason: Translation and Its Dyscontents*. New York: New Directions, 2005.

Racy, A. J. *Making Music in the Arab World: The Culture and Artistry of Ṭarab*. New York: Cambridge University Press, 2004.

Ramaḍān, Bilāl. “Intiqādāt ḥādah li-‘*Sayyidāt al-qamar*’ awwal riwāyah tafūz bi-jāʾizat Mān Būkar al-ʿalamiyyah.” *al-Yawm al-Sābiʿ*, May 27, 2019. https://www.youm7.com/story/2019/5/27/4260408/انتقادات-حادة-لـسيدات-القمر-أول-رواية-تفوز-بجائزة-مان

Rancière, Jacques. *Dissensus: On Politics and Aesthetics*. Translated by Steven Corcoran. New York: Bloomsbury Academic, 2015.

Rastegar, Kamran. *Literary Modernity between the Middle East and Europe: Textual Transactions in Nineteenth-Century Arabic, English, and Persian Literatures*. New York: Routledge, 2007.

Reynolds, Dwight F. “A Thousand and One Nights: A History of the Text and Its Reception.” In *Arabic Literature in the Post-Classical Period*, edited by Roger Allen and D. S. Richards, 270–291. New York: Cambridge University Press, 2006.

Reynolds, Susan Salter. Review of *I'jaam: An Iraqi Rhapsody* by Sinan Antoon, translated by Rebecca C. Johnson and Sinan Antoon. *Los Angeles Times*, June 17, 2007. https://www.latimes.com/archives/la-xpm-2007-jun-17-bk-discoveries17-story.html.

Rice, Edward. *Captain Sir Richard Francis Burton: The Secret Agent Who Made the Pilgrimage to Mecca, Discovered the Kama Sutra, and Brought the Arabian Nights to the West*. New York: Charles Scribner's Sons, 1990.

Riker, Martin. “A Ramshackle Modernity.” Review of *The Time Regulation Institute* by Ahmet Hamdi Tanpinar, translated by Maureen Freely and Alexander Dawe. *New York Times*, January 3, 2014. https://www.nytimes.com/2014/01/05/books/review/the-time-regulation-institute-by-ahmet-hamdi-tanpinar.html?searchResultPosition=3.

Robinson, Douglas. *The Translator's Turn*. Baltimore, MD: Johns Hopkins University Press, 1991.

——. *Who Translates?: Translator Subjectivities Beyond Reason*. Albany: State University of New York Press, 2001.

Roper, Geoffrey. "Aḥmad Fāris al-Shidyāq and the Libraries of Europe and the Ottoman Empire." *Libraries & Culture* 33, no. 3 (1990): 233–248.

——. "Fāris al-Shidyāq and the Transition from Scribal to Print Culture." In *The Book in the Islamic World: The Written Word and Communication in the Middle East*, edited by George Atiyeh, 209–231. Albany: State University of New York Press, 1995.

Rosenman, Ellen Bayuk. *Unauthorized Pleasures: Accounts of Victorian Erotic Experience*. Ithaca, NY: Cornell University Press, 2003.

Ruhl, Sarah. *100 Essays I Don't Have Time to Write: On Umbrellas and Sword Fights, Parades and Dogs, Fire Alarms, Children, and Theater*. New York: Farrar, Straus and Giroux, 2014.

Rushdie, Salman. *Shame*. London: Jonathan Cape, 1983.

Ryding, Karin. *A Reference Grammar of Modern Standard Arabic*. Cambridge: Cambridge University Press, 2005.

Sacks, Jeffrey. *Iterations of Loss: Mutilation and Aesthetic Form, Al-Shidyaq to Darwish*. New York: Fordham University Press, 2015.

Said, Edward W. "Embargoed Literature." *The Nation*, September 17, 1990, 278–280.

——. *Orientalism*. New York: Vintage Books, 1994.

——. "The World, the Text, and the Critic." In *The World, the Text, and the Critic*, 31–53. Cambridge, MA: Harvard University Press, 1983.

Ṣāliḥ, Sharīf. "'Ashr naṣā'iḥ lil-fawz bi-jā'izat 'al-Būkar.'" *Al-Nahār*, May 12, 2015, 32.

Saussy, Haun. "Comparative Literature: The Next Ten Years." In *Futures of Comparative Literature: ACLA State of the Discipline Report*, edited by Ursula K. Heise, 24–29. New York: Routledge, 2017.

——. *The Ethnography of Rhythm: Orality and Its Technologies*. New York: Fordham University Press, 2016.

——. "Exquisite Cadavers Stitched from Fresh Nightmares: Of Memes, Hives, and Selfish Genes." In *Comparative Literature in an Age of Globalization*, edited by Haun Saussy, 3–42. Baltimore, MD: Johns Hopkins University Press, 2006.

Sawa, George. *Music Performance Practice in the Early 'Abbāsid Era: 132–320 AH / 750–932 AD*. 2nd ed. Ottawa: The Institute of Mediaeval Music, 2004.

Scarry, Elaine. *The Body in Pain: The Making and Unmaking of the World*. New York: Oxford University Press, 1985.

Schjeldahl, Peter. "Casualties." Review of *Theater of Operations: The Gulf Wars 1991–2011* at MoMA PS1, New York City (November 3, 2019–March 1, 2020). *The New Yorker*, December 2, 2019, 70–71.

Schleiermacher, Friedrich. "On the Different Methods of Translating." Translated by Susan Bernofsky. In Venuti, *The Translation Studies Reader*, 43–63.

Sedgwick, Eve Kosofsky. *Touching Feeling: Affect, Pedagogy, Performativity.* Durham, NC: Duke University Press, 2003.

Seigworth, Gregory J., and Melissa Gregg. "An Inventory of Shimmers." In Gregg and Seigworth, *The Affect Theory Reader*, 1–25.

Selim, Samah. "The Narrative Craft: Realism and Fiction in the Arabic Canon." *Edebiyat: Journal of M.E. Literatures* 14, nos. 1–2 (2003): 109–128.

Sells, Michael. *Approaching the Qur'an: The Early Revelations*. Ashland, OR: White Cloud Press, 1999.

Shamma, Tarek. "The Exotic Dimension of Foreignizing Strategies: Burton's Translation of the Arabian Nights." *The Translator* 11, no. 1 (2005): 51–67.

———. *Translation and the Manipulation of Difference: Arabic Literature in Nineteenth-Century England*. Manchester: St. Jerome Publishing, 2009.

Shannon, Jonathan H. "Emotion, Performance, and Temporality in Arab Music: Reflections on Tarab." *Cultural Anthropology* 18, no. 1 (2003): 72–98.

Shklovsky, Victor. "Art as Technique." In *Russian Formalist Criticism: Four Essays*, translated by Lee T. Lemon and Marion J. Reis, 3–24. Lincoln: University of Nebraska Press, 1965.

Shūmān, Hilāl. *Līmbū Bayrūt*. Beirut: Dār al-Tanwīr, 2013.

Shusterman, Richard. *Thinking through the Body: Essays in Somaesthetics*. New York: Cambridge University Press, 2012.

Silcox, Beejay. "The First Arabic Novel to Win the International Booker Prize." Review of *Celestial Bodies* by Jokha Alharthi, translated by Marilyn Booth. *New York Times*, October 21, 2019. https://www.nytimes.com/2019/10/21/books/review/celestial-bodies-jokha-alharthi.html.

Smith, Rachel Greenwald. *Affect and American Literature in the Age of Neoliberalism*. New York: Cambridge University Press, 2015.

Snaije, Olivia. "The Politics of Translation: 'Arabic Literatures in Europe.'" *Publishing Perspectives*, October 26, 2019. https://publishingperspectives.com/2019/10/politics-of-translation-arabic-literatures-in-europe-frankfurt-2019-show-daily.

Sontag, Susan. *On Photography*. New York: Penguin, 1977.

Spinoza, Benedictus de. *Ethics*. Translated and edited by Edwin Curley. London: Penguin Books, 1996.

Spivak, Gayatri Chakravorty. *An Aesthetic Education in the Era of Globalization*. Cambridge, MA: Harvard University Press, 2012.

———. *A Critique of Postcolonial Reason: Toward a History of the Vanishing Present*. Cambridge, MA: Harvard University Press, 1999.

———. "The Politics of Translation." In Venuti, *The Translation Studies Reader*, 312–330.

Stanton, Anna Ziajka. "Eyes on the Prize: The Global Readability of an IPAF-Winning Modern Arabic Novel." *Middle Eastern Literatures* 24, no. 1 (2021): 20–39.

———. "Feeling the Grammar: Literary Translations of the Dual Inflection in Arabic." *Philological Encounters* 4, nos. 1–2 (2019): 26–54.

Staten, Henry. "Tracking the 'Native Informant': Cultural Translation as the Horizon of Literary Translation." In *Nation, Language, and the Ethics of Translation*, edited by Sandra Bermann and Michael Wood, 111–126. Princeton, NJ: Princeton University Press, 2005.

Steedman, Carolyn. *Dust*. Manchester: Manchester University Press, 2001.

Steiner, George. *After Babel: Aspects of Language and Translation*. New York: Oxford University Press, 1975.

Steingass, F. *The Student's Arabic-English Dictionary: Companion Volume to the Author's English-Arabic Dictionary*. London: Crosby Lockwood and Son, 1884.

Stewart, Kathleen. "Worlding Refrains." In Gregg and Seigworth, *The Affect Theory Reader*, 339–353.

Stoler, Laura Ann. *Race and the Education of Desire: Foucault's* History of Sexuality *and the Colonial Order of Things*. Durham, NC: Duke University Press, 1995.

Storace, Patricia. "After Rabelais." Review of *Leg over Leg* by Ahmad Faris al-Shidyaq, translated by Humphrey Davies. *TLS*, November 18, 2015. https://www.the-tls.co.uk/articles/private/after-rabelais/.

Stratton, Allegra. "2007 Is America's Deadliest Year in Iraq." *The Guardian*, December 31, 2007. https://www.theguardian.com/world/2007/dec/31/usa.iraq?CMP=share_btn_link.

Ṣuwayliḥ, Khalīl. "Riwāʾīyūn bi-lā jawāʾiz . . . riwāʾīyūn mansīyun." *Al-Akhbār*, January 18, 2016. http://ar.theasian.asia/archives/29887.

Tageldin, Shaden. *Disarming Words: Empire and the Seductions of Translation in Egypt*. Berkeley: University of California Press, 2011.

———. "The Returns of Theory." *International Journal of Middle East Studies* 43 (2011): 728–730.

Tanoukhi, Nirvana. "Rewriting Political Commitment for an International Canon: Paul Bowles's *For Bread Alone* as Translation of Mohamed Choukri's *Al-Khubz Al-Hafi*." *Research in African Literatures* 34, no. 2 (2003): 127–144.

"Theater of Operations: The Gulf Wars 1991–2011." https://www.moma.org/calendar/exhibitions/5084.

Tīfāshī, Aḥmad al-. *Nuzhat al-albāb fī-mā lā yūjad fī kitāb*. Edited by Jamāl Jumʿah. London: Riyāḍ al-Rayyis, 1992.

Toler, Michael A. "The Ethics of Cultural Representation: The Maghribi Novel in English Translation." *The Journal of North African Studies* 6, no. 3 (2001): 48–69.

Toorawa, Shawkat. "A Corpus, Not a Canon (Nor an Anthology): Creating a 'Library of Arabic Literature.'" *Journal of World Literature* 2 (2017): 356–376.

Traboulsi, Fawwaz. "Ahmad Faris Al-Shidyaq (1804–87): The Quest for Another Modernity." In *Arabic Thought beyond the Liberal Age: Towards an Intellectual History of the Nahda*, edited by Jens Hanssen and Max Weiss, 175–186. New York: Cambridge University Press, 2016.

Trivedi, Harish. “Translation and World Literature: The Indian Context.” In *Translation and World Literature*, edited by Susan Bassnett, 15–28. New York: Routledge, 2019.

Troxell, Jenelle. “Torture, Terror, Digitality: A Conversation with Tony Cokes.” *Afterimage* 43, no. 3 (2015): 20–25.

Tymoczko, Maria. “Western Metaphorical Discourses Implicit in Translation Studies.” In *Thinking through Translation with Metaphors*, edited by James St. André, 109–143. New York: Routledge, 2014.

Updike, John. “Satan's Work and Silted Cisterns.” Review of *Cities of Salt* by Abdelrahman Munif, translated by Peter Theroux. *The New Yorker*, October 17, 1988, 117–121.

Vasseleu, Cathryn. *Textures of Light: Vision and Touch in Irigaray, Levinas and Merleau Ponty*. New York: Routledge, 1998.

Venuti, Lawrence. “Genealogies of Translation Theory: Jerome.” In Venuti, *The Translation Studies Reader*, 483–502.

———. “Hijacking Translation: How Comp Lit Continues to Suppress Translated Texts.” *boundary 2* 43, no. 2 (2016): 179–204.

———. *The Translator's Invisibility: A History of Translation*. New York: Routledge, 1995.

———. *The Translator's Invisibility: A History of Translation*, 3rd ed. New York: Routledge, 2018.

Venuti, Lawrence, ed. *The Translation Studies Reader*, 3rd ed. New York: Routledge, 2012.

Versteegh, C. H. M., O. N. H. Leaman, and J. E. Bencheikh. “Maʿnā.” In *Encyclopaedia of Islam, Second Edition*, edited by P. Bearman et al. Leiden: Brill, 2012. https://referenceworks.brillonline.com/entries/encyclopaedia-of-islam-2/mana-COM_0659.

Versteegh, Kees. “The Development of Argumentation in Arabic Grammar: The Declension of the Dual and the Plural.” *Zeitschrift für Arabische Linguistik* 15 (1985): 152–173.

Wadud, Amina. *Qur'an and Woman: Rereading the Sacred Text from a Woman's Perspective*. New York: Oxford University Press, 1999.

Walkowitz, Judith. *City of Dreadful Delight: Narratives of Sexual Danger in Late-Victorian London*. Chicago: University of Chicago Press, 1992.

Walkowitz, Rebecca. *Born Translated: The Contemporary Novel in an Age of World Literature*. New York: Columbia University Press, 2015.

Warhol, Robyn. *Having a Good Cry: Effeminate Feelings and Pop-Culture Forms*. Columbus: Ohio State University Press, 2003.

Weinstein, Emily. “Letter Imperfect: Dreams from Prison in an Orwellian Iraqi Novel.” Review of *I'jaam: An Iraqi Rhapsody* by Sinan Antoon, translated by Rebecca C. Johnson and Sinan Antoon. *Village Voice*, June 13–19, 2007, 55.

Wellek, René, and Austin Warren. *Theory of Literature*. New York: Harcourt, Brace and Company, 1942.

Williams, Gordon. *Shakespeare's Sexual Language: A Glossary*. London: Continuum, 1997.

Williams, Mark. "In Algeria the Biggest Cultural Event Is a Book Fair." *The New Publishing Standard*, October 20, 2019. https://thenewpublishingstandard.com/2019/10/20/in-algeria-the-biggest-cultural-event-is-a-book-fair-will-the-algiers-ibf-break-its-2–3-million-visitor-record-this-year-with-its-focus-on-young-authors/.

Williams, Raymond. *Marxism and Literature*. New York: Oxford University Press, 1977.

Wood, James. "Lifelines." Review of *Celestial Bodies* by Jokha Alharthi, translated by Marilyn Booth. *The New Yorker*, October 14, 2019, 78–81.

"World Lite." *n+1* 17 (2013). https://nplusonemag.com/issue-17/the-intellectual-situation/world-lite/.

Wright, Thomas. *The Life of Sir Richard Burton*. 2 vols. London: Everett and Co., 1906.

Wright, W. *Arabic Grammar*. 3rd ed. Mineola, NY: Dover Publications, 2005.

Yargo, John. "More Steps Than the Stairway of a Minaret." Review of *Leg over Leg* by Ahmad Faris al-Shidyaq, translated by Humphrey Davies. *Los Angeles Review of Books*, May 10, 2014. https://lareviewofbooks.org/article/steps-stairway-minaret-humphrey-davies-translation-faris-al-shidyaqs-leg-leg/.

Zachs, Fruma. *The Making of a Syrian Identity: Intellectuals and Merchants in Nineteenth Century Beirut*. Leiden: Brill, 2005.

INDEX

Aboul-Ela, Hosam, 4–5, 16, 38–39
About Baghdad, 134–35
Abu Dhabi International Book Fair, 146
Abu Ghraib prison photographs, 115
Abu-Haidar, Jareer, 94–96
Abu-Zeid, Kareem James, 153–55, 195n52
adab, 19–20, 68–69
Adūnīs (Adonis), 69
aesthetics: *ʿajamī*, 119; of Arabic literature, 5–6, 14–16, 20–21, 80, 132–33, 142, 149–51; of English, 7, 11, 51–53, 98, 129; experience of, 5, 30–31, 44, 66, 72, 114, 116–17, 119, 129, 138–39; of *lafẓ*, 33, 35–36, 38, 44–45, 47–48; of the *muthannā*, 94–95, 97; of *sajʿ*, 70–71; *ṭarab* and, 75–76, 78; translation methods and, 12–14, 26, 36, 84, 86–87, 141; worldliness and, 3, 7, 17, 19, 21, 26, 87, 111, 137
affects, defined, 18, 26, 78, 116–17, 127–28, 132, 156
Agamben, Giorgio, 120
Ahmad, Aijaz, 188n70
Ahmed, Sara, 18, 90, 156
ʿajamī, 118–19, 136
Al-Bagdadi, Nadia, 52
Albazei, Saad, 122, 123
Alf laylah wa-laylah ("Arabian Nights" stories), 5, 57, 63, 65; Burton's editions of, 61–62, 67; literary features of, 58, 64–65, 73–74; *sajʿ* in, 68–70; translations of, 8, 57–58; as world literature, 58, 79. See also *The Book of the Thousand Nights and a Night*; *The Book of the Thousand Nights and One Night*
Algiers International Book Fair, 193n30
Alharthi, Jokha. *See* al-Ḥārithī, Jūkhah
Allan, Michael, 19–20
Allen, Roger, 10, 140, 143
Al-Nakib, Mai, 133
Al-Nowaihi, Magda, 16
Al-Shidyaq, Ahmad Faris. *See* al-Shidyāq, Aḥmad Fāris
ʿAlwān, Muḥammad Ḥasan (Mohammed Hasan Alwan), 150
Amer, Sahar, 74
Anderson, Benedict, 143
Antoon, Sinan. *See* Anṭūn, Sinān
Anṭūn, Sinān, 6, 134–35; self-translation and, 135–37, 191n98. See also *I'jaam*; *Iʿjām*
Appadurai, Arjun, 144
Appiah, Kwame Anthony, 61
Apter, Emily, 22–24, 38–41, 144
"Arabian Nights" stories. See *Alf laylah wa-laylah*
Arabic alphabet, 6, 54, 94, 101, 104–6, 119, 121, 123–25, 131
"Arabic Booker," 145. *See also* International Prize for Arabic Fiction (IPAF)
the Arabic novel, 52, 144, 146–47, 149, 150
Arab-language classes enrollment, U.S., 155
Arab Spring, 162n7
Asad, Talal, 53, 117

ʿĀshūr, Raḍwā (Radwa Ashour), 52
Austin, J. L., 47
Ayoub, Dima, 15, 35

Baalbaki, Ramzi, 31
Badiou, Alain, 129, 139
Bahoora, Haytham, 136
Bakhtin, Mikhail, 102
Bal, Mieke, 186n16
Barakāt, Hudā (Hoda Barakat), 153
Barīd al-layl (*Voices of the Lost*) (Barakāt), 153
Barthes, Roland, 79, 89
Bassnett, Susan, 83, 102, 135
Baudrillard, Jean, 115
al-Bayān wa-al-tabyīn (al-Jāḥiẓ), 87–88
Bayoumi, Moustafa, 117–18
Beecroft, Alexander, 164n34
The Bell Jar (Plath), 107–8
Bellos, David, 24, 167n97
Bengio, Ofra, 121–22
Benjamin, Walter, 22–24
Berlant, Lauren, 92, 109
Bermann, Sandra, 40, 164n37
Blanc, Haim, 93
Bloom, Harold, 81
The Book of the Thousand Nights and a Night (translation by Burton), 6; critical reception of, 76–77, 79; enduring legacy of, 57–59; eroticism in, 62, 72–74, 76–77, 79; foreword to, 64, 70, 74–75, 177n39; Obscene Publications Act and, 77; Payne's translation compared to, 59, 67–68, 70–73; plagiarism and, 58–59, 63, 66–67, 80; profitability of, 63, 74; *ṭarab* and, 75–78; as world literature, 58–59, 76, 81
The Book of the Thousand Nights and One Night (translation by Payne), 58–59, 63–65, 67–68, 70–73
Booth, Marilyn, 10, 15, 150–53, 155–56
Borges, Jorge Luis, 57
Boulanger, Pier-Pascale, 165n43
Boullata, Issa, 10
Bourdieu, Pierre, 18, 116
Boyden, Michael, 135
Brennan, Teresa, 18, 132
Brennan, Timothy, 144
Briggs, Kate, 89
Brodie, Fawn, 80, 175n22
Brouillette, Sarah, 143
Brustad, Kristen, 93, 97
Burton, Richard Francis, 6, 176n26; annotations by, 61–62, 67; *The Book of the Thousand Nights and a Night* foreword by, 64, 70, 74–75, 177n39; circumcision and, 60–61, 175n22; cosmopolitanism of, 61; eroticism and, 62, 72–74, 76–77, 79; fictional depictions of, 174n1, 175n23; Huntington Library bust of, 56–57; Payne's correspondence with, 64; plagiarism and, 58–59, 63, 66–67, 80; *ṭarab* and, 75–79; on translation as "labor of love," 163n30; translation of *sajʿ* and, 68, 70–71. See also *The Book of the Thousand Nights and a Night*
Bush, George W., 126, 128, 134–35, 185n3
Butler, Judith, 90, 110–12

Cairo International Book Fair, 148
Casanova, Pascale, 164n34
Cassin, Barbara, 23–24
Caton, Steven, 175n23
Celestial Bodies. See *Sayyidāt al-qamar*
de Certeau, Michel, 108
Cheah, Pheng, 142
Chen, Mel Y., 98
Cheney, Dick, 128
Chouman, Hilal. *See* Shūmān, Hilāl
Cokes, Tony, 117–18
Cole, Peter, 12
Colla, Elliott, 12, 74, 155
The Collector of Worlds (Der Weltensammler) (Troyanov), 174n1
Conrad, Joseph, 56
content. See *maʿnā*
Cooperson, Michael, 70
The Corpse Washer. See *Waḥdahā shajarat al-rummān*
Creswell, Robyn, 2, 12–13, 52, 75
Croft, Jennifer, 89
Cusk, Rachel, 110–11

Dallal, Jenine Abboushi, 15, 144
Dames, Nicholas, 17, 78–79
Damrosch, David, 22, 57, 141
Dauphinée, Elizabeth, 115
Davies, Humphrey, 5, 27; *Leg over Leg* translation reviewed, 27–28, 48, 50–51, 54–55; translator's afterword by, 49. See also *Leg over Leg or, The Turtle in the Tree, concerning The Fāriyāq*; *al-Sāq ʿalā al-sāq fī mā huwa al-Fāriyāq*
De Bleeker, Liesbeth, 135

Deleuze, Gilles, 3, 17, 123
Derrida, Jacques, 38, 81, 122
The Devil Drives (Brodie), 80
Dimock, Wai Chee, 54
Dolar, Mladen, 65
domesticating translations, 10, 28, 168n7
Driver, G. R., 105
dual grammar. See *muthannā*

"El Aleph" (Borges), 57
El-Ariss, Tarek, 14–15, 18–19, 39, 52, 80, 127–28, 138
Emirates Airline Festival of Literature, 152–53
Evil.16 installation (Cokes), 117–18

Farwell, Byron, 79
Fī sūq al-sabāyā (*The Beekeeper*) (Mīkhā'īl), 150
foreignizing translations, 10–11, 28, 153–54
form, 20–21, 33. See also *lafẓ*
Foucault, Michel, 84
Frānkishtāyn fī Baghdād (*Frankenstein in Baghdad*) (Sa'dāwī), 150
Franks, Tommy R., 127
Friedmann, Jessica, 111
Furani, Khaled, 7

Galland, Antoine, 58
Gerhardt, Mia, 69
Ghazoul, Ferial, 73, 140
globalization: Arabic literature in English translation and, 2, 144–45, 152–53; world literary system and, 143–44
Greenblatt, Stephen, 53–54
Gregg, Melissa, 25, 80
Guattari, Félix, 3, 17, 123
Gulf Wars. *See* Iraq Wars

Hafez, Sabry, 34
Hanoosh, Yasmeen, 136
Harb, Lara, 5, 31, 170n23
al-Ḥarīrī, Abū Muḥammad al-Qāsim ibn 'Alī, 69–70
al-Ḥārithī, Jūkhah (Jokha Alharthi), 150–53
Hartman, Michelle, 10, 11, 54
Hassan, Waïl, 2, 37, 40, 135
Heidegger, Martin, 168n104
Heinemann African Writers Series, 140
Helmreich, Stefan, 48
Hodder, Mark, 174n1
Horta, Paulo Lemos, 59, 61–62
Huntington Library, 56–57, 61–62, 66–67
Hussein, Saddam, 113, 116, 121
Hutchins, William, 150

Ibn Khaldūn, 162n17
Ibn Manẓūr. See *Lisān al-'Arab*
Ibrahim, Abdallah, 69
I'jaam (Anṭūn), 6; aesthetics in, 115–16, 129–31; critical reception of, 133–34; depictions of Iraqi pain in, 115–16, 119, 127–28; footnote usage in, 130; self-translation and, 135. See also *I'jām*
Imru' al-Qays, 94, 96
International Prize for Arabic Fiction (IPAF), 145–49, 153, 192n15
Iraq Wars (1990–1991 and 2003–2011), 6, 185n3; American abuse of prisoners during, 115, 117–18; American rhetoric during, 128–29; Iraqi fatalities in, 113–15, 126–27, 185n4; *Theater of Operations* exhibit and, 113–15
Ismail, Sherif, 170n35
Issa, Rana, 29, 51
I'jām (Anṭūn), 6, 114, 120–21; aesthetics in, 122–23, 125–26; depictions of Iraqi pain in, 119, 123, 127–28; politics of, 122, 132; wordplay in, 120–21, 125, 130. See also *I'jaam*

Jābir, Rabī', 154
Jacquemond, Richard, 19, 166n75
al-Jāḥiẓ, Abī 'Uthmān 'Amru ibn Baḥr, 36–41, 87–88, 112
Jakobson, Roman, 94, 102, 183n39
Jameson, Fredric, 133, 188n70
Jaquette, Elisabeth, 150, 153–55
Jauss, Hans Robert, 190n90
al-Jā'izah al-'Ālamiyyah lil-Riwāyah al-'Arabiyyah (IPAF). *See* International Prize for Arabic Fiction
Jā'izat al-Malik 'Abd Allāh bin 'Abd al-'Azīz al-'Ālamiyyah lil-Tarjamah. *See* King Abdullah Bin Abdulaziz International Award for Translation
Jā'izat al-Multaqā lil-Qiṣṣah al-Qaṣīrah al-'Arabiyyah. *See* AlMultaqa Prize for the Arabic Short Story
Jā'izat al-Shaykh Zāyid lil-Kitāb. *See* Sheikh Zayed Book Award
Jā'izat Katārā lil-Riwāyah al-'Arabiyyah. *See* Katara Prize
Jerome (Saint), 13–14

Johnson, Barbara, 90–91, 107, 111
Johnson, Rebecca C., 33, 43–45, 52, 147; as co-translator of *I'jaam*, 6, 114, 135–36. See also *I'jaam*
Johnson-Davies, Denys, 140–41, 152
Joyce, James, 107–8
Junge, Christian, 43
al-Jurjānī, 'Abd al-Qahir, 31, 38, 170n23

Kabbani, Rana, 62, 79
Kapchan, Deborah, 32, 42
Kareem, Mona, 15
Katara Prize (Jā'izat Katārā lil-Riwāyah al-'Arabiyyah), 145
Keen, Suzanne, 127–28
Kennedy, Dane, 77
Keynes, Quentin, 67
Khalīfah, Khālid (Khaled Khalifa), 150
Kīlīṭū, 'Abd al-Fattāḥ (Abdelfattah Kilito), 37, 39, 40
King Abdullah Bin Abdulaziz International Award for Translation (Jā'izat al-Malik 'Abd Allāh bin 'Abd al-'Azīz al-'Ālamiyyah lil-Tarjamah), 145
Kitāb al-ḥayawān (al-Jāḥiẓ), 36–38
Kouloughli, D. E., 31
Kristeva, Julia, 111

LaBelle, Brandon, 65
lafẓ, 5; acoustics of, 30, 33, 42, 47, 97; aesthetics of, 30–31, 33, 35, 38, 44, 48; al-Jāḥiẓ on, 36–37; al-Jurjānī on, 31, 38, 170n23; *ma'nā* contrasted with, 30–31, 35–36, 39–40, 43, 45, 48; in the Qur'an, 31; translatability of, 40–42, 48; as untranslatable, 36–41
Lane, Edward, 62
Lebanese civil war (1975–1990), 91–92, 101, 104, 106, 108
Leg over Leg or, The Turtle in the Tree, concerning The Fāriyāq (al-Shidyāq), 5, 27; critical reception of, 27–28, 48, 50–51, 54–55; translator's afterword to, 49. See also *al-Sāq 'alā al-sāq fī mā huwa al-Fāriyāq*
Leighton, Angela, 29–30
Levinas, Emmanuel, 88, 181n17
Levine, Caroline, 21
Levine, Suzanne Jill, 58
Lewis, Philip, 26, 99
Lezra, Jacques, 23
Library of Arabic Literature, 28, 55, 169n14
Lienau, Annette Damayanti, 118–19
Limbo Beirut. See *Līmbū Bayrūt*
Līmbū Bayrūt (*Limbo Beirut*) (Shūmān), 6, 88; critical reception of, 181n19; crossword puzzles in, 101–3, 106–8; maternal ethics and, 89–90, 92, 100–1, 104, 106–8; May 2008 conflict represented in, 91, 108–10; the *muthannā* in, 91–100
Lisān al-'Arab (Ibn Manẓūr), 31, 40, 106
literariness. *See* aesthetics
literary prizes: Arabic novels and, 146–47, 149–50; established in the Arab world since 2000, 145–46, 192n16; readership of Arabic literature and, 148–52; translated Arabic literature winning, 150–52
Liu, Lydia, 4, 11
Locke, John, 18
Love, Heather, 16–17
Lovell, Mary, 77, 175n22
lughah, 5, 30–31, 162n17

Maḥfūẓ, Nagīb (Naguib Mahfouz), 1, 146
Makdisi, Saree, 63
Malallah, Hanaa, 113, 120
Man Booker International Prize, 150–51, 194n38
maqāmah, 34, 68, 146
al-Mashshā'ah (*Planet of Clay*) (Yazbik), 150
Masmoudi, Ikram, 120, 126, 133
Massumi, Brian, 18, 78, 84, 112, 116–17
Mawsim al-hijrah ilā al-shamāl (*Season of Migration to the North*) (Ṣāliḥ), 140
Mawt saghīr (*Ibn Arabi's Small Death*) ('Alwān), 150
al-Mawt 'amal shāqq (*Death Is Hard Work*) (Khalīfah), 150
ma'nā, 5; *lafẓ* contrasted with, 30–31, 35–36, 39–40, 43, 45, 48; translatability of, 39–40
Ma'rūf, Māzin (Mazen Maarouf), 150
McManus, Anne-Marie, 149–50
The Mehlis Report. *See Taqrīr Mīhlīs*
Meschonnic, Henri, 12, 165n43
Metcalf, Edwards, 56
Mīkhā'īl, Dunyā (Dunya Mikhail), 150
Minor Detail. *See Tafṣīl thānawī*
Mitchell, W. J. T., 105
Modern Language Association, 155, 166n77
Montgomery, James, 28, 36
Moretti, Franco, 22
Morgan, Benjamin, 78–79
motherhood, 89–91, 110–111
Moukheiber, Karen, 78

Mountains of the Moon, 174n1
Mufti, Aamir, 5, 10
AlMultaqa Prize for the Arabic Short Story (Jāʾizat al-Multaqā lil-Qiṣṣah al-Qaṣīrah al-ʿArabiyyah), 145
al-Musawi, Muhsin, 66, 146
muthannā (dual grammar), 6; acoustics of, 93, 95–97; aesthetics of, 94–95, 97–99; Arabic poetry and, 94–95; body parts and, 92–93, 97; English versions of, 93–94, 182n38; the Qur'an and, 95–97; translation of, 98–100

Naaman, Mara, 19
Naguib Mahfouz Medal for Literature, 192n16
Nahda (Nahḍah) period, 34
Nancy, Jean-Luc, 45
Newton, Adam Zachary, 7
Ngai, Sianne, 138
novels. *See* the Arabic novel
Nukāt lil-musallaḥīn (*Jokes for the Gunmen*) (Maʿrūf), 150
Nussbaum, Felicity, 63

Omri, Mohamed-Salah, 14, 38, 146
Orientalism: Burton and, 61, 75–76; reception of Arabic literature in the U.S. and, 1, 4, 14, 134

Pannewick, Friederike, 122, 123
Payne, John, 62; Burton's correspondence with, 64; Burton's plagiarism of, 58–59, 63, 66–67, 80; translation of *saj*ʿ and, 70. See also *The Book of the Thousand Nights and One Night*
Peled, Mattityahu, 43, 44
Penjweny, Jamal, 113
Penzer, Norman, 80
Personal Narrative of a Pilgrimage to El Medinah and Meccah (Burton), 175n26
Pierpont, Claudia Roth, 133–34
Plath, Sylvia, 107–8
Polizzotti, Mark, 22–23, 85
postcolonial theory, 4, 14
Preston, Theodore, 69–70
Price, Leri, 150
prison literature, 120, 126, 133–34
prizes. *See* literary prizes
Probyn, Elspeth, 24, 131, 188n65
publishing industry, U.S., 1–3, 9, 146, 153
Puchner, Martin, 58, 174n10
Puig de la Bellacasa, María, 7

Qualey, Marcia Lynx, 151
the Qur'an, 31, 39, 71, 97, 106

Rabassa, Gregory, 89, 163n30
Racy, A. J., 75, 76
Rancière, Jacques, 115–16, 131
Rastegar, Kamran, 34–35
readership: of Arabic literature in the U.S., 1–3, 15–17; of Arabic literature in Arabic, 148–50
Rice, Edward, 61
Robinson, Douglas, 12, 85–87
Roper, Geoffrey, 35
Rosenman, Ellen Bayuk, 77
Ruhl, Sarah, 111
Rumsfeld, Donald, 128, 188n54
Rushdie, Salman, 57

Sacks, Jeffrey, 25–26, 48
Saddam City (Saʿīd), 134
Said, Edward, 1, 3–4, 61
*saj*ʿ, 6, 68–71
Ṣāliḥ, al-Ṭayyib, 140
al-Sāq ʿalā al-sāq fī mā huwa al-Fāriyāq (Leg over Leg or, The Turtle in the Tree, concerning The Fāriyāq) (al-Shidyāq), 5; aesthetics of *lafẓ* in, 33, 35–36, 38, 44–45, 47–48; Library of Arabic Literature edition of, 27–29, 53, 55, 169n14; *maʿnā* in, 30–31, 33, 43–45, 47; lists in, 33, 43–44, 49, 51; publication history of, 33–35, 52–53, 168n1; sound in, 29–30, 32, 41–49, 54. See also *Leg over Leg or, The Turtle in the Tree, concerning The Fāriyāq*
Saussy, Haun, 66, 141–42
Sawa, George, 76
Sayyidāt al-qamar (*Celestial Bodies*) (al-Ḥārithī), 150–52
Saʿdāwī, Aḥmad (Ahmed Saadawi), 150
Saʿīd, Maḥmūd (Mahmoud Saeed), 134
Scarry, Elaine, 123
Schleiermacher, Friedrich, 167n96
Scott, Jonathan, 58, 62
Seale, Yasmine, 58
Sedgwick, Eve Kosofsky, 25
Seigworth, Gregory, 25, 80
self-translation, 135, 137
Sells, Michael, 95
September 11th attacks, 2, 129
El Shakry, Hoda, 97
Shame (Rushdie), 57
Shamma, Tarek, 66, 71–72, 75
Shannon, Jonathan, 76

Sharjah International Book Fair, 193n30
Sheikh Zayed Book Award (Jā'izat al-Shaykh Zāyid lil-Kitāb), 145
Shiblī, 'Adaniyyah (Adania Shibli), 150
al-Shidyāq, Aḥmad Fāris (Ahmad Faris Al-Shidyaq), 5, 34, 51–52; authorial commentary by, 33–34, 43, 170n31. See also *al-Sāq 'alā al-sāq fī mā huwa al-Fāriyāq*
Shklovsky, Victor, 33
Shūmān, Hilāl (Hilal Chouman), 6, 88–102. See also *Līmbū Bayrūt*
Shusterman, Richard, 84, 86, 87
Sībawayhi, 30
Smith, Rachel Greenwald, 17
somaesthetics, 86–87, 111
sonority, 45, 54–55
Sontag, Susan, 115
Spinoza, Baruch, 18
Spivak, Gayatri Chakravorty, 7, 10–11, 38, 89, 164n37, 182n22
Staten, Henry, 11
Steedman, Carolyn, 60
Steiner, George, 13
Steingass, Francis Joseph, 62
Stewart, Kathleen, 26, 142
The Strange Affair of Spring-Heeled Jack (Hodder), 174n1
structure of feelings, 128–29

Tafṣīl thānawī (*Minor Detail*) (Shiblī), 150
Tageldin, Shaden, 8–9
Tales from the Arabic (Payne), 58, 67
Tanoukhi, Nirvana, 10
Taqrīr Mīhlīs (*The Mehlis Report*) (Jābir), 154
ṭarab, 75–79
Theater of Operations exhibit, 113–15, 117–20
thick translation, 35
third world, 129, 133, 144
Three Percent initiative, 2
Tolstoy, Leo, 27
Toorawa, Shawkat, 28
Traboulsi, Fawwaz, 170n31
Troyanov, Iliya, 174n1
Tymoczko, Maria, 13–14

al-'Ukbarī, 'Abdallāh ibn al-Ḥusayn, 97
untranslatability, 1, 7, 13, 23, 90, 108, 142; *lafẓ* and, 38–40; *saj'* and, 70

Vasseleu, Cathryn, 88
Venuti, Lawrence, 10, 23, 28, 66, 83–84, 89, 118, 168n7

Wadud, Amina, 96–97
Waḥdahā shajarat al-rummān (*The Corpse Washer*) (Anṭūn), 137–38
Walkowitz, Judith, 77
Walkowitz, Rebecca, 23, 163n28
Warhol, Robyn, 17
Warner, Marina, 27
Warren, Austin, 33
Weiss, Max, 150
Wellek, René, 33
Williams, Raymond, 128
Wood, Michael, 23, 164n37
Words Without Borders, 195n52
world literature: Arabic literature as, 5, 12, 19–20, 26, 28, 79–80, 141–44, 146, 154; Burton's *Nights* as, 58–59, 76, 81; definitions of, 22, 40, 143; English and, 6, 10–12, 53, 152; reading and, 18, 57, 76, 78, 137
Wright, Jonathan, 150
Wright, Thomas, 59, 61, 63–64, 80
Wright, W., 45–46

Yazbik, Samar (Samar Yazbek), 150

Zachs, Fruma, 34

Anna Ziajka Stanton is Caroline D. Eckhardt Early Career Professor of Comparative Literature and Assistant Professor of Comparative Literature at the Pennsylvania State University. She has published articles in the *Journal of Arabic Literature*, *Philological Encounters*, the *Journal of World Literature*, the *Cambridge Journal of Postcolonial Literary Inquiry*, and *Middle Eastern Literatures*. Stanton is the translator of Hilal Chouman's *Limbo Beirut*, which was longlisted for the 2017 PEN Translation Prize and shortlisted for the 2017 Saif Ghobash Banipal Prize for Arabic Literary Translation. She has been an editor at the *Journal of Arabic Literature* since 2014.

www.ingramcontent.com/pod-product-compliance
Lightning Source LLC
Chambersburg PA
CBHW020405080526
44584CB00014B/1187
* 9 7 8 1 5 3 1 5 0 3 2 2 2 *